Wit and Wisdom

Other Books from Bright Leaf

Wit and Wisdom

THE FORGOTTEN

LITERARY LIFE OF

NEW ENGLAND VILLAGES

JOAN NEWLON RADNER

BRIGHT LEAF
BOOKS THAT ILLUMINATE
Amherst and Boston
An imprint of University of Massachusetts Press

Wit and Wisdom has been supported by the Regional Books Fund,
established by donors in 2019 to support the
University of Massachusetts Press's Bright Leaf imprint.

Bright Leaf, an imprint of the University of Massachusetts Press,
publishes accessible and entertaining books about New England.
Highlighting the history, culture, diversity, and environment of the region,
Bright Leaf offers readers the tools and inspiration to explore its landmarks
and traditions, famous personalities, and distinctive flora and fauna.

ISBN 978-1-62534-738-1 (paper); 739-8 (hardcover)

Designed by Deste Roosa
Set in Dante and Mr Eaves
Printed and bound by Books International, Inc.

Cover design by adam b. bohannon
Cover photos: (front) *The Gordon farmstead. Albion Gordon, his wife Harriet, and
possibly his sister Maria stand in the front yard.* Undated photograph.
Private Collection; (top right) detail from first page of "Report of last
Lyceum," *Toll Bridge Journal* 6, no. 3, March 12, 1870. Courtesy of the author.

Library of Congress Cataloging-in-Publication Data
Names: Radner, Joan Newlon, author.
Title: Wit and wisdom : the forgotten literary life of New England villages
/ Joan Newlon Radner.
Description: Amherst : Bright Leaf, An imprint of University of
Massachusetts Press, 2023. | Includes bibliographical references and
index.
Identifiers: LCCN 2022044966 (print) | LCCN 2022044967 (ebook) | ISBN
9781625347381 (paperback) | ISBN 9781625347398 (hardcover) | ISBN
9781685750299 (ebook) | ISBN 9781685750305 (epub)
Subjects: LCSH: Lyceums—New England—History—19th century. |
Lyceums—New
England—Newspapers—History—19th century. | Community life—New
England—History—19th century. | Lectures and lecturing—New
England—History—19th century. | Debates and debating—New
England—History—19th century. | New England—Humor—History—19th
century.
Classification: LCC LC6551.N38 R34 2023 (print) | LCC LC6551.N38 (ebook)
| DDC 374/.8097409034—dc23/eng/20221116
LC record available at https://lccn.loc.gov/2022044966
LC ebook record available at https://lccn.loc.gov/2022044967

British Library Cataloguing-in-Publication Data
A catalog record for this book is available from the British Library.

In memory of
Leo Marx
whose enthusiasm for this project meant the world to me
and
Roberta Chandler and Irene Dunham
who honored the intricate delights of local history

The North Fayette Lyceum

The North Fayette Lyceum now commences once again,
Right willingly we'll help it by the use of tongue & pen,
We will take the parts assigned us and no duty will we shirk,
The labor will be pleasant for our hearts are in the work.
All ye people come and join us from the region round about,
We shall welcome your assistance please take hold and help us out,
We would make our programme varied as has ever been our wont,
Be not afraid and stay not back but come right to the front.
Full well do we remember all the good old jolly times,
When the past Lyceum papers teemed with fun and jokes & rhymes,
How we all kept so good natured mid the flying shafts of wit
Not a continental did we care how hard we might get hit.
And when the question was discussed, it was not thought a sin,
If each and every disputant tried hard his case to win,
If language oft got twisted and reason set aside,
If appeals were made to passion, to prejudice & pride.
In maintaining the Lyceum we can help in divers ways,
Its supporters in past seasons have deserved the highest praise.
Let us hope that in the future it may flourish more and more,
And its influence be greater than it e'er has been before.

from the *Firefly*, paper of the
North Fayette (ME) Lyceum, c. 1887

CONTENTS

CONTENTS

AUTHOR'S NOTE

About the conventions of this study: I have quoted generously from the lyceum papers, wishing to invoke the writing styles and the disparate voices of those long-ago villagers. Quotations from lyceum papers are always presented in italics to suggest the handwriting so essential to these texts. Except in cases where the meaning might be unclear, I have preserved the writers' irregular punctuation and occasionally variable spelling.

FIGURE I. Cover, *Toll Bridge Journal* 6, no. 3, March 12, 1870. Collection of the author.

THE TREASURE IN THE ATTIC

It was a sweltering August afternoon and I was sticky and covered with dust. One more summer of emptying the home in Fryeburg, Maine, where my great-grandmother, Maria Eliza Gordon Adams, had spent her last years. The house had to be sold, and it had fallen to me, the only available adult descendant, to sort through centuries of furniture, crockery, linens, books, tools, and all the rest that my packrat Maine family had accumulated. I had finally reached the attic, capacious repository of everything that the generations could neither discard nor use. Broken clocks, keys without locks, empty pasteboard boxes that might come in handy someday, old-fashioned machinery, obsolete schoolbooks—and paper. So much yellowed paper, in heaps and boxes and dresser drawers. Letters, diaries, ledgers, maps, magazines, scrapbooks, commonplace books, newspaper clippings, my grandmother's college essays. Too much to read that dusty afternoon, but treasure for the future. Like a good packrat, I brought empty boxes, loaded them up, and carried them down the steep, narrow stairs to be stored elsewhere.

Years later, in search of family history, I opened one of those boxes of miscellaneous loose papers from the Fryeburg attic. On top was a jumble of literary compositions, their characters as diverse as their handwriting. I saw

The Afterglow.
Suggested by a sunset off Mt. Kearsarge.
The sun is descending low,
And o'er the mountain height
Streams a warm and crimson glow
With a soft, rich purple light.

followed by

Local Brevities.

Mr Fred Farington while in Saco recently was mistaken for a member of the last Legislature and arrested. He was charged with burglary, arson, conspiracy, embezzlement, sedition and false pretenses.

Well, I thought, Great-Grandma had an odd hobby! And then, as I turned over the yellowed pages in the box, some of them stuck together. No, they were *sewn* together with a few stitches at the left margin. I lifted out the small gathering. What a strange cluster! Pages of different sizes—long ledger sheets, scraps of copybook pages lined and unlined, letter paper, even some small square bits of odd paper, all in various hands. Had it not been for the stitching, I would never have imagined these shards were related.

At first, the cover page looked blank. Then a spidery, faint pencil heading caught my eye:

Toll Bridg Journal
Vol. 6, No. 3
March 12th, 1870.

FIGURE 2. Cover detail, *Toll Bridge Journal* 6, no. 3, March 12, 1870. Collection of the author.

Toll Bridge I knew: the neighborhood at the northern edge of Fryeburg surrounding the crossing of the old course of the Saco River, just south of the Lovell town line. Home of my great-grandmother, Maria Eliza Gordon, before she married. (Later, in her widowhood, she had lived in that house in the village whose attic I had emptied.) But Toll Bridge was a completely rural small farming neighborhood, its only public building the one-room red schoolhouse. A *journal*? A newspaper? Impossible.

I opened the cover—and was captivated. Reading the first piece, *"Report of last Lyceum,"* was like stepping into a time machine. Suddenly my great-grandmother and her neighbors were alive before me, teasing, listening, arguing, laughing, bringing the warmth of good fellowship to a cold winter evening. I wasn't sure what they were talking about. I didn't know all the characters. I didn't understand their jokes. But I read on. Alien as I was, I couldn't miss the unusual quality of the gathering: serious commitment to whatever was going on, laced with a spirit of fun. That revelation launched me into a long quest for more such "journals" and "lyceums," for more traces of such genial winter gatherings of men and women, young and old, farmers and intelligentsia, selectmen and schoolchildren. Finally, I uncovered a long-forgotten tradition that had spread creative joy across rural northern New England for most of the nineteenth century. This book tells that story.

Lyceum papers
Lyceum record books
Both papers and record books

MAINE

VERMONT

Kenduskeag
Embden
Veazie
Carthage
South Levant
East Bethel
Beans Corner, Jay
North Fayette
West Danville
East Cabot
Wrightsville
South Bethel
Vergennes
Landaff
Toll Bridge, Fryeburg
NEW
HAMPSHIRE
Tunbridge
West Plymouth
South Freeport

NORTH

East Andover
Duttonsville
Franklin Village
Webster
Chester
South Acworth
Westminster
Antrim
Bow Lake Village
Dublin
Fremont
Mont Vernon

Atlantic Ocean

Heath
MASSACHUSETTS
Shirley

Northbridge

RHODE
ISLAND

50 MILES
100 KILOMETERS

CONNECTICUT

BLACKMER MAPS

MAP 1. This map marks the sites of lyceums whose surviving papers and record books I have consulted and referred to in this study. Because the survival of these documents is so rare, the locations on this map should not be taken as an accurate representation of the distribution of the rural lyceums, which were dotted very densely throughout the region.

Wit and Wisdom

This project began by chance, with my discovery of the tattered *Toll Bridge Journal* of March 12, 1870, in the attic of my great-grandmother's house in Fryeburg, Maine. I was drawn into that puzzling bundle of handwritten literary compositions—prose and poetry, sober essays and wry reportage, biblical parodies and jokes. As I unriddled the nature of the *Journal* (a story I will tell in chapter 1), I discovered not only a window into my ancestors' daily lives but also an entrance into a once powerful, now forgotten wintertime institution in nineteenth-century rural New England: the village lyceum. Although I had been at home in the rural landscape of my New England ancestors and loved the inventive grace of their old connected farmsteads, I had given little thought to their daily lives—particularly their lives in the winter. Until the *Toll Bridge Journal* launched my investigations, I assumed that deep snowdrifts and long, dark winter evenings would have isolated families in their scattered farms, reducing life to the necessities of woods work, livestock care, domestic toil, and school attendance. I knew almost nothing about the wintertime social life of northern farmers, and I certainly had no inkling of what that Maine attic later revealed to me: that those hardworking farm families had developed and maintained a regular, community-wide, entertaining tradition of intellectual and literary endeavor. Neighbors gathered for their Toll Bridge Lyceum every Saturday evening during the winter months, bent on improving their mental abilities through formal debates, literary composition, and public speaking. Bent, too, on courting, teasing, and enjoying one another's company.

Such a well-established tradition, with its own complex handwritten journal, could not, I thought, be unique to a single small neighborhood in Maine. My first inquiries to nearby town historical societies were met with puzzlement, but slowly, as I expanded my quest throughout New England, copies of similar manuscript papers from other lyceums began to turn up in regional, state, and local archives, in private collections, and even in other attics. The village lyceum tradition, with its debates and journals, had passed out of living memory, but it was not so deeply buried that its bones could not occasionally surface. It became evident that those bones were scattered widely. One of my first respondents was Matthew Thomas of the Fremont (NH) Historical Society, who sent me copies of two issues of the handwritten *Poplin Herald* from December 16, 1879, and February 17, 1880, *"edited every Tuesday by the Fremont Literary Society"*—issues with very much the same mix of wit and wisdom, the same love of biblical parody and verbal humor, that I'd found in the *Toll Bridge Journal*. Identical practices from two different small villages, a decade and a hundred miles apart, in an era of slow travel: direct influence was improbable. The tradition must have been widespread.

A range of sources have helped me flesh out the picture of that tradition, which endured in wintertime in northern New England from the 1830s into the 1890s. Diaries—beginning with my own great-grandmother's—occasionally mention attendance at local lyceums. Sketches of lyceums in poetry or prose often occur in the manuscript papers themselves. Memoirs and early town histories give general descriptions of village lyceums. Local columns in regional newspapers reported on local lyceums, mentioning participants, topics of debate, lyceum papers and their editors, and the formation of new lyceums. Some authors reflected expansively on the virtues of the tradition:

> The lyceums and the debating clubs of the farming towns are a greater force than those who participate in them imagine. . . . They are the bellows that blow the sparks of thought once ignited. Thought tells. Thought pays. . . . A great many people will be the brighter and better after this season of improvement. One night a week at the reading club or the lyceum will foot up an astonishing total gain at the end of the winter. (*Lewiston [ME] Journal, c. 1880*)

Period fiction set occasional scenes in village lyceums, giving further evidence of the social and emotional environment of those gatherings. Lyceum record books, whose hard covers and stitched bindings have helped them survive and pass into many historical archives, present the fullest formal information: constitutions, bylaws, lists of founding members, and minutes that report dates, officers, agendas, debate topics and speakers, paper editors' names, and information about other activities. Evidence continues to come to light through increasingly available online full-text resources, but I believe that my research has reached what Ronald Zboray and Mary Zboray, in bringing their own archival searches to a close for *Everyday Ideas*, have felicitously named the "point of redundancy."[1]

These homegrown neighborhood associations existed at the opposite end of the spectrum from the commercial and more urban productions of the lyceum movement that specialized in subscription lectures by traveling notables.[2] Both traditions emerged from and supported the nineteenth century's national passion for self-education, oratory, and improvement, but the village lyceums were embedded in their small communities in distinctive ways. Organized by local people, they gave active public speaking roles to men and women who were diverse in age, occupation, social status, and education. They gave paramount value to face-to-face discussion and engagement with ideas. "*We are social beings,*" wrote a correspondent to the Dublin, New Hampshire, lyceum paper in 1841: "*We need the speaking eye and the listening ear to enable us to go on with success.*" Audience volunteers as well as appointed local speakers took part in the debates. In addition, all participants were encouraged to compose literary pieces for the lyceum's paper, which was compiled by the editor (most often a woman, designated "editress") and then read aloud at each meeting.

The varied lyceum activities were a seasonal performance of community, eagerly anticipated as winter approached and the long, dark evenings released farmers from their summer labors. In November 1889, the editor of the *Gazette,* the handwritten paper of the South Bethel (ME) Debating Society, looked toward winter and laid out local options:

> "The melancholy days" have surely come at last, and we think the poet has fitly termed them thus for surely nothing can be more desolate and cheerless than the present forbidding landscape.
>
> Everything seems wrapped in silence, cold and austere as though in anticipation of the coming winter. Occasionally, however Nature relaxes her stern features in a smile and then we enjoy a pleasant day as only one can that lives in almost dread of the change to follow.
>
> Not that the people of Poverty Hollow intend to den up this winter though, by any means, for there are the Lyceums and Circles, the dances and the "Stormy Day Association" held in the black-smith shop, to call us out even if there were no other attractions to keep us from taking a four months nap.
>
> We hope the members of the Debating Society will "wake up" and move our meetings along lively this winter; and tell the South Bethel Sewing Circle to keep up good courage for as "Betsy Spriggins" says "We air goin' to have that agin," for the boys are all hungry at the thoughts of those Circle suppers and the girls though they don't eat anything are equally interested.[3]

Although these rural associations had a range of names—debating clubs or societies, literary associations, clubs, unions, and even, most elaborately, societies for mutual or mental improvement—they most commonly called themselves lyceums. Throughout the century, as Joseph F. Kett has pointed out, *lyceum* was a broad term denoting "a literary club of almost any description."[4] The name gained considerable favor thanks to its appealing allusion to classical learning—specifically, to the Lyceum garden in ancient Athens where Aristotle met his pupils. But it earned even greater cachet in the United States after 1826, when Josiah Holbrook's enormously successful American Lyceum got its start in Millbury, Massachusetts.

Thus, when the adult citizens of the little village of Dublin, New Hampshire, established a debating society in 1824, they called it the Dublin Literary Society; but on October 7, 1836— after the American Lyceum had established wide popularity— they voted to rename their association the Dublin Lyceum.[5]

I have focused my research on rural Maine, New Hampshire, Vermont, and Massachusetts because these states were the most densely dotted with village lyceums over the longest range of time and because the tradition spread from this region. Commenting in 1886 on the nineteenth-century diaspora of "the rural inhabitants of New England" across the upper Midwest, Edmund Steadman described them as "seeming almost a race by themselves. . . . This hive of individuality has sent out swarms, and scattered its ideas like pollen throughout the northern belt of our States."[6] Certainly lyceums—not only subscription lecture series but also rural debating societies— were pollinated all along the "Yankee Runway" from upstate New York to Minnesota and Kansas; their meetings are noted occasionally in regional newspapers throughout the century. Settlers in the western states re-created institutions that evoked their eastern homeplaces. Reverend James Hill exulted in the virtues of the lyceums established by a Maine member of the "Iowa Band" of New England missionaries who settled in the west in 1843: "As Samson found the honey, so these lyceums discovered talent where it would be looked for least . . . [and] developed a social group and a communal intellectual life."[7] When they could, emigrants maintained direct connections with New England. A column in the Greenfield, Massachusetts, Gazette and Courier announced that one of the debaters at the local Zoar Lyceum would be "R. D. Sanford of Iowa, a native and former resident of an adjoining town."[8] Although I have not pursued such research in this project, investigation of the institution of village lyceums during the western migration might yield interesting insights.

Debating had been a widespread improvement activity in civic and academic societies in America since well before the Revolutionary War. The forensic exercises of the village lyceums were descendants of this heritage. Rural speakers often debated the same philosophical and political topics that students were discussing in colleges and academies, and they saw their engagement with these subjects as expressions of their essential roles as concerned citizens. Manuscript papers in the rural lyceums complemented the debates. To be sure, handwritten newspapers were a widespread pastime in the nineteenth century, a family hobby (witness *Little Women*) and also popular at gatherings such as Sunday schools, common schools, and temperance lodges. But the village lyceum papers are distinctive in their variety of tone and authorship. In them we listen to rarely heard, diverse voices of the community. The few surviving papers offer hundreds of examples of the creations of village writers, who composed the best pieces they could in order to appeal to the literary tastes and social needs of their neighbors. We hear serious voices, concerned about the brevity of life, the uncertainty of farming, the wisdom of migrating to the new mill towns or to rock-free western acres. We hear poets praising the beauty of the local landscape, the virtues of the community, the joys and tribulations of the lyceum itself. We eavesdrop as villagers manipulate dozens of literary genres to comic effect, teasing one another about questionable behavior, imprudent decisions, and, most of all, the ups and downs of courting. We note the frequent paro-dies of journalistic conventions in which villagers obliquely appraise values expressed in the contemporary press. The authors' contributions demonstrate not only the breadth of what they read but also how deeply their literary experience had formed their view of the world. The dazzling mixture of tones and genres in each paper gives a vivid impression of village-wide conversation and interaction.

Although the lyceum papers are invaluable records, their study has presented quite a few challenges, not the least of which has been finding the actual documents. They were not meant to survive, and most have not. Editors wrote one

copy—just one. Its "circulation" was only aural; once the editor
had read it aloud to the assembled lyceum, the written text had
fulfilled its function and could be discarded. Because no lyceum
maintained an archive of its papers, no complete set of issues
from any season has come to light. A random few of what
must have been thousands of individual lyceum papers have
been preserved in state, local, and personal collections. Those
few can be hard to locate even in historical archives, where
they may be camouflaged in collections of "family papers" or
"miscellaneous poetry/literature." The surviving papers were
probably kept as mementos by individual editors and wound
up (like the *Toll Bridge Journal*) in family attics, judging from
the fact that the issues I have seen often come in clusters of
two or three or four with scattered dates, all attributed to the
same editor or to editors in the same family. Papers stored at
home might have been reread from time to time by the editors,
their friends, or families as a way of revisiting particular compositions or remembering the community moment that had
called them forth. In his diary for February 15, 1843, T. P. Mason
of Dublin, New Hampshire, notes a visit to his friend Jonas
Piper, occasional editor of the papers of the Young People's
Society for Mutual Improvement: "Was very interested in
looking over the 'Posts' and 'Scrap gatherers' which he has
in keeping—a very pleasant evening." Beyond such private
occasions, individual lyceum papers had no ongoing audience.

I have found and worked with some seventy mostly intact
papers (see appendix A), augmented by disassembled pieces of
others and copious collateral evidence. This is an unavoidably
random sample, not representative of the distribution of the
tradition either temporally or geographically. For instance, I
have seen only two papers, five issues in total, from Vermont,
but columns in the Vermont press attest to prolonged state-
wide occurrence of lyceums with papers. Moreover, I have
seen no papers from any state written between 1860 and
1875, even though accounts in reliable sources such as diaries,
lyceum record books, and the commercial press confirm that

the tradition continued throughout that period. As further papers come to light, they may fill in these gaps.

The lyceum authors did not expect anyone beyond their immediate neighbors to hear their compositions. I am sometimes painfully aware that I am not their intended audience. Part of my problem is ignorance. Most of the time I cannot identify the people hidden by nicknames and sly allusions or the authors writing behind the customary veil of anonymity. I am unfamiliar with the local events and relationships suggested by the writers' words. Added to my lack of information is a significant aesthetic and cultural gap. To me, reading in the twenty-first century, not all of the amateur literature in these lyceum texts is equally engaging, and some is disturbing. Some pieces are clumsy, some poems prosodically challenged. I cringe at the obsolete gender images and the grating racial stereotypes. I am tempted to look away from pieces revealing a long-dead taste for the sentimental and picturesque and from local poets' enthusiastic deployment of stock images. My modern tastes move me toward other elements of the lyceum papers: satire and clever pastiche, masterful deployment of verbal wit, writing that even centuries later reveals the twinkle in its author's eye. I labor against these preferences, striving to see the literary landscape whole so as not to misrepresent the papers and their manifold purposes.

Village lyceum papers were ephemeral. Precisely because they were not intended to survive, we must pay earnest attention to their original oral nature.[9] Each was created and read aloud for a specific community at a specific moment; meanings inhere not in the written text alone but in the text as a sign (though nowadays hard to read) of performance in context. The papers occupy the borderline between speech and writing. The editor would have spoken every word, every phrase—whether nimble or lumbering, humorous or solemn; whether composed by a local lawyer or a schoolchild. Although some pieces might have been criticized, all were heard, making the papers a collective testimonial to the lyceum's core values of improvement and solidarity. As I pay heed to every element in a paper, to the paper in the spoken panoply of the lyceum's activities, and to the lyceum in the evolving identity of the small nineteenth-century village, I gain immense respect for the energy and determination, the wit and wisdom, of my ancestors.

Like the Toll Bridge Lyceum in Fryeburg, Maine, rural lyceums throughout New England took their place among other social and educational occasions created by villagers in the wintertime. A whirl of activity resisted the cold and isolation of the scattered farmsteads. Gatherings ranged in formality from casual visiting, to dances, circles, parties, fundraising suppers, dramatic entertainments, and wedding-anniversary celebrations. Sunday church services were supplemented by prayer meetings on weeknights. Temperance societies and meetings were popular. Neighbors took part, as my great-grandmother did, in improving educational events such as singing schools, often conducted for a period of weeks by traveling music masters, writing schools at which itinerant champion writers taught local people the finer aspects of penmanship, and homegrown "spelling schools"—spelling bees—for old and young. The rural lyceums represented the pinnacle of intellectual challenge and variety.

Rural and urban lyceums adapted differently to their particular social and economic environments, and the heyday of the American Lyceum ended earlier in the century than did the democratic debating societies and homegrown literary exercises of the small villages. Although rural lyceum members were well aware of the national lecture lyceum movement, they did not emulate it and sometimes even poked fun at it (as in the *Toll Bridge Journal*'s sly allusion to subscription lectures in "*Notice of a scientific Lecture upon the subject of Hogology*"). Though the rural lyceums did not sell subscriptions or sponsor lectures by traveling notables, they did share with the urban system a passion for the cultivation of the mind combined with convivial entertainment and social opportunities. As with the urban lectures, too, attending the rural lyceums was a popular courtship activity. Angela Ray's comment is applicable to lyceums of all sorts throughout the country: "The word *lyceum* embodied the paradoxes of playful learning and serious fun."[10]

I begin my exploration into the village lyceum tradition with the fuller story of my discovery that it existed. Chapter 1 traces my puzzled encounter with the pieces of the *Toll Bridge Journal,* so deliberately arranged in what nevertheless seemed to be an incoherent jumble of topics and tones and genres. Reading through the *Journal,* unraveling its allusions and its place in its community, was a process that began with guesswork and finally required handwriting analysis, genealogical research, and crucial clues from my great-grandmother's laconic diary and other local documents. From this nose-to-the-paper investigation, I step back, in chapter 2, to provide a broad overview of the village lyceum tradition as it occurred in New England from the 1830s to the 1890s: how rural people established their winter lyceums, conscientiously wrote constitutions and bylaws, and structured their meetings to accommodate the community. Although most of the founders were young adults, a wide range of local residents bent on self-improvement and sociability took enthusiastic part: men and women of all ages, older schoolchildren, farmers and skilled craftsmen, and the few village intelligentsia. The central exercise of each meeting was a formal debate, and chapter 3 locates this tradition in the longstanding American passion for self-education through the cultivation of debating and oratory. Taking seriously their roles in the developing nation, rural debaters grappled with matters of national policy, general philosophy, history, and ethics as well as with local issues. Contemporary commentators recognized the village debating societies as a primary means of developing the mental skills needed for success in business, public service, the professions, and citizenship in general.

Chapter 4 considers the position of women in the lyceums. Although debating itself was marked as a masculine activity, women played significant roles in the rural associations' work of improvement, often serving as debate judges and critics and, as the century advanced, occasionally even taking part in the debates. Although they were junior partners in the lyceum, women usually took the lead in editing and presenting the paper. Chapter 5 examines the complexities of this role, which gave the editor or editress significant satisfaction as well as local influence but also created significant challenges. It required ingenuity to persuade neighbors to write pieces for the paper. If local contributions were insufficient, editors had to create their own compositions or sometimes adapt pieces published elsewhere in order to fill out the pages. In an era when women rarely spoke at public events, some village women found it intimidating to read the paper to a community audience. Yet many accepted the responsibility, encouraged by the belief that the intellectual improvement to be gained from writing and reading was comparable to the benefits of public debating.

Saturated in literature from childhood, village authors modeled their various creations for the lyceum papers on what they read in the Bible, school primers, books, almanacs, newspapers, and magazines. Chapter 6 surveys the impressive range of rural literary ability. Although they were silent on partisan politics and sectarian religion, lyceum authors wrote on major national issues from women's roles to slavery, from temperance to the Gold Rush; they expressed their profound Christian faith; they discussed matters of ethics and conduct; and they expressed their delight in their own community. Even when lyceum authors or editors incorporated commercially published pieces into the papers, they often modified them to include local characters, places, and attitudes. And they loved humor. Almost all lyceum papers embedded serious pieces in a creative matrix of jokes, teasing, and multiple forms of verbal wit.

Chapter 7 focuses on one major model for the lyceum papers: the commercial press. Rural lyceum papers seem to be almost the antithesis of commercial newspapers. Handwritten, they looked nothing like newspapers, were performed aloud to a group rather than read silently by individuals, and were primarily produced and edited by women. Nevertheless, they engaged with the conventions and intentions of nineteenth- century journalism in multiple ways. Lyceum editors felt that they shared the public-spirited mission claimed for the contemporary press. However, many lyceum pieces imitated journalistic genres with obvious irony or parody, suggesting the villagers' cosmopolitan awareness of national culture as well as their resistance to what the popular press stood for: the increasing dominance of mass industrialization, the market economy, and urban values.

In chapter 8 I tackle the importance—and the difficulty—of actually *hearing* the papers nowadays, of treating them not as texts to be encountered on the page but as evidence of significant performances of community. Even writing a piece for the paper in private was a social act, as the writer imagined its reception by well-known listeners. The convention of authorial anonymity might trigger guessing games among listeners, but it also enabled a kind of literary cross-dressing as men and women sometimes wrote in the styles of each other's gender. Some transgressive features of the papers suggest the carnivalesque. Editors composed their papers in distinctive ways to suit oral performance; as they read, presenting the diverse voices of individual authors, they echoed back to the community its own complex identity.

Finally, chapter 9 delineates the end of the rural lyceums. Lyceum authors often predicted that their villages and values would endure; they rejected the century's growing image of the decline of New England. Villagers had strategically designed their lyceums—and also their gracefully interconnected farm buildings—to proclaim and maintain their conservative way of life. By the 1890s, however, production of lyceums as well as of those ingenious farmsteads was waning as national economic and educational developments became too strong to withstand. Although the evolving local Granges matched the neighborhood sociability of the lyceums and debating continued as an activity in academies and colleges, the village lyceums ceased to meet, were recollected with nostalgia for a generation, and then vanished from view. Rediscovering this communal, joyful tradition, revisiting a world in which people often truly listened to one another, feeling again the sincerity with which old and young dedicated themselves to mental improvement, we must admire their dedication to wit and wisdom.

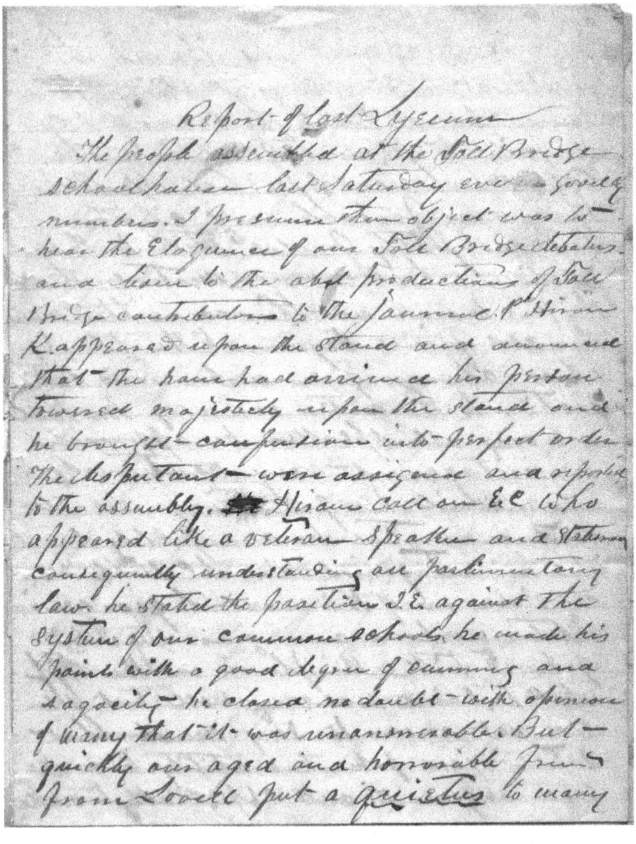

FIGURE 3. First page of *"Report of last Lyceum,"* Toll Bridge Journal 6, no. 3, March 12, 1870. Collection of the author.

"REPORT OF LAST LYCEUM"

Discovering a Forgotten Institution

As I opened the *Toll Bridge Journal*, that puzzling bundle of sober essays and wry reportage, biblical parodies and jokes, the title of the first piece, *"Report of last Lyceum,"* baffled me. If newspaper production—a *Journal*—seemed unlikely in the Toll Bridge hamlet, certainly a "Lyceum" was even more improbable. The only nineteenth-century lyceums I had heard about were those urban and largely antebellum institutions that featured subscription lecture series by traveling notables. As I read on, however, I learned about a very different community tradition.

> *Report of last Lyceum*
> *The people assembled at the Toll Bridge schoolhouse last Saturday eve in goodly numbers.*

The schoolhouse? I thought. A meeting place for adults?

> *I presume their object was to hear the Eloquence of our Toll Bridge debaters, and lisen to the abel productions of Toll Bridge contributors to the Journal.*

Evidently this "Lyceum" was some kind of neighborhood debating society. And the *Journal* I held had been created by *"Toll Bridge contributors"* (were the local farmers also authors?) and apparently had been read aloud so that the people could *"lisen"* to it. The *"Report"* went on:

> *1st Hiram K. appeared upon the stand and anounced that the hour had arrived his person towered majesticly upon the stand and he brought confusion into perfect order.*

I didn't know who *"Hiram K."* was, but I could not miss the author's sly wink about his *"person."*

The account continued.

> Hiram call[ed] on EC who appeared like a veteran speaker and
> statesman consequently understanding all parlimentary law.
> he stated the position I.E. against the system of our common
> schools. he made his points with a good degree of cunning and
> sagacity—he closed no doubt with opinion of many that it
> was unanswerable. But quickly our aged and honorable friend
> from Lovell put a quietus to many of his chosen points and
> discussed the question at length with great ability.

So the topic of the debate was *"the system of our common schools."* But this author was not interested in what had been said—only in *how* it had been said, and by whom. This writer seemed to be a seasoned critic of forensic technique.

> Then came Asa O. Pike to the re[s]cue of E. C. who failed to
> present the question in the light which was expected Mr Pike
> spoke very forc[e]able and clear but completely failed to stick
> to the question which is very essential otherwise they fail to
> make out their case. Then came our old friend Seymour to
> the floor which always gives unbounded satisfaction to the
> entire assembly Mr Hobbs is a very able speaker he approaches
> his antagonist very cautiously & and assails his points with
> unmistakable evidence untill he completely demolishes his
> antagonist Mr S. C. Hobbs we consider one of the most logical
> concise debaters we have among us.

Debating was evidently long established in Toll Bridge, long enough for the participants to have developed individual styles and acquired reputations. The author's arch tone returned in a headlong comic riff about a local character:

> My Friend John F took the floor on the Aff what he said was
> very well but John did not mean to say much but I tell you

> *John has ability to make good arguments and especially to*
> *make funy ones but John was tired he labored 1/2 day at the*
> *Caucus to secure his favorite candidates for Town Officers so*
> *he is fully exonerated for his deficiency by being somewhat*
> *elated by his success in being nominated to Office but I must*
> *return to my subject.*

Humor—but also pride in the competence of the debaters:

> *The speakers severally returned as before stated and completely*
> *demolished the question on both sides. I think if we could of*
> *had a stienographer present it would been worth while to*
> *have laid some of those arguments before the legislature for*
> *they are now to work on this matter. Well Enoch sumed up*
> *in a few words and submitted it to the President Hiram arose*
> *in all his majesty and said that question was ably managed*
> *on both sides but should be obliged to give it to the negative.*

The debate was over. What would come next? Apparently, the expected event was the reading of the *Toll Bridge Journal*, important enough to mention even in its absence.

> *Our journal was omitted on account of the negligence of some*
> *of our contributors but we trust this week will fully pay for*
> *waiting*
>> *Thus ended the Lyceum and may I hope it will prove*
> *profitable to all who attend I was very much pleased to observe*
> *the good order which prevailed throughout the entire evening I*
> *now close this report hoping all our meetings may be as good.*

My mind was whirling with questions and impressions. The anonymous writer's report had made me an eavesdropper on an intimate community. No need to give full names where all are known. *"Hiram K.," "E. C.," "our old friend Seymour,"* and *"my Friend John F"* were lovingly skewered—indeed, the sly vignettes seemed to be a major purpose of the piece. All the focus was on the quirks and foibles of the disputants, but nothing seemed to be vicious. This *"Report"* appeared to be a roast of friends, a performance not to tear down the fabric of community but to celebrate its resilience. I could not identify either the debaters or the author. Like most of the other pieces I found in this odd, stitched-together bundle, the *"Report"* was unsigned.

As I read through the next pages of the *Journal*, looking for clues, the puzzles multiplied. The second piece, written in a beautiful hand on a 3½-by-4¼-inch scrap of paper sewn by its corner into the gathering, had a headline that sounded like the lead-in to an article in a newspaper's farming column but instead was followed by names and obscure allusions.

No certainty in Hogs
we have for witnesses
J. W. R. Farrington
Isaac Abbott
Wm. G. Walker
Albion P. Gordon
All feel bad but Ripley
says they are not to blame

FIGURE 4. Detail, *Toll Bridge Journal 6*, no. 3, March 12, 1870. Collection of the author.

Next, in a spidery hand on two pages of letter paper, came an earnest moral essay signed, unhelpfully, *"Uncle J—"*:

Virtue.

Virtue is a subject which deserves evry man's attention. It consists in doing good, and in speaking truth; the effects of it, therefore, are advantageous to all mankind, and to one's self in particular. . . .

In pencil, on the back of the final page of *"Virtue,"* in a different hand, I found two jokes:

*A man entered a printing office to beg a paper for said he we
like to read news papers but our neighbors are too stingy to
take one*

    *do you retail things here remarks a boy to a cleark in a
contry store. yes sir Well, retail my dog then*

On the next page I spotted the handwriting of the *"Report of
last Lyceum"* author, but this time he was turning his wit on
the hog-raising topic:

Notice ~

*Dr. Franklin L. Hobbs would announce to the people of Toll
Bridge and vicinity that he will deliver a scientific Lecture upon
the subject of hogology at this school house on Monday evening
next commencing at half past eleven o'clock and lecture twenty
one minutes precisely. During the Lecture the learned Dr will
look like and act out, the hog as natural as life. tickets $5.00.
Albion P. Gordon William G. Walker, Hiram K. Hobbs and
J. W. R. Farrington will be admitted free out of sympathy
for them, on account of the losses and trouble they have had
in the cultivation in the cultivation of this most interesting
animal. To any young man, who will testify under oath at the
door, that he is paying his attentions to any one with serious
intentions of getting married and keeping a pig, a deduction
of three cents will be made*

    *Children, double price. If at the close of the lecture, any
person is not fully satisfied that he has received his money's
worth, he can have the privilege of finding as much fault as
he likes, but the money positively will not be refunded. John F.
Hobbs is respectfully requested not to be present as he might
consider the lecture personal.*

Oh, this was esoteric. I certainly saw the bones of the joke—
the play on the nineteenth-century fondness for subscription

scientific lectures (perhaps thumbing the Toll Bridge nose at the *other* kind of lyceum), the deliberately exaggerated ticket price, the parody legalese in the (non)refund policy, the cheerful taunt at John F. Hobbs—but I knew that I was an outsider and that this spoof was not intended for me. Several farmers had evidently experienced trouble raising hogs, but I had no idea why this was funny.

A few more clues would appear, but not for several pages. First came a most diverse series of pieces about relations between the sexes. *"Men's Vanity,"* an earnest essay seemingly from a woman's point of view, argued that men are even more vain than women, with far less justification. This was followed by a homegrown poem, *"Sam's Soliloquy,"* ostensibly spoken by a man whose marriage prospects had been ruined (*"nothing left but misery and that is all for me"*) by his clumsiness when courting: *"up to Mr. Walker['s] I tumbled down the stairs."* The next piece, brief and perfunctory, offered a (perhaps ironic) juxtaposition:

Love Something

That man alone is happy who has something to love, truly and sincerely. If he has no wife nor children, he may be attached to a dumb creature a bird or a dog. . . . Few men who have some object to love turn out to be depraved and wicked. They who have nothing to love, are often outcasts from society, and die miserably at last.

Another essay followed, by a different hand, presenting an enthusiastic if hackneyed view of *"The True Wife,"*

the light whose rays serve to illuminate man's pathway in life. She is a companion given by God to smooth the rough road to eternity and make happy the transitory existence allotted to mortal man in this ever changing world.

By this point I had come to expect dizzying changes of tone in the *Toll Bridge Journal,* and the next page, a smaller scrap of paper, did not disappoint:

Conundrums
What kind of curency does Maria Gordon deal in.
(ans) Harrimans—poor cash
(Harriman Poor Cash)

At last, my great-grandmother Maria Gordon had appeared—but I had no idea what she was being teased about. Then a second conundrum, equally opaque:

Why is E. C. Farrington an unsuccessfull hunter
Ans because he hunts orter shoots coon and gets ducks

I found more clues to this second riddle later in the *Journal*, but two more pieces on the hog disaster came next. First was a lengthy and elaborate biblical parody, in the same hand as *"Report of last Lyceum,"* headed *"The last Epistle of John to the people of Toll Bridge."* *"Dearly Beloved,"* began the preacher / author, calling on his auditors: *"He that keepeth a pig, let him hear, and he that ever intendeth to keep a pig, let him hear."* Neighbors gained biblical stature: *"one Joseph, the son of Joseph of the tribe of Frye,"* *"Albion whose sir name is Gordon of the tribe of Harry."* Castigating unbelievers who had ignored his warnings that *"evil days would surely come upon you"* from *"foolish speculations in pork and in swine,"* the preacher expertly manipulated the registers of his jeremiad:

> *Verily, verily did I not write unto you again, my dearly beloved*
> *when the Deacon boiled his little piggies and did ye not laugh*
> *me to scorn saying we will not have this John to rule over*
> *us. And did not ye take unto you one Frank of the tribe of*
> *Hobbs a false prophet and a boaster, who said himself to be*
> *somebody, and who said unto you, "Come unto me all ye that*
> *have sick hogs and I will heal them, for I am a mighty healer*
> *and physician and what I do not know is not worth knowing."*
> *. . . And now it came to pass that Albion's swine died.*
> *Then Albion lifted up his voice and wept. Then was heard the*
> *voice of lamentation and weeping, Albion weeping for his hogs*
> *and would not be comforted because they were not. Thus was*

fulfilled the prophecy, the desolation of the pig pen spoken of by the prophet John. Then Albion said now I know John was indeed a prophet, henceforth I will believe on him and have nothing more to do with the unclean things

Shifting tone again, a small scrap of paper in the same hand as "*No certainty in Hogs*" introduced a sarcastic recipe in the style of newspaper columns on household economy:

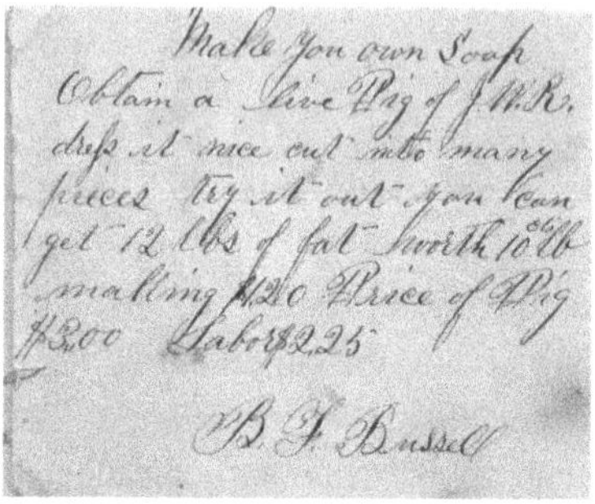

Make you[r] own Soap
Obtain a live Pig of J. W. R.
dress it nice cut into many
pieces try it out you can
get 12 lbs of fat worth 10 cts lb
making $1.20 Price of Pig
$3.00 Labor $2.25
            B. F. Bussell

FIGURE 5. Detail, *Toll Bridge Journal* 6, no. 3, March 12, 1870. Collection of the author.

The final piece sewn into this *Journal*, headed "*March 9th 1870*," summed up all of the local "*newes*" of the week in a set of jogtrot verses in Maria Gordon's unmistakable handwriting:

All around the wide creation
E'er you roam or where may be
You will find in every station
something new the eye will see
Or the ear which is in relation
Will commit some newes to me

First our Hiram though no jockey
Swaped his horse for an old grey nag
Though the nag was not buckey
Yet of his worth he did not brag
            Then after a close examineation
                        In relation

To the deseas of the glanders[1] it was unfurled
Which to Hiram was one of the wonder[s] of the world

Next our General Joseph Whelocke Ripley
Went to Trues and a pig did bye
And when he came home though no wais tiply
Closed the pig safe in the stye

He next saw the pig was failing
And was not biger than a bee
And to True kept complaining
For selling selling a pig that he could not see

True though cunning yet stayed some frisky
Took from the General many a dig
And at last sent him one pint of whiskey
Which fairly settled with him for the pig

Then Frank Buswell thought he would try it
Swapt his horse to loose or win
Soon got sick and recanted by it
Paid for the saddle and lost the gin

Then he swapt his watch with Ripley
For the pig he had of Trues
When on his pins the pig was so tipley
It made Frank have the blews

Then Frank the poor pig did slawter
Dressed him of his side to win
And says with True and Ripley he will not barter
Without at first he gets the gin

Then Enoch C. the mity hunter
Started out just at noon
Went in persuit of a fine young orter
Came in contact with a slye old coon

While in the chase up and down the river
The coon plaid stratergem just like dice
And Enoch found himself all in a shiver
Bodily fishing under the ice

Poor Enoch has at last found his boon
And getting out of the river has showed his pluck
He says that there is fun hunting orter & coon
But joy by fishing in the watter for a duck.

Another blunder was mentioned for the first time: Hiram—seen earlier as president of the lyceum—had traded his horse for a diseased *"old grey nag."* Then the summary poem yielded yet more details of the hog story: how the various trades took place, involving swaps of whiskey, gin, a horse, and a watch. Finally, I found clues to the earlier conundrum teasing E. C. Farrington—evidently a dig about a hunting misadventure. Out checking his traps for an otter (I noted the regional phonetic spelling *"orter"*), Farrington had taken off across the frozen river in pursuit of a raccoon and had fallen through the ice (*"fishing in the watter for a duck"*). Quite a week!

Could the *Toll Bridge Journal* be a window through which I could look into my great-grandmother's community? I saw some of the general topics I would have expected in a nineteenth-century rural neighborhood: farming, hunting, social morality, schooling (the debate topic), courting, marriage, and bachelorhood—but also, to my surprise, intellectual skill and oratorical prowess. I could hear distinct voices. Eight different hands, and thus eight individual writers, were represented in volume 6, number 3, two of them in more than one item. It was clear from the order and nature of the pieces in that issue that neither I, more than a century later, nor any other outsider (even a contemporary) could be the intended audience for the *Toll Bridge Journal*. Although I needed the clues from all five relevant pieces to puzzle out the hogs episode, the *Journal*'s audience must have known the story from the start to appreciate the changes rung on it by different authors. This journal did not communicate the local news; the neighborhood grapevine had already done that. It converted that news into entertaining literature.

I wanted to see Maria's world more clearly. I made my way laboriously through the pieces of this miscellaneous journal, teasing out the hints of stories, matching names and nicknames—and, in two cases, handwriting—as best I could to make a list of the players. I consulted census data, local genealogy and history, and maps. The picture of the *Toll Bridge Journal*'s neighborhood began to take shape.

I started by identifying the debaters named in the opening *"Report."* They were all male, solid citizens, adults ranging in age from thirty to fifty-eight, most of them relatives of my great-grandmother. They included a member of the state legislature ("E. C.," Enoch C. Farrington, age thirty-five), the East Fryeburg postmaster (businessman Asa O. Pike, age forty-four), one of the three Fryeburg selectmen (Seymour C. Hobbs, age fifty-eight), and a lawyer from the neighboring town of Lovell (John F. Hobbs, age thirty). Of the men named in the article, the president of the lyceum, Hiram Kelsey Hobbs, age thirty-one, had the least public prominence. The roster of men involved in the hogs episode added more solid citizen neighbors: Fryeburg farmers James Wheelock Ripley Farrington (a former Union Army general, age sixty-one), Isaac Abbott (age forty-four), Franklin L. Hobbs (Abbot's neighbor, age forty-five), William G. Walker (a deacon, age thirty-three), and Albion P. Gordon (age thirty-four), Maria Gordon's older brother and head of the household in which she and her parents resided. What writer, I wondered, had had sufficient status to tease these men?

And then a stroke of luck. Some other writings by John F. Hobbs, the Lovell lawyer, turned up in the collection of the Lovell Historical Society, and their handwriting matched three of the items in the *Toll Bridge Journal*: the *"Report of last Lyceum,"* the *"Notice"* of the *"scientific lecture upon the subject of hogology,"* and *"The last Epistle of John to the people of Toll Bridge."* The wry author of those droll pieces now had a name, and his comic strategy was distinctive. He had created himself as a character in each of his pieces: in the first, a self-satisfied office seeker and flawed debater; in the second, perhaps a relative of a pig, as *"he might consider the lecture personal"*; and in the third, the smug *"prophet John,"* a pompous, preaching know-it-all. Self-deprecating humor, then as now, is much appreciated in rural New England, and it would have been an especially apt tactic for a lawyer, who, with physicians and clergymen, would have belonged to the neighborhood's tiny intelligentsia. To claim respect for his status would have isolated John Hobbs from his neighbors; to laugh at himself and his pretensions would have cemented his kinship. The canny lawyer preempted the arguments of the opposition.

Maria Eliza Gordon, whose handwriting established her as the author of the *Journal*'s final teasing verses, was twenty-one years old and single in March 1870, living in the family farmhouse in Toll Bridge. Her name had been mentioned only once in the sewn-together *Journal* I had found, but her older brother Albion was a central player in the hog story, and the document had been stored in Maria's attic. Clearly, the Gordon family had some strong connection to the lyceum and the *Journal*, but I needed to know more. By itself, the conundrum in the *Journal* told me nothing about Maria.

> What kind of curency does Maria Gordon deal in.
> (ans) Harrimans—poor cash
> (Harriman Poor Cash)

Then a box from that Fryeburg attic yielded another treasure: Maria's little diary for 1870, laconic but crucial. I turned to it for clues.

Not yet married or engaged to be, Maria, by her own diary's account, had a lively social life. Even in harsh winter weather, nearly every evening brought visitors to the family farm, and enough visitors meant a party. "Bill Walker and Amelia and Ally came up and Sam and Owen Abbott and John came down. We had to dance a little" (Thursday, February 3). Sometimes she sounded like a giggly schoolgirl. When her friend Eliza Wiley came for an overnight visit, she wrote, "I hope it won't storm tomorrow and Eliza and I shall have a beau: won't it be neat?" (Saturday, January 8). But as she reported the next day, they were disappointed: "Eliza and I have been over to Uncle Wilson's. We didn't have any beaux" (Sunday, January 9).

Maria certainly played the field. The *Journal's* riddle punned on the names of three of the young men whose company she enjoyed. She saw a good deal of eighteen-year-old John Harriman, who was living as a farm laborer at the home of her neighbor Henry Walker. A frequent visitor, he came over for a dance party at the Gordon house on January 18 ("Had a neat time," Maria told her diary). Twenty-year-old Laroy Poor, who lived next door to Maria's friend Eliza in nearby Sweden, Maine, was another favored companion, as

FIGURE 6. The Gordon farmstead. Albion Gordon, his wife Harriet, and possibly his sister Maria stand in the front yard. Undated photograph, with a note on the back: "What 'the Farm' looked like *after* 1870 with shed connecting house to stable." Private collection.

was Cassius Pike of East Fryeburg (the "Cash" mentioned in the conundrum).

> *Laroy was here today went home about 8 o'clock P.M. Cassius*
> *Pike came in here a little while. He is real neat. He says take*
> *the will for the deed. (Kiss). (Sunday, January 30)*

The anonymous Toll Bridge author of the conundrum was tweaking Maria about her flirtatiousness—and was probably justified.

Maria's 1870 diary made it clear that she was indeed involved in the lyceum and the *Journal*.

> *Had a Lyceum tonight quite a lot there. Annie Pray and I had*
> *a neat time. I am intending to read the Paper next Saturday*
> *evening. Didn't have any tonight. (Saturday, February 5)*

So the "Paper"—the *Toll Bridge Journal*—could be "read" (aloud, evidently) by a woman at the lyceum, and Maria would be responsible for the next performance. Her role meant enough to her that she mentioned it among her characteristically terse diary entries and chronicled the steps along the way. Her responsibilities during the week before she read the paper apparently included both writing her own pieces and collecting compositions from other *"Toll Bridge contributors to the Journal"* (as the *"Report of last Lyceum"* put it):

> *I went down to Kelsey's tonight: (meeting). Went to bed about 1*
> *o'clock. I had a very pleasant time, wrote a peice for the paper.*
> *(Monday, February 7)*

> *I got some peices for my paper. (Thursday, February 10)*

When the anticipated reading took place, Maria reported it (with her usual succinctness) among the other notable social and meteorological events of the day.

> *Rec'd a letter from Lizzie. Stormed this morn. Cleared off before*
> *noon. Sullivan and Frank and Bell and Gustie Wiley came over*

here. Had a very good Lyceum. I read the paper. Palmer Walker
buried today. (Saturday, February 12)

Maria was not the only Toll Bridge woman involved with the
paper. Apparently responsibility for production of the *Journal*
rotated in the neighborhood.

Eliza read the paper at the Lyceum. Wind blew like fury
the first of the evening. Wasn't many people at the Lyceum.
(Saturday, February 26)

Maria's diary mentioned no men in connection with reading
or preparing the paper.

Maria seems to have kept the written *Journal* at her home
after the lyceum rather than, perhaps, passing it around in
the community or placing it in some hypothetical lyceum
archive. On Sunday, February 27, she wrote "Sam Frye in here
and stopped to dinner. I read my paper to him." (This would
probably have been the paper she had created for the February
12 lyceum.) I noticed that she had *read* it *to* Sam; she didn't hand
him the issue for his own perusal. Perhaps it was important
that the paper be an aural experience?

Evidently the Toll Bridge Lyceum was a regular Saturday
event in the winter months, for it was noted in Maria's diary
through the middle of March, even by omission. "Didn't have
any Lyceum" (Saturday, February 19). She remarked on her
attendance. "I came over to the Lyceum" (Saturday, March 5).
And when she didn't go, she indicated why. The death of her
cousin Willard Barker on Saturday, March 12, kept her away.
"Cassius Pike came up this morning and told us of Willard's
death. I didn't go to the Lyceum."[2]

The diary made it clear that the weekly winter lyceum was
not the only community event that Maria Gordon enjoyed.
Like most rural New Englanders, she loved social occasions—
year round, but particularly on long winter evenings. Her
diary chronicled a dazzling array of events. Winters brought
casual gatherings for fiddling and dancing and sledding, for-
tunetelling and euchre, endless visiting and overnight stays

with friends—but also more formal, if homegrown institutions. All occasions, even those that were ostensibly educational, gave her social opportunities. Her 1870 diary mentioned several wintertime "spelling schools" (essentially, adult spelling bees); usually she commented "Had a nice time" and once "lots of people and we had lots of fun" (Tuesday, January 11). When one of the ubiquitous traveling writing masters came to Toll Bridge in early March and offered a month-long "writing school"—a course for adults in improving handwriting—Maria attended regularly and again found social bonuses in the occasion. "I went to the writing school and saw Laroy and I was pleased. He was neat as a pin. I hope we shall make a go of it" (Tuesday, March 22).

Like the lyceums, spelling and writing schools took place in the evening at the Toll Bridge schoolhouse. During the day Maria kept school in the same building. Like many unmarried young women in New England at the time, Maria taught at the nearby one-room schools—usually at the Toll Bridge schoolhouse where she herself had been educated, but she also occasionally hired out to schools in nearby districts and boarded with local families. By 1870 she had been teaching school for at least four years—possibly, ever since she herself had finished her own studies at the Toll Bridge school. Her diary entries about teaching school ran in habitual veins: how she traveled to school in bad weather, whether or not she had kept school on a particular day, when she "commenced" and finished school terms, her eager anticipation of the end of the term. Never was there any mention of pedagogy or any indication that she thought of teaching as either a profession or a particular intellectual challenge; it was simply a job, an expected role. Her testimony validates Margaret Nelson's analysis of women's school teaching in the nineteenth century as often a rite of passage, a signal that a woman "had completed her own education and was now ready for marriage."[3]

To judge from her diary, Maria found school teaching most notable for its social pleasures—again, education mixed with amusement. Only one kind of school-day event received any mention: visiting. She noted the periodic inspection calls of the local school committee, but her major interest was in the frequent social visits. Friends and neighbors seem to have stopped by the schoolhouse every few days; some even stayed for hours, though Maria did not mention how they passed their time (observing? assisting? chatting?).

> *Hazen and Gustie Wiley called to the schoolhouse. (Friday, January 14)*

> *Enoch Farrington and Charlotte into school this P.M. (Saturday, January 29)*

And on an especially busy day:

> *All the neighbors were into school this afternoon. Had quite a good time. (Tuesday, March 1)*

FIGURE 7. Toll Bridge schoolhouse, District 13, Fryeburg, Maine. Undated photograph. Courtesy of the Fryeburg Historical Society.

She seems to have judged these school visits by their social value:

> *Had company in school but they want [weren't] of much*
> *account so I won't say anything about them. (Saturday, Jan-*
> *uary 8)[4]*

Some events recurred weekly in Maria's diary. During term, she kept school Monday through Saturday unless prevented by weather or illness. Lyceums came every Saturday evening, though only in the winter months; she mentioned none in 1870 between mid-March and December. On many Wednesday evenings throughout the year she attended "circles," each time at the home of a different family in the neighborhood.

> *I went to the circle with Frank Barker up to Thomas McIntires.*
> *We had a nice time. Lots of pretty folks there. Rode home in*
> *a sleigh. (Wednesday, January 26)*

> *I went to the circles. Had a splendid time. Laroy was there he*
> *and I went over to see Mother. Had a pleasant walk. We had*
> *a nice chat. (Wednesday, March 23)*

Beyond generalities ("nice time," "pretty folks") and the mention of a few neighbors and beaux, Maria did not describe the circles in her diary. But in that box of miscellaneous manuscripts from the Fryeburg attic I found a piece—in John Hobbs's handwriting and very likely written for another issue of the *Toll Bridge Journal*—headed *"Toll Bridge Jan 21st 1869,"* in which the writer proposed *"to give you a succinct account of the circle which assembled at Mr Charles Chandlers on Wednesday last."* In a familiar, friendly, and arch tone, the writer painted a vivid picture of young people's courting and social life.

> *First when your contributor arrived the First Table was partak-*
> *ing of the repast which was provided by the several members*
> *of the circle. . . .*

> *The table was again spread and the younger craft appeared*
> *with an exceedingly good appetite all striving to ascertain by*
> *the victuals who was the best Cook.*

But the *"younger craft"* were not solely intent upon the menu.

> *Second When your contributor arrived the young people was*
> *all congregated in the sitting Room enjoying a social chat more*
> *especially Hiram who had Hannah Chase in close proximity*
> *and talking all the soft language that he was master of pres-*
> *ently he changed his base of action by an onslaught on Gustie*
> *Wiley which he conducted with his accustomed shrewdness*
> *and won laurels in the undertaking.*[5]

(Here was another dart directed at Maria's bachelor cousin Hiram Kelsey Hobbs, at whose *"majestic person"* the writer of *"Report of last Lyceum"* had chuckled.)[6]

> *Third After supper they commenced to play. Charlotte filled*
> *the house Flora Temple like with her beautiful voice seconded*
> *by Hirams base [sic] which made a beautiful air which caused*
> *the assembled multitude to choose their partners quick and*
> *kiss with a good deal of gusto.*[7]

As new guests arrived, the party became more enthusiastic (*"caused by the addition of girls"*) and *"things passed off in splendid style."* The writer made roguish allusions to *"a horrible conspiracy . . . contrived to take place in a certain play and it was fully developed Oh shame where is thy blush."* (As with the hog-disease episode in the March 12 *Journal*, no doubt the listeners of this piece were already in on the joke.) Lively description of the young people's maneuvers to evade their parents and travel home with particular escorts was followed by expressions of thanks to the circle's hosts, Mr. and Mrs. Chandler, and *"Also to our efficient Collector Mrs Hattie G. Gordon."*

That phrase brought me around again to the lyceum, the probable audience for this piece. Hattie Gordon—Albion's wife, Maria's sister-in-law—acting as the week's editor of the *Toll Bridge Journal*, must have been collecting pieces for the paper at the circle. The account of the circle meeting at the Chandlers' house put one more small piece into my puzzle about the *Journal*: the maintenance of the neighborhood's literary endeavors was woven into social gatherings. This friendly community of farmers, courting youth, and neighbors was, at the same time, a community of authors, bringing their compositions to *"our efficient Collector"* in hopes of hearing them read to the lyceum on the following Saturday evening.

By the time I had made my way through the stitched-together issue of the *Toll Bridge Journal* and the account of the circle, meanwhile poking into genealogy, census data, maps, and Maria Gordon's diary for clues, I had glimpsed an energetic, sociable neighborhood surrounding my great-grandmother's family. I had discovered, in the Toll Bridge Lyceum, fellowship among young and old, men and women—fellowship marked not only by an established tradition of teasing but also by moral and social beliefs so seriously shared that they, too, gained equal public hearing in the *Journal*. From the articulate writing in the *Journal* I had gained respect for the quality of education provided in the common schools—whatever critiques might have been leveled at the system by those 1870 debaters and however little the project of teaching might have delighted the young Maria Gordon. I had admired a culture of adults weaving together forensics and courting, play and self-improvement. I had witnessed a community that tolerated its members' flaws and blunders—indeed, that celebrated them as occasions for public literary comedy, perhaps to take the sting out of blunders or to administer lighthearted warnings about misbehavior that, in a close neighborhood, might otherwise have festered uncomfortably. Most impressive of all was how the existence of the *Journal* testified to rural people's commitment to writing of all sorts and genres and to a belief that their own daily lives could be the stuff of literary composition.

CHAPTER 2

"A CROWN OF WISDOM WEAVE"

The Rural Lyceum Tradition

Our Lyceum we love so well,
That from our homes we joy to come,
Though storms and tempests round us swell,
And winds our distant mountains hum.
'Tis here we'll educate our minds
And here, a crown of wisdom weave,
And here we hope some good to find
Upon this merry Christmas eve.

—*Experiment* (Landaff, NH) 2, no. 6,
December 24, 1852

The Toll Bridge Lyceum turned out to be typical of hundreds of village societies scattered across Maine, New Hampshire, Vermont, and rural Massachusetts—the first hint of a huge array. Those societies were quintessentially local; perhaps it would be more accurate to call them neighborhood lyceums because members' homes tended to cluster in the vicinity of the one-room schoolhouses in which they held their meetings. They belonged to the hill towns, the hamlets of scattered farmsteads, the out-of-the-way districts rather than the bustling commercial town centers.[1] (Characteristically, Maria Gordon's lyceum was in the Toll Bridge neighborhood at the northern edge of Fryeburg, not near the town's business center.) Sometimes lyceum writers acknowledged this remoteness with ruefulness, pride, or deadpan humor. *"We meet on a cold & bleak spot,"* acknowledged a Dublin, New Hampshire, writer.[2] A piece submitted to an 1849 lyceum paper in tiny East Andover, New Hampshire, included this wry geographic summary:

> *East Andover occupies a central position among several locali-*
> *ties on either side in fact four roads here meet at right angles so*
> *that it has a direct communication with places of importance*
> *in all directions, Portland and London on the east Boston*
> *& Rio Janerio on the south Buffalo & Astoria on the west*
> *Stewartstown and Quebec on the north.*

The writer went on to catalogue the population of East Andover
with seemingly straightforward local statistics:

> *East Andover has nearly the form of a square being 1½ miles in*
> *extent on either side consequently it contains 2¼ square miles.*
>   *It has a population 200 there being about 89 to the square*
> *mile. The number of legal voters is 50 about ½ Democrats 310*
> *Whigs and 15 Free soil men. It contains 44 dwelling houses*
> *which accommodate 49 families 45 married men and 46 mar-*
> *ried ladies 10 widows 2 widowers 6 ladies and 7 gentlemen on*
> *the cold side of thirty 13 bright marriagable girls 10 young gents*
>   *It has one doctor 1 lawyer 1 law student 3 ministers 4 Esqrs*
> *2 Colonols 1 major 4 captains 4 practical shoemakers several*
> *occasional workers 8 carpenters and cabinetmakers 1 mill right*
> *2 millers 2 tanners 1 stone cutter 1 bricklaer 2 coopers 1 sailor 3*
> *job takers 2 blacksmiths 1 gunsmith 1 silver smith 1 merchant 1*
> *clerk 1 postmaster 3 section men 3 seamstresses 1 dress maker 1*
> *dealer in marble 2 hunters 1 traveling periodical and book agent*
> *3 local newspaper agents 3 California adventurers 1 collier 1*
> *horse trader 20& [?] farmers.*[3]

With a few adjustments—and allowing for the probability that
individuals might practice multiple vocations—this reckoning
might be typical of most of the villages that generated lyceums.
Precise demography is elusive today, however, because the
lyceum memberships did not fall within politically delineated
boundaries.

Although neighbors of different ages took part in the rural
lyceums, young adults were the prime movers. The men and
women who signed the pledge at the beginning of the 1870

constitution of the West Plymouth (NH) Literary Association—
indicating that they were the founders—ranged in age from
twelve to twenty-five. Eager for social occasions on the long
winter evenings, caught up in the national passion for self-
improvement, and well aware of the advantages of combining
intellectual life with opportunities to meet the opposite sex,
youths in farming hamlets regularly threw their energies into
"getting up" lyceums. "Aren't we going to have a Lyceum this
year?" asked the editor of the *Bridgton (ME) News*—a commercially published newspaper—in December 1858.

> Thanksgiving with its bodily enjoyment is over and we
> should now make preparations for more deeply rational
> and intellectual amusements. In a village like this, there
> are always people who eschew dancing and want more
> excitation than our ordinary daily life affords. The lecture
> room and the debating club meet these wants. . . . We
> are essentially social beings, and when we bring our
> individual heats and lights together, we help one another
> with our personal magnetisms and provoke thoughts by
> our inevitable antagonisms.[4]

Surviving record books show a remarkable uniformity in
the way in which lyceums were established and conducted.
No doubt founding documents were shared, exchanged, and
imitated in neighboring villages and carried from place to
place by travelers, but published handbooks were also readily available to prescribe and model all stages of a lyceum's
development. Charles Morley's popular *Guide to Forming and
Conducting Lyceums, Debating Societies, &c.* (1841) opens with
"Directions for Forming Societies":

> You who wish the advantages of a Lyceum or Debating
> Society in your village or town either for your own or
> others' benefit, call on your neighbours, propose the
> subject, state the objects of such a society, and obtain
> as many as you can to co-operate with you in this noble
> work. Appoint a meeting to organize a society—either

state to the audience the importance of such an institution or prevail on a clergyman, or some other influential individual, to do it—appoint a committee to draft a
constitution, or have one already prepared.[5]

Lyceum members, who loved narrating the histories of
their associations, sometimes embellished their founding
mythology. This tongue-in-cheek account of the origins of
the Literary Society of Fremont, New Hampshire, appeared
in that lyceum's paper in 1879:

First chapter of Chronicles

*In the year 1877 it entered into the heart of one Johnithan
whose sir name is Robinson, to start a Literary Society, to
make more liberal provisions for the strengthening of the
understanding of the people in the town of Fremont. The
people immediately assembled themselves to gather into their
tent for instruction, and the result was a determinating to
find a temple whereunto the people might assemble to have
their ideas sharpened.*

*Now they employed a score of men, and commanded them
to erect a wing to the temple and they did as they were commanded and overlaid it with brass which shined like unto gold
exceedingly rich. Now when the temple was finished it was
noised abroad, and commandments were sent out through all
the town of Fremont and regions around about, Saying "come
all ye who take an interest in the cultivation of the understanding of the people, up to the Temple and have it dedicated unto
the purpose for which it is used." Behold at the appointed time
people were seen coming from the east and from the west, up
to the temple, till it was filled to an overflow and after much
speaking the multitude dispersed each one to their own house,
and the fame of it went out through all the country around.[6]*

The records of the West Plymouth Literary Association nar-
rate its organizing meeting with scrupulous and formal detail.

West Plymouth February 11th 1870

The Literary Association Meeting Opened at 6.1–2 [6:30] o'clock. . . . Mr. Ansel Davis was chosen as Moderator by Ballot. Mr. Chas. Drake to act as Secretary. Then the rest of the officers as follows by Nomination: Mr. Frank Jackson President Mr. George Clark Vice President. Mr. James Morse Editor. In the absence of the Ladies two Editors were chosen, Mr. Orrin Davis as the other. The Editors were Elected by Ballot. Mr. Chas. Drake was appointed to make out the Constitution and Bylaws with power to substitute another to help him Mr. Chas. Morrill was substituted. Voted to take up a collection to purchase a blank book for the use of the Secretary and get the rest in paper. The collection ammounted to fifty seven cents wich was handed to Mr. Clark to purchase the same. Voted that each one on becoming a member should pay five cts. Voted that we should furnish our own lights. Voted that every member should write a piece for the paper. Voted that each one should invite as many of their friends to join us as they wished to. Voted that we meet at Mr. Morrill's next Wednesday. Adjourned at 8.1–2 o'clock.

C. E. Drake, Secretary

The first organizing step for any lyceum was to create a formal constitution. The officious formalities of government had strong appeal. *"Our first Lyceum,"* wrote a member of the West Plymouth Literary Association, *"commenced on the 11th of February 1870 with Chas. Morrell as chairman under a constitution and bylaws that would cover several pages of foolscap, which were of the strictest kind but after a few evenings we became so united that we were convinced that a great many of them were needless and so they remain a dead letter to this day."*[7] Templates for constitutions and bylaws abounded. Morley's manual opened with one and even suggested a generic preamble:

> We, the undersigned, believe with the wise man, that "Wisdom is the principal thing; that she is more precious

than rubies; and that all things that can be desired are not
worthy to be compared with her;" and in order to store
our minds with it, and for mutual improvement, as well
as the diffusion of useful knowledge, we form ourselves
into a Society for these noble purposes; and agree to be
governed by the following Constitution and By-laws.[8]

Each actual lyceum shaped its constitution somewhat differently, but all were variations on the standard theme.

Those who took the initiative to "get up" a lyceum—to
write the constitution and bylaws, to lead meetings—were
a predictable group. Some of the men who took the most
conspicuous parts—that is, were mentioned in the regional
newspapers or listed as founders, officers, or debaters in lyceum
record books—were village leaders or youths who may have
aspired to future prominence. Although most of the forty-
one signatories of the 1870 constitution and bylaws of the
West Plymouth Literary Association were in their teens and
twenties, three older members had already served as town
selectmen, and the younger members included several children of selectmen, a state legislator, and town clerks as well
as four future selectmen. When the Fremont Literary Society
was founded in the fall of 1877, its organizers were young men
in their twenties and thirties. Alden F. Sanborn, chosen as the
first president, was twenty-two years old at the time and still
lived and worked on his father's farm; in later years he served
as selectman, town moderator, state legislator, school superin-
tendent, and tax collector. Andrew J. Brown, age twenty-three
at the time and likewise farming with his father, later became
town postmaster. Cyrus Gove, age thirty-three, a wheelwright,
was also an active member of the Fremont community, serving on the first board of library trustees, as supervisor for the
voting checklist, and as town auditor. (Other founders, no
doubt connected with Gove, also were in the carriage-making
business—Clarence A. Cilley, age twenty-three, a carriage
painter, and George and Charles Whittier, ages thirty and
thirty-six, both wheelwrights.)

Village democracy was not entirely comfortable with the elite ambitions of the lyceum organizers. Maintaining balance between the desire for intellectual improvement and the belief that improvement should be available to all was not easy, as the founders of the West Plymouth lyceum discovered when they tried, at the outset, to keep their meetings exclusive.

> One of the features of the past was, that we should have our gatherings private, that is, no one but that had the password and signal could be admitted and so a guard was chosen to admit the members but at one time the door was forced, Ben Butler style, owing of course to insufficient police regulation, and being denied our rights we retired to a private house and were not molested any further that evening.
>
> Of course such tradegies could not be countenanced a great while and either we must read the riot act and enforce the law or open the door and let every one in which we did thinking no doubt that discretion was the better part of valor.[9]

Such ill-fated attempts at exclusivity were rare; rural lyceums, even those connected to local academies, generally opened their meetings to the public. There might be detractors. *"Thus blest are we in pure delight / Secluded from the scoffers sight,"* wrote the editors of Landaff, New Hampshire's, lyceum paper, describing the pleasure of attending the meetings despite some local derision.[10] Joining and participating in lyceums was a matter of individual choice and responsibility. *"When we have an opportunity to learn what will do us or others good and we let those opportunities pass unimproved, we are criminal in such neglect,"* the organizers of the South Freeport (ME) Mutual Improvement Society proclaimed, encouraging neighbors to join the new association.[11] Catherine Kelly observed that, in rural areas, where well-to-do and poorer people knew one another as neighbors, class differences rarely became sources of strife, thanks to "an etiquette of social proximity."[12]

Winter lyceums in fact attracted a spectrum of the population that extended well beyond the politically or professionally ambitious. The majority of the attendees were members of farm families, leavened by the families of merchants and "mechanics"—skilled craftsmen such as blacksmiths, cabinet-makers, coopers, carriagemakers, and the like. Local clergy, lawyers, schoolteachers, and doctors often took part in the debates or delivered occasional lectures. Yet the intelligentsia were not exempt from a little democratic ribbing, as this example from the record book of the Shirley (MA) Institute, December 31, 1867, demonstrates: "Essay by Rev. Seth Chandler [a long-time member]. On Motion of Rev. E. Robbins, voted to extend a vote of thanks to the Rev. Mr. Chandler for his clean collar & wristbands, together with the main body of his Essay. (Carried unanimously.)" Participation below the "middling" classes was rare. Unless they were offspring of local farmers, laborers and servants rarely took part, paupers never. Given the demographic homogeneity of the northern New England hamlets, it is not surprising that Anglo-Americans prevailed in the lyceums. But the lyceum was recognized as a path to improvement; and in a few villages adjacent to mining or manufacturing areas, children of immigrants were mentioned in the lyceum proceedings. In the West Rutland (VT) Lyceum in 1860, for instance, one active participant was thirteen-year-old Eddy O'Brien. According to the census, his father was an Irish stonecutter, and his two sisters were domestic servants.

The energy to establish and sustain a lyceum generally came from young and mainly unmarried men, so it is no surprise that they saw the participation of women as crucial to the success of their societies. In the lyceum record books the opening membership rolls were usually signed by "Ladies" as well as "Gentlemen." Sometimes women were involved as founders; sometimes their participation was solicited soon afterward. The December 12, 1857, bylaws of the Chester (VT) Village Lyceum state that "any male may become a member," but also stipulate that "the President shall weekly appoint two ladies to prepare and read an original paper at the next regular meeting." A mere week later, on December 19, the lyceum members passed their first amendment: "Any lady may become a member of this society by signing the constitution and shall have the privilege of voting."[13] Occasionally tensions between the sexes were more obvious. When the youthful male founders of the Dublin (NH) Young People's Society for Mutual Improvement gathered in 1837 to draw up a constitution, they apparently neglected to invite "the ladies" to join in this activity. A "stormy debate" among the organizers resulted, and the lapse was noted with painstaking apologies in a subsequent history of the society:

> At length however a meeting was called for the purpose of organizing a Society and adopting a Constitution. But it so happened that in notifying this meeting which was done verbally the individual neglected particularly to request the ladies to attend. This omission was not because the gentlemen were determined to transact all the business themselves without even consulting the wishes of the ladies (who were expected to constitute a very important portion of the Society both with respect to numbers and ability) nor was it because their presence would be undesirable but an opinion was entertained that it would be more agreeable to them to be excused from taking a part in the laborious duties of legislation and it was thought that they would not be disposed to find fault with such a Constitution as the gentlemen might adopt provided it required nothing unreasonable of them. Whether the wisest course was taken may perhaps admit of a question but it was a course dictated by no bad motives.[14]

Women members moved into greater and greater responsibilities in the lyceums as the century wore on.

Just as participants of both sexes were essential to the rural lyceums, so, too, were young and old. In 1878 the editor of the *Monitor*, the manuscript paper of the East Cabot (VT) Debating Club, boasted of his lyceum's intergenerational history:

> *The Father of Sixty was often followed by the son of Twelve and openly criticized in debate. Each one was eager and earnest in dabate, and anxious that their side should win. Old*

oriters that had lain dorment since the war came quickly to
the front, and so lofty were their flights in oritory that the
rocks by the wayside wept tears of frost in reverance to them
as they passed on their way home, and the school boy searched
all the old books for facts to use in argument, and thus our
Lyceum became a success.

Intergenerational lyceum activity in Dublin, New Hampshire, followed an unusual path. The young adults of Dublin established the Young People's Society for Mutual Improvement in 1837 in response to the success of what Thaddeus Perry Mason, its first president (at age twenty), referred to in his diary as "the old people's society"—the Dublin Lyceum. Young and old people's societies were complementary from the start: they met in alternate weeks, and their members often attended both events. By early 1838 they were taking part in each other's debates and contributing to each other's papers.

Single young men and women of marriageable age, young married couples, older school pupils, and older men in the community made up the active body of the typical rural lyceum; in addition, older women, married or single, might serve as editors of the paper. Mrs. Katie Shaw, age twenty-five, editress of the January 22, 1877, issue of the *Veazie (ME) Light*, humorously directed her editorial not only to *"Ladies, Gentlemen, boys, girls, & babies too (if there are any here),"* but also to *"particularly the Village Doctor, the village schoolmaster, the village Barber, the village Blacksmith & all the village Coopers."* Record books document the age range of lyceum participants. In Fremont, the supporting elder citizen of the group—not mentioned as a founder but nonetheless chosen as vice president—was Jonathan A. Robinson, age fifty-six, a prominent businessman who owned mills and was also involved in the carriage business. At the first meeting of the Fremont Literary Society, a senior Congregationalist minister was asked to make the opening address. The demographics in Fremont were not unusual among village lyceums: community elders lent support, while the work of organizing fell to younger men. Because siblings within a household tended to attend the lyceum together, younger children were often present. Among the forty-one signatories of the 1870 West Plymouth Literary Association constitution and bylaws were multiple siblings from seventeen different families. Two ten-year-old boys were included, each attending in the company of his father. Membership was open to older common-school pupils. *"No person shall become a member of this Society who is not over twelve years of age,"* declared article 10 of the 1861 Constitution of the Denmark (ME) Lyceum, but there was never an upper limit. The roster of that lyceum does indeed include a couple of twelve-year-olds, but members' ages ranged up to sixty. The forty-six identifiable participants in the 1888–89 activities of the small Union Debating Club of West Deerfield, Massachusetts, spanned the ages of ten to seventy but their average age was twenty-eight. Of these forty-six, ten were women: two wives, ages twenty-nine and thirty-six, attending with their husbands, and eight single women and girls between ten and twenty years of age. The advantages of intergenerational membership were often explicitly appreciated. The Thornton, New Hampshire, correspondent to the *Grafton County Journal* commented:

> The Mad River Literary society held its weekly meeting. . . . One feature in the weekly gatherings is prominent, the old and young take an active part in the exercises, which are kept up to a high standard; for nothing vulgar or debasing is tolerated, and in fact the people that meet and take part are not of that stamp. Their aim and purpose in meeting together is improvement, to inculcate morality, virtue, and religion. (February 7, 1880)

Despite the serious intentions they so often piously intoned, other motives also animated lyceum-goers. Alice Cary's short story, "The Grand House and Its Owner," brings to life the assembly gathered in anticipation of the start of a lyceum:

> It was the custom to hold in the "brick schoolhouse," of winter evenings, what were termed "debating societies,"

the which all the heads of families about, sometimes accompanied by their sons and daughters, attended. . . .

What a din there was in the house! Big boys whispering half aloud to each other; young ladies talking in a low key; the old men comparing notes as to the size and value of favorite colts, the quantity and quality of wheat harvested the last summer, or discussing politics and religion; the young men as yet remained about the door, whittling the fence, or trying the mettle of one another's horses.[15]

Neighborhood lyceums generally met in the local schoolhouse, a space that was secular and nonsectarian and emblematic of mental improvement and democratic opportunity. As the Reverend DeWitt Talmadge rhapsodized in 1860 in the *Maine Teacher and School Officer,*

The Schoolhouse.—The schoolhouse is the symbol of the people's culture. For defense, it is better than fortifications of rock, better than batteries to guard the harbors, than armies to defend our treasuries, than navies to guard our seas. More learned institutions may and ought to be established, but the schoolhouse must never be neglected.[16]

Schoolhouses were not ample spaces, but they were well loved nonetheless. In 1865 a reporter for the *Vermont Record* presented a paean to "An Old Fashioned Lyceum," writing from what he evidently felt was a more modern, sophisticated, urban perspective. He was startled to notice how well the audience attended both to the proceedings and to social opportunities.

We can conscientiously advise any one who wishes to see a bona-fide old fashioned lyceum, to step into Centerville school-house some pleasant Monday evening and take a seat near the door where he can be sure of an occasional breath of fresh air. We had the pleasure of being present at a recent meeting of this society, and confess that we were agreeably disappointed in the general appearance of the assembly, and the evident interest manifested in the exercises.

The paper, edited and read by ladies, the declamations, and the debate, all commanded commendable attention, and all who took active part, either by appointment or voluntarily, did so with that apparent good faith and preparation, which is the real life of such an institution. The little school-room was crowded to its utmost capacity, in the regular Yankee style, with the ladies on one side and the gentlemen on the other—thus affording ample opportunity for that innocent pastime,—"casting sheep's eyes," among the younger and more impressible portion of the audience. It is a matter of serious regret that there are not better accommodations for the lyceum, for it is an institution which cannot fail to exert a healthful influence in a community, and which merits the hearty support it evidently receives.

The Vermont reporter noted that the behavior of the young boys needed monitoring.

(N.B. Nervous old bachelors, and old maids who are inclined to faint or be hysterical, are seriously advised not to visit the Centerville Lyceum, because the boys who are present in large numbers, will applaud anything that gratifies them, or touches their risibles, with the most vociferous stamping and clapping,—the shrillest whistles, and the most demoniacal yells. Young America revels in a babel of noises, and don't like to be defrauded of its right to applaud, but the officers of the lyceum ought to control its irrepressibility a little.)[17]

Edward Calver quotes the 1867–72 record book of the Heath, Massachusetts, lyceum: "Whether the cause [of the behavior] was cold feet, monotony, or enthusiasm, 'On the motion of Rev. W. H. Adams it was voted that the stamping of feet as demonstrations of applause be ruled out of order.'"[18]

Given the youth of some of the members, keeping order in the lyceum could sometimes be a challenge. The cover sheet of one of the issues of the *Firefly*, paper of the North Fayette, Maine, lyceum, states its terms: *"A still house & no peanut cracking."* The constitution-happy founders of lyceums attempted to legislate proper behavior. "Any member guilty of indecorum may be expelled by a vote of 2⁄3 of the members present at any legal meeting."[19] Most of the evidence points to young schoolboys as the indecorous culprits. In Enoch Emory's 1872 novel *Myself: A Romance of New England Life*, the narrator, a native of "a sparsely populated town in the interior of New Hampshire," presents a lively scene from his boyhood in a chapter entitled "How we mobbed the 'Jeffersonian Atheneum and Jackson Debating Club,' and what came of it." Because the schoolboys in the debating society did not have "sufficient employment," "we took to mischief," he explains, first placing nutshells under chairs so that they cracked loudly, then throwing and snapping shells at the chairman and speakers during the sessions. Finally, the major disrupters were turned out of the building.[20] Reporting on a meeting of the West Plymouth Lyceum in 1880, the *Grafton County Journal* correspondent ended his account with a wry allusion to such behavior. The question for debate, he reported, was "Resolved, That corporal punishment should be abolished in our homes and in our schools. James Penniman and N. D. Melven made some strong points in favor of abolition, but their young opponents, Charles Drake and Charles Chase gained a favorable decision from the judges. The corps of small boys in the rear of the hall may be accountable in some measure for this decision."[21] Papers hinted at other behavioral issues as well. A concluding editorial in the Dublin paper, *Ladies' Miscellany*, sniffed, *"We know that great improvement can be made if the right course is pursued. In order to do this we are not to come here to see, and be seen, & in addition to this, spend our time in whispering, but it is highly necessary that we should take an interest in the various exercises."*[22]

West Plymouth [NH]   Dec 11th 1879

The meeting was oppened by the
President J. A. Penniman
report was read by the Secretary

Extemporaneous Debate Question
Resolved that Education prevents
crime.

      Fred McIntosh } Affirmative
      N. D. Melvin }
Disputants
      Orrin Fletcher } Negative
      J. S. Blodgett }

      {L. S. Gordon
Judges {T. J. Adams
      {Mrs. S. M. Morse

Merits of Argument decided in
favor of the Affirmative.

Recitation by Gracie McIntosh

Intermission of 15 minutes

Declamation by C. E. Quincy
entitled Curfew must not
ring tonight

The Gem of the Valley was read
by the Editress Miss Mary Sargent

      Officers for the next
evening

For President   F. P. Morse
"   Secretary   C. H. Perkins
"   Editress   Mrs. S. M. Morse

      C. H. Perkins
         Secretary

As with constitutions and bylaws, the order of business in rural lyceums was similar everywhere, as documented in the record books passed from secretary to secretary. The gathering opened with the reading of the proceedings of the previous meeting. Various minor literary exercises might occur in different parts of the evening, including select readings, declamations and recitations (performances of memorized oratorical or literary texts), or prepared theatrical dialogues. Suitable texts were readily available in contemporary anthologies and in school readers. Lyceum members might also read essays of their own composition. Occasionally, distinguished men in the community or visitors—ministers, lawyers, doctors—were invited to deliver lectures. Brief musical performances could also be part of the proceedings. The centerpiece of the evening, however, was the "discussion" of the "question"—a formal debate on a resolution that had been announced at the previous meeting. Generally two assigned discussants on the affirmative and negative spoke first, and then the question was thrown open to arguments by volunteers from the audience. Decision was rendered by the president, by a board of judges, or by a vote of all present. (Sometimes two decisions were rendered: one on the merits of the argument, the other on the merits of the question.)

Meeting of Kenduskeag [ME] Literary Association, Town Hall, Kenduskeag, Oct. 18th 1884

Meeting called to order by President. The records of previous meeting were read and accepted. A collection was taken for the expenses of the society which amounted to $1.02. Miss Banks was appointed critic for next meeting. Having no other business on hand—proceeded to the discussion of the question—Resolved that the works of art are more pleasing than those of nature, which was opened by W. C. Spratt, on the affirmative. After listening to remarks on the negative, by T. W. Hodsdon,

the question was continued on the affirmative by Annie
Edgerly, on the negative by Fred Jenkins. As the other
disputants were not prepared, the question was opened
to the house, and Nellie Harvey and Miss Banks spoke
on the negative. Moved and seconded that the discussion
go back to disputants and remarks were again made by
the first gentleman on each side of the question, after
which it was decided by vote in the negative.

Recess.

The remaining entertainment was as follows. Song,
entitled "Grandfathers Mule" by Ernest H., Fred Dolliver,
Kilburn Sweet, Lillie Spratt, Emma Hall, and Edna Harvey.
Reading of paper by Mrs. Shaw and Mr. Brady. Song by
Mr. and Mrs. Frank Harvey and Nellie. The report of programme by Ex. Com., and also that of critic being read
and accepted, voted to adjourn.

Toward the end of the meeting, the paper—an eagerly
anticipated highlight of the evening—was read aloud by its
editor. In some lyceums a "critic" was appointed to comment
on any shortcomings in the evening's exercises. Finally, the
resolution for the next meeting's debate was announced; the
next disputants, paper editor, and other participants were
chosen; and the lyceum was adjourned—releasing the attendees to their next social event: choosing the company for their
journeys home.

> And when 'twas finished and all was o'er
> We've lingered bashfully around the door
> And when that one of all the rest
> Had kindly granted our request
> Then up the horseback chill and bleak,
> We quickly turned our willing feet.[23]

From my examination of contemporary sources, I would
estimate that, had they wished, inhabitants of any small village

in northern New England could have attended a lyceum weekly, or at least fortnightly, during the winter months, either in their own hamlet or in one nearby. Lyceums in neighboring districts often supported each other. The West Gilsum, New Hampshire, columnist reported to the *Cold River Journal,* "Last Wednesday eve, several of the lyceum members paid a visit to the lyceum at the south part of the town. They have but just started, but are thoroughly in earnest, and the question, Resolved, That the Mechanic has benefited this country more than the Professional man, was discussed with more than ordinary ability."[24] Visitors from nearby neighborhoods were expected. Zuar Jameson of Irasburgh, Vermont, commented in his diary one night, with some disappointment: "Our lyceum was only an ordinary affair there were no persons from the other district to assist in the debates. . . . Our next one is to be on Tuesday evening so that we may go the common Wednesday to their Lyceum."[25] Some people not only attended but also took responsible part in more than one lyceum. In the winter 1861–62 season, several residents of Athol and Petersham, Massachusetts, served as officers in three separate groups: the Bennett Hill Lyceum in Petersham and the New Sherburne Literary Association and the Union Lyceum in school district 9 in Athol. Elbridge G. Chamberlin, a fifty-five-year-old farmer in Petersham, not only occupied several leadership positions but also, on occasion, edited the paper in each of the three. Although most lyceum attendees were drawn from a close neighborhood, some enthusiasts willingly traveled up to twenty miles—in the winter!—to take part.[26]

It was fortunate that people were disposed to travel some distance to visit lyceums because individual neighborhood lyceums did not always continue from year to year. The long gaps between winter seasons no doubt facilitated dissolution. The leaders might have moved to another town, married, had children, gone to war or taken up factory work or headed west; local associations for causes such as temperance or abolition might have consumed time and energy that would otherwise have gone into support of the lyceum. Lyceum maintenance in particular neighborhoods tended to be sporadic—a series of foundings and re-foundings over time, as a previous lyceum was remembered and reestablished. The *Grafton County Journal* (December 6, 1879) concluded a long description of a meeting of the West Plymouth Lyceum with the comment, "This is the third season that the people of West Plymouth have succeeded in keeping up the lyceum and they deserve much credit for their energy." That lyceum's paper, the *Gem of the Valley*, reported in 1878 that, since their inception in 1870, *"our Lyceums have been held from year to year with the exceptions of a few seasons, when from a lack of interest and not, as we believe, from a lack of talent they were discontinued."*[27] Lyceum record books often continued through several different renewals. The South Acworth, New Hampshire, record book shows that the lyceum started and stopped several times between 1850 and 1868, and each iteration involved creating a new constitution and frequently renaming the paper. The Tunbridge (VT) Lyceum record book runs from 1838 to 1844; toward the end of this period attendance became increasingly sparse until, at the last meeting, the minutes report that "not being members present sufficient to constitute a quorum the meeting adjourned sine die."[28] Some lyceums proved to be more durable than others. According to William Heywood, the Westminster (MA) Lyceum continued for at least twenty years, up until the Civil War. "The breaking out of the war turned the thoughts of the public into other channels, and claimed its energies for the promotion of other objects. As a consequence, the lyceum disappeared from view and was never in its old and proper form re-established, other agencies and activities coming in to fill, in part at least, the place it once so honorably occupied."[29]

Many other village lyceums, however, continued through the Civil War years despite massive disruptions, not least of which was the large number of young men from the northeast who enlisted and were lost. The war crisis was often the focus of debates. In February 1862, the Vergennes (VT) Lyceum debated *"Resolved,* That the Government should emancipate the slaves as the speediest way of ending the war." In April

1862, the Brandon (VT) Lyceum took up the question "*Resolved,
That immediate emancipation is our true national policy.*"
Debaters argued over difficult questions, often before rapt
audiences. For instance, when the Westminster West (VT)
Lyceum considered in February 1863 "that it would promote
the interest of the United States and the world, to at once
acknowledge the independence of the southern confederacy,"
the *Bellows Falls Times* reported that "so great was the interest
that they had an audience of some two hundred and fifty and
the contest was kept up for two nights on the same subject,
till half past ten o'clock."[30]

Establishing and maintaining a lyceum was laborious, but it
was a task embraced again and again by rural New Englanders,
wherever they happened to be, throughout the nineteenth
century. Northern troops carried lyceums into the Civil War
itself. The *Barre (VT) Gazette* informed readers that Reverend
Francis B. Perkins, formerly of Montague (in Bridgewater,
Vermont) and now chaplain in Vermont's Tenth Regiment,
had instituted not only prayer meetings, spelling schools, and
a singing school in the regiment but also Thursday evening
meetings of the Tenth Regiment Lyceum.[31] Like those other
institutions, the lyceum evoked home, normalcy, the community identities and connections that the young soldiers wanted
so dearly to maintain and defend. It would be hard to overstate
New Englanders' delight in their lyceums' blend of literary
performance, sociability, and organizational ritual.

CHAPTER 3

"THE GREAT WORK OF SELF-CULTURE"

Learning through Debate

Well did the sturdy farmer answer the traveler's
half contemptuous query, as to what were our
productions, "Well our land is rough and our soil
poor, so we build school-houses and raise men!"

—Reverend J. L. Merrill,
History of Acworth (NH) (1869)

Debating societies were nothing new in nineteenth-century
America. After English replaced Latin in the collegiate study
of rhetoric in the mid-eighteenth century, elocution—"the
science of delivery"—became an important academic subject.
Self-education and academic curriculum went hand in hand.
College students began to organize extracurricular literary
and debating societies focused on essay writing, forensics,
and oratory. Students at Harvard organized a debating society
as early as 1720; other clubs came along after 1750, including
the Linonia Literary and Debating Society at Yale and the
Cliosophic Society and American Whig Society at Princeton.
John Adams and Thomas Paine attributed their success as orators to such associations. By 1815 debating societies existed on
almost all college campuses, and many sponsored subsidiary
undertakings such as orations, recitations, dramatic skits, the
reading of compositions, and literary magazines.[1]

As academies were founded rapidly in New England in the
latter half of the eighteenth century, secondary students, too,
organized extracurricular forensic societies on the collegiate
model. In 1798 students at Leicester Academy in Massachusetts
created a Social Fraternity "calculated to promote the art of

speaking, and impress on the mind a sense of verbal propriety."
The constitution proclaimed that "the stated exercises of the
Society shall consist in composition, forensic disputation, and
declamation"; these tasks were to be apportioned to members
strictly in alphabetical order, by last name. The proceedings of
the Social Fraternity were to be kept secret, and no spectators
were admitted.

Out-of-school adults also took part in debating societies
to improve their oratorical and literary abilities. During the
colonial period literary clubs on the English model developed
in the larger coastal cities, serving an elite group of educated
men (often urban civic leaders or their sons) who wished
to polish their already accomplished rhetorical and literary
skills. In the early nineteenth century voluntary associations
for mutual improvement—the descendants of the colonial
societies—spread through the towns and cities of the northern
states. Typical was the Dracut (MA) Mutual Debating Society,
founded in 1829 and comprising "the most prominent and
influential men in the town."[2]

The antebellum period saw debating societies multiply all
over the country, open to a wide and not necessarily well educated public that wished to develop their minds. In December
1821, for instance, twenty-five young apprentices from local
businesses in Hallowell, Maine, organized a debating society to discuss "ingenious and useful subjects." Catching the
wave of the democratic desire for mental improvement, Josiah
Holbrook (perhaps building on his experience as a student at
Yale) founded the Millbury (MA) Lyceum in 1826 and went
on to establish the American Lyceum in 1831.[3] The lyceum
movement multiplied rapidly; Angela Ray estimates that,
by 1839, 4,000 to 5,000 lyceums had been established in the
United States. This popular national institution began as a
mutual education society that encompassed libraries, public
lectures, and debates, but by the 1840s it had become associated
more with prominent speakers and top-down instruction by
subscription—the lyceum circuit, the lyceum lecture system—
than with mutuality.

The quest for mental development extended well beyond the cities and major towns that supported the lecture lyceum circuit. In secondary schools in the countryside students routinely organized serious debating societies as extracurricular activities. Even when participation was restricted to students, the meetings of school forensic societies were almost always open to public attendance. Student societies often welcomed the participation of townspeople, and in some cases the participants were so interwoven that it is hard today to distinguish school from village lyceums. The East Andover (NH) Mountain Club, a village association, moved into the Highland Lake Institute when that academy was founded in 1850, and it served students as well as the community.[4] In October 1868, the pupils of the Dublin (NH) High School and their teacher established the Young People's Literary Association, which continued in the village at least until 1882 and became the Dublin Literary Association. In later years, the association's paper, the *Gazette*, was edited by older women in the community.[5] According to Lynne Benoit-Vachon, the same interpenetration of local and academic participation obtained at Limington Academy in Maine in midcentury: Catharine McArthur, a local woman who was not a student at the academy, was one of the editors of the debating club's newspaper. "The contents of the paper are miscellaneous pieces written by the scholars of the Academy and various other individuals," she wrote in a letter to her brother William.[6] The project of education in nineteenth-century America was less formal in its boundaries than it is today, and—as with the rural associations—it was often a matter of individual or community initiative.[7]

Democratic self-education was a major theme of the nineteenth century. Timothy Dwight, the president of Yale from 1795 to 1817, famously declared that republican America had "no peasants. . . . The ascent to better circumstances and higher stations is always open."[8] In the antebellum period no profession or occupation required an advanced or even a college degree; and among the middle and farming classes, young people were often unable to take much time away from family work for schooling. "The pursuit of knowledge under difficulties" was so much the norm that it was seen not as a detriment to education but as an ideal of life-long learning.[9] The epigraph from Joseph Abbott that opened all issues of the *Maine Normal*, a journal "Devoted to the Family and The School" that began publication in 1866, was typical: "The most successful student that ever left a school, or took his degree at college, never arrived at a good place to stop in his intellectual course." Indeed, one of the prime arguments for the necessity of common-school education was, in the words of a Vermont writer, that "the discipline of our common-schools qualifies our youth to profit by other means of public instruction."[10] Teachers were enjoined to keep this goal in view. When she proclaimed that "the initiation of the pupil into the great work of self-culture, by forming habits of earnest, persevering, and self-reliant exertion, is an important part of the teacher's mission," one Boston teacher envisioned her own part in an exalted educational chain:

> The whole school system is but a preparatory course of training for the great normal school of life, where friends, relatives, and promiscuous society are the teachers, and an all-wise Providence and a vigilant conscience, the disciplinarians; and the whole of life is but a period of self-education for the life to come. The teacher who fulfils her mission, desires her pupils not only to do well in school, but to do well through life; and strives to make them feel the necessity of their own earnest exertion and coöperation, if they would acquire an education that will prepare them for the great work of self-culture.[11]

The same sentiments were sometimes echoed in the papers of the rural lyceums:

How to educate one's self

The idea that schools are indispensable in acquiring knowledge is without foundation. All persons however situated may gain wisdom and knowledge every day, may add new treasures to

the intellect as often as earth revolves. . . . If any would educate
themselves they must be dependant on no teacher, minister,
doctor or lawyer; but must be all of these to themselves.[12]

Echoing the accepted wisdom and reflecting widespread
practice, the first issue of the *Vermont School Journal and Family
Visitor* featured an article on "Clubs and Associations" urging citizens to form societies for "individual and aggregated
improvement."[13] Reading and conversation were encouraged as
informal ways to increase individual knowledge, but oratorical
occasions of all sorts, and particularly debating societies, which
gave the opportunity to practice oratorical skills, were most
highly regarded. Oratory was intimately connected to the moral
as well as mental development of a speaker. Rhetoricians drew
no boundaries between the moral, emotional, and intellectual
qualities requisite for effective public speaking. According to
the 1857 manual *How to Talk*, those qualities were "good sense,
sound judgment, a strong sense of right, lively emotions, quick
perceptions, and clear and vivid conceptions, a powerful will,
perfect self-command, good taste, an adequate command of
language, the strictest mental discipline, and the highest culture
in every department of learning, and particularly in the art
and science of elocution."[14] American belief in the efficacy of
debating was grounded in the theories of Isaac Watts, whose
1741 treatise *The Improvement of the Mind* continued to be a staple
of American schools into the next century. Watts presented a
detailed analysis of forensic practice:

> XV. It must be confessed, there are some advantages to
> be attained by academical disputations. It gives vigour
> and briskness to the mind thus exercised, and relieves the
> languor of private study and meditation. It sharpens the
> wit and all the inventive powers. It makes the thoughts
> active, and sends them on all sides to find arguments and
> answers both for opposition and defence. It gives oppor-
> tunity of viewing the subject of discourse on all sides,
> and of learning what inconveniences, difficulties, and
> objections, attend particular opinions. It furnishes the

soul with various occasions of starting such thoughts as otherwise would never have come into the mind. It makes a student more expert in attacking and refuting an error, as well as in vindicating a truth. It instructs the scholar in the various methods of warding off the force of objections, and of discovering and refelling the subtle tricks of sophisters. It procures also a freedom and readiness of speech, and raises the modest and diffident genius to a due degree of courage.[15]

Oratory was not simply a talent to be cultivated and applauded; since the early republic it had been seen as a social and moral service to the community, to justice, and to the maintenance of democratic values. John Quincy Adams told his students "that by the eternal constitution of things it was ordained, that liberty should be the parent of eloquence; that eloquence should be the last stay and support of liberty."[16] A common topic for lyceum debate was "Resolved, That the power of Eloquence is greater than the power of Wealth."[17] Authors of nineteenth-century manuals of elocution and debate pointed to the cultivation of public speaking through debating as the means by which men might raise themselves in life.

LYCEUM and DEBATING Societies, are admirable Associations for the improvement of mind, and cultivation of talent, for public or private speaking. Franklin and Roger Sherman, (the one a PRINTER, and the other a SHOE-MAKER,) rose from obscurity to great eminence, and usefulness, by their own efforts: so may we, by using the proper means. It was in a Debating Society, that Lord Brougham first displayed his superior talents and unrivalled eloquence; and there, also, Henry Clay, the greatest American orator, commenced his brilliant career. A word to those who would be wise is enough.[18]

Debating was conventionally seen as essential preparation for the professions—law, government, the ministry. But some saw the virtues of debating skills more broadly. Ralph Waldo Emerson argued that the United States had particular need for eloquent speakers "in our commercial, manufacturing, railroad, and educational conventions" as well as in "the service of science [and] the demands of art."[19] By the mid-nineteenth century, claims about the connections among oratory, forensics, and national identity had developed a decidedly homegrown flavor. *Beadle's Dime Debater* asserted,

> The Debating Society is an American "institution." It flourishes here as naturally as corn, and like corn needs only to be cultivated in any locality to yield gratefully. It is true that such a mode of improvement as the Debating Society is known in Great Britain; but it is not indigenous there: like corn, potatoes, tobacco, maple sugar, Peter Parley, and Webster's Elementary Spelling Book, it was transplanted from Yankee soil.[20]

Like those in towns and cities, the village debating societies were established by citizens zealous for improvement. Their statements of purpose broadcast high goals and expectations. In the winter of 1850, the citizens of the little village of South Acworth, New Hampshire, gathered together to found the South Acworth Association for Mental Improvement. Echoing national ideas about rhetorical associations, the preamble to the association's constitution outlines the high, serious, and ambitious beliefs that lay behind the venture:

> Whereas the general diffusion of intelligence is of vital importance, and whereas it is the surest safeguard of republican principles and the most efficient means for the suppression of vice, error & crime, and whereas we the citizens of Sth. Acworth believe there is no way better calculated to preserve such results than by an interchange of sentiments & opinions: we do therefore agree to form ourselves into a society the object of which shall be the improvement of the various faculties of the mind.[21]

The "Mental Improvement" in the association's name encompassed faculties both moral—suppressing "vice, error & crime"—and intellectual. Importantly, this improvement was a social process, to be attained through "interchange of sentiments & opinions"—through communal interaction, not solitary study. The methods were communal and the goals were not only personal improvement but also, ultimately, the betterment of society as a whole. This social mission was often explicit in the charters of village lyceums, as, for instance, in the 1839 preamble to the constitution of the South Amherst (MA) Lyceum, which aimed "to increase the happiness and promote the well-being of the community."[22] In 1888 the new Pomfret (VT) Lyceum invited villagers to join, announcing that "all those who care to improve morally and intellectually are cordially invited to help us."[23] Lyceum participants commented on the efficacy of their debating societies. In his 1853 diary, young Edwin Harris Burlingame recorded his impressions of the lyceum at Barre (VT) Academy:

> [October 6] Tonight attended lyceum. . . . The tendency of the Lyceum lectures and the like is, I think, good; it calls out those who would otherwise spend the same time in idle amusement or lounging about some place of resort, and presents knowledge to them in a way at once agreeable and useful. The Lyceum also fits us to speak in public so that when called upon to act our part in the great drama of life, we may not shrink back afraid or unable to express our sentiments to the mass.[24]

Rural debating societies appeared in popular fiction. Edward, the eponymous young man in John N. Norton's *The Boy Who Was Trained Up to Be a Clergyman* (1854), prepares himself for a clerical career by honing his skills in composition and declamation and speaking at the local debating society. In Mrs. N. P. Lasselle's *Hope Marshall, or, Government and Its Offices* (1859), a poor young couple go to a village and start a debating society, thus bringing healthful influences to the ignorant. Lizzie

Doten's *My Affinity* (1870) presents a town whose inhabitants are intelligent and well informed thanks to a number of societies, including the Lyceum, the Young Men's Literary Society, and the Debating Society.[25] Debating societies also played a stock role in temperance novels. In these formula fictions, which often portrayed upstanding young men led astray by the availability of drink and the blandishments of drinking companions, participation in a debating society served as a marker—though an inadequate protection—for social and personal virtue. Poor, doomed Fred Hill in Francis Dana Gage's *Elsie Magoun, or, The Old Still-House in the Hollow* (1867) started out as "a boy of great spirit, and of much personal beauty, and a favorite throughout the town. He was the finest scholar in school, the best talker at the debating club." But, alas, "he would not allow that he could not drink as much egg-nog, or toddy, at a husking frolic as any one. He drank and became mad, and went forth a wanderer from the home of his childhood." The local barroom lures even upstanding older citizens such as Squire Murdock, "the stanch friend of morality and virtue in the debating society." That demon rum can corrupt even the best and the brightest testifies to its power. In T. S. Arthur's *Woman to the Rescue, a Story of the New Crusade* (1872), an entire debating society is destroyed by the attractions of Jimmy Hanlan's new saloon.

> One after another of the smartest young men lost interest in the meetings and stayed away. If you sought for them, you would be very sure to find them at Jimmy Hanlan's. The less gifted members of the society failed to bring out the usual audiences, and naturally the debating society, which had been so large a source of improvement and pleasure, languished.

The saloon's addition of a billiard table "was a *coup de grace* to the reading clubs and debating society; from that time they were things of the past." In the end, of course, the praying women win out—but there is no mention of reinstating the debating society.[26]

Even children's literature modeled the establishment of literary societies. Through the narration of a boy named Tom

Truit, Mrs. E. E. Boyd's novel *The "P.D.S."* (1873) presents a fictional account of the founding of the Pen Dipper Society, a boys' literary club, which meets in Tom's family's sitting room, with his mother (who, in the boys' view, is "just splendid") as an honorary member. Tom is president (the boys draw lots), and the details of the formation of the society mimic adult lyceums: they chip in to buy the record book and pay five cents a month each so they can buy another when that one is filled. They offer to pay for the light, but Mother donates it; she also "teaches" by asking questions when she's asked for help. Even the constitution the boys compose is a juvenile version of the typical lyceum format. "Article II. The object of this society is to mentally improve the minds of boys, and teach them to be literary, also to be orators." One boy writes a composition on "Men and Boys" in which he opines:

> There is not enough trouble taken with boys, and that is the reason there are so many men without brains. If all the boys were encouraged to get up societies like this one of ours, there would be some chance for great men in the future; but instead of that, most people laugh and say, "Young America,"—"Starting out to make donkeys of themselves," and all that sort of thing. . . . If every boy belonged to a society like the Pen Dipper, there wouldn't be any danger of their turning out bad.

The editor of the local paper is so impressed by the P.D.S. members that he pays a strong compliment: if "any business-man" were to see their work, "he would be sure to want a boy from the society."[27]

The literacy curriculum of the common schools emphasized elocution and prepared children specifically for the speaking modes common in the public lives of New England villagers.[28] Educational theorists propounded declamation as the means of advancement in a democratic nation "where the poorest and humblest boy may aspire to be the richest and greatest man in the nation." Speaking and writing were allied arts, closely connected in the classroom. "While the boy is learning to express his thoughts upon paper, he can be taught to declaim well, which is in itself little more than a physical accomplishment; and as he ripens into a good writer, he will readily unite the two attainments, and become an earnest debater."[29] Schools not only taught the speaking arts to children but also produced public events—exhibitions and sometimes school lyceums—that prepared children for adult oratorical occasions. A Maine common-school teacher wrote to the *Maine Normal* to share with novice teachers his success in having his students organize a Friday afternoon "Literary Society" for readings, declamations, and debating:

> At first, many of the pupils could get no further than "Mr. President—I think—I think"; but with true Yankee pluck and with encouragement, they soon were able to discuss, in a creditable manner, any question propounded to them. At the end of the term they voted to have a public meeting and invite their friends. The occasion was gratifying to all, and on Fridays, of the following term, persons visited the school who could not be induced to come at any other time.[30]

E. Foster Bailey remembered his first debate at the Fitchburg, Massachusetts, lyceum in 1843 as a nerve-wracking rite of passage: "On the night of the meeting the hall was well filled, and I was anxious as to my personal fate being fearful of a breakdown, as it was my first attempt to face an audience in debate."[31]

The culture of oratory united the small village with the large nation, not only in a shared belief in the virtues of public speaking and debating but also by way of the specific questions selected for debate. Of the forty-eight questions debated in the Duttonsville (VT) Union Lyceum between 1841 and 1845, fully half concerned matters of national policy.[32] Proportions seem to have been similar throughout the century in other village debating societies. Members discussed abolitionism, the responsibilities of elected legislators, capital punishment, imprisonment for debt, rates of interest, foreign immigration, mail delivery, itinerant electioneering, temperance policy, international copyright, states' rights, protective tariffs, women's suffrage, and common schools. Such topics called for study and for attentive reading of the national press. To discuss them was to be an aware, responsible citizen of the nation.

More general philosophical questions were also common in the debates. Is ambition a vice or a virtue? Is novel reading injurious to the mind and morals? Is the human mind more influenced by art than by nature? Does a life of celibacy contribute more to the happiness of mankind than a life of matrimony? In the Duttonsville Union Lyceum about one-third of the topics debated were of this nature. A few common questions required historical research—for example, evaluating the reign of Napoleon Bonaparte or weighing the virtues of Christopher Columbus, "discoverer" of America, against those of its "defender," George Washington. Some village lyceum meetings addressed state and local issues. Duttonsville debaters questioned whether the Vermont militia should be paid during peacetime; in 1872, Felchville villagers argued whether "it is morally wrong, and bad financial policy, for Vermont capitalists to lend their money West, rather than in their own State."[33]

Occasionally the lyceums took up immediate local matters. Village debate topics lived up to the proclamation in *Beadle's Dime Debater* that "it is one of our inalienable rights to discuss every question affecting our welfare, from the powers of the Constitution down to the powers of the town pump, and one of our assumed rights to argue all questions of morals, religion, economy and jurisprudence."[34] When the Wilton (NH) Lyceum discussed the resolution "that the town, in refusing to appropriate five hundred dollars for the use of the library, acted wisely," the regional newspaper not only carried a long account of the debate but also, in the following week's edition, printed a letter to the editor arguing the issue further.[35] Even general topics could have significant local resonance. Most dramatically, a murder was said to have been inspired by the South Franklin, Massachusetts, lyceum's 1859 debate on the question "Resolved, that every married man should be at least ten years older than his wife." Jonathan Wales, age twenty-eight, had been engaged to sixteen-year-old Susan Whiting until she broke the engagement. At some point after the lyceum debate he ambushed and shot her to death as she was walking home from a party with a young man from a neighboring town. The Lyceum Association of South Franklin publicly rejected the general speculation that Wales had been driven to desperation by lighthearted jesting during the debate, pointing out that the topic had been proposed by a friend of his and approved by Wales himself and that the motive of the debate had been "to prove by argument that a difference of ten or twelve years in the ages of husband and wife, instead of militating against domestic happiness was a thing rather to be desired than otherwise."[36]

Many of the same national and philosophical questions were discussed repeatedly over time in different towns and villages. Forensic manuals printed not only sample arguments, but also extensive lists of suggested questions for debate. *Beadle's Dime Debater* lists 113 "Subjects for Discussion," many of which appear in the records of village lyceums.[37] Topics were also carried from place to place by word of mouth or transferred from high school and academy debating societies to village lyceums. Zuar E. Jameson of Irasburgh, Vermont, an avid debater, noted with chagrin in his diary on January 20, 1856, that "our lyceum came off at the usual time and I got beat in the debate. . . . I was disappointed in this result as I had discussed this question twice before [in lyceums elsewhere] and got the decission in my favor."

With the age-old scorn of the urban sophisticate for the supposed bumpkin, writers occasionally made fun of the pretensions of rural debaters, as in the arch jibe in the *Pittsfield (MA) Sun's* report about the village of Windsor's new debating society:

> A debating society was formed last week with James White president, vice president H. C. Cleveland, secretary Grove E. Converse. Subject for debate this week Wednesday evening, Resolved, that man depends more upon the animal kingdom than upon the vegetable

kingdom. We suppose that after they get started they
will decide questions that have puzzled wise heads for
centuries, at the rate of one a week.[38]

The "Our Funny Box" column in the Milford (MA) Enterprise
joked, "An Eastern debating society is trying to settle which
is the hardest to keep, a diary or an umbrella."[39] Novelists also
found rural debating societies good fodder for humor. Seeking
to illustrate a point about having to make an impossible choice,
a character in Oliver Bell Bunce's A Bachelor's Story tells an
anecdote about a young farmer "whose matrimonial and agricultural tendencies were perplexed by certain economical
considerations, appertaining to each, and who, in consequence,
gravely submitted to the village Debating Society this problem:
Which is most, a barn or a wife?"[40]

Lyceums embraced humor even about their own proceedings. The institution was so well known that it spawned
parodies that were sometimes performed at actual lyceum
meetings. One popular spoof, "Jimtown Lyceum," portrayed
an entire meeting from call-to-order to adjournment, poking
fun at recognizable elements of the tradition. Minutes of the
previous meeting "reported" that

> on motion of Joseph Hobbs, it was resolved that there be
> no courting done during the performances. On motion
> of Barney O'Donnell, it was resolved that there be an
> interval of fifteen minutes each evening, so as to give the
> gentlemen an opportunity of asking to escort the ladies
> home. On motion of Amanda Cobb, it was resolved
> that the boys who crack hickory-nuts at the meetings
> be dispensed with.

When the announced (but hardly traditional) question for discussion, "Is promiscuous dancing sinful?," came up for debate,
the appointed disputants made every mistake in the forensics
book, rambling about toothaches, rat traps, and the shabby coat
of the impecunious local preacher, scrambling their sentences

to hilarious effect, playfully threatening the opponent, and only occasionally touching on the assigned question.[41] A reading of "Jimtown Lyceum" was mentioned appreciatively as part of the entertainment at the West Plymouth (NH) Lyceum on February 13, 1880 (*Grafton County Journal*, February 20, 1880).

Despite the jokes, there was little doubt about the value of rural lyceums. To the question announced for debate at the Skowhegan and Bloomfield (ME) Lyceum in November 1842— "Can every young man of mediocracy of talent, become a good public speaker?"—the common answer, from remote hill towns to urban centers, would have been in the affirmative.[42] Young men, citizens believed, should at least strive for this goal. "A good Debating Society," commented one New Hampshire town historian, "strengthens the intellect, sharpens the logical powers, creates tact, and often awakens even the apparently dull and stupid to a fair amount of zeal and energy."[43] Even rural farm boys might aspire to the professions, provided they took part in the local lyceums. As "Mrs. Kirkland" put it in the *American Agriculturalist* of New York in 1845,

> There is hardly any country village so small and unam-
> bitious, as not to have its debating society or its literary
> effort of some kind. Many a young man who has had
> good success in life, has ascribed the figure he has been
> able to make in court, or his reputation as a teacher, or
> his acceptableness in the pulpit, to an early opportunity
> for practice in his native village, and the taste for litera-
> ture which naturally grows with such efforts.[44]

Nor were the virtues of the debating societies limited to those who aimed for professional status. Wilson Palmer's memoir of his boyhood in Candia, New Hampshire, painted the salutary effects of the Candia Lyceum in broad strokes:

> The Candia Lyceum, as it was way back in the years
> of the calendar, has been a help to me in all my school
> and journalistic life, and I am positive that it has been a

decided help to those boys who now occupy the pulpit, and to those who have made their mark in the legal profession. And it has been a substantial aid, as well, to the boys who have remained at home on the old farm and to the girls who took an active part therein. To be able to speak in public, and to discuss before an intelligent audience matters of current interest, is an accomplishment that everywhere counts.[45]

After the early nineteenth century, the notion of improvement was almost never described analytically, either in village lyceum documents such as the South Acworth constitution or in popular treatises. Metaphor and hyperbole prevailed over realistic assessment, as in Charles Morley's paean:

The Lyceum and the Debating Society are among the best means for the improvement of talents and the discipline of the mind. . . . If the marble is rough, the Debating School will polish it and bring to light its inherent beauty. It is the refiner's fire; it burnishes and purifies the fine gold, brings order out of confusion, light out of darkness, and beauty out of deformity; yea, it transforms pebbles into diamonds.[46]

Even the nineteenth-century textbooks on oratory and elocution did not usually explain in any detail how their subjects improved the mind; that they did so was simply assumed. C. P. Bronson's *Abstract of Elocution and Music* did provide a brief analysis of the benefits of the study of oratory, explaining that its principles "are well calculated, to accustom the mind to the closest investigation and reasoning; thus affording a better discipline for the scientific, rational, affectuous faculties of the mind, than even the study of the Mathematics; for the *whole* man is here addressed, and all his mental powers, and all his acquirements, are called into requisition." But Bronson concluded with a metaphorical leap like Morley's: "This system is a fiery ordeal, and those who pass through it, *understandingly* and *practically*, will come out purified as by fire."[47] Though the villagers tended to speak of the improvement to be gained from lyceums in more homegrown, agricultural metaphors—"replenish[ing] our mental store," "the brain won't yield until 'tis tilled"—they, too, avoided specific articulation of the personal and vocational skills to be gained.[48] The very generality of these statements of mission held out the benefits of lyceums to all, young and old, less and more educated, rich and poor, farmer and mechanic, artisan and professional, and—though this had interesting complexities—male and female. Although debating was understood to be a masculine endeavor, the village lyceums offered women significant public responsibilities.

CHAPTER 4

"THE LADIES HAVE NOBLY
RESPONDED"

Women in the Lyceum

The only danger now is, that she may overstep the bounds
which modesty and delicacy prescribe, and come forward
upon that arena of strife which ought to belong exclusively
to man. . . . The bold and fearless spirit with which men
enter public discussion and controversy well becomes
them, but it should excite our admiration without provok-
ing to emulation. The paths that are open to us are many,
but they lie along "the cool, sequestered vale."

—Mrs. Louisa C. Tuthill,
The Young Lady at Home and in Society (1869)

In the formal debates central to their lyceums, rural communities embraced not only a long national tradition of self-culture
but also the assumptions about gender roles upon which that
tradition was built. Eloquence, oratory, and debate were all
explicitly male arts, often discussed and portrayed in military
metaphors. "If I should make the shortest list of the qualifi-
cations of the orator," wrote Emerson, "I should begin with
manliness." Even the stance of the public speaker should bespeak
martial heroism: "The orator must ever stand with forward
foot, in the attitude of advancing. . . . His speech is not to be
distinguished from action. . . . It is action, as the general's word
of command, or chart of battle is action." An author writing
about "Popular Eloquence" brought the image to an extreme:
"It is only the impassioned and vehement language of eloquence
that arrests and subjugates the multitude." Popular manuals
also emphasized the agonistic nature of debate. According to
Beadle's Dime Debater, the "office of the Debating Club" was
"to spring questions for mental antagonisms."[1]

American rhetoric made it almost unimaginable that debating in a public lyceum could be a female activity. "In a mixed company," Reverend J. M. Austin urged young women, "avoid, if possible, all contentions and disputes, especially on exciting topics. If carried to any extent, they lead to the exhibition of improper feelings, and generally cause the disputants, and the whole company, to become unhappy."[2] As American public speech changed over the course of the nineteenth century to become increasingly vigorous and vulgar, women were more and more discouraged from entering the public arena.[3] Antebellum conduct books urged them to constrain themselves even in private gatherings. "Avoid studiously every approach to pedantry, or an effort to shine in conversation," advised Margaret Coxe's *Young Lady's Companion*.[4] Sarah Josepha Hale quoted Jean de La Bruyère: "The spirit of conversation consists less in displaying your own powers than in developing those of others."[5] Rules for each sex were dramatically different. Consider the strictures in one 1852 conduct book. Men were to avoid aggressiveness:

> Hold no one by the button, when talking.
> Punch no one in conversation. . . .
> Engross not the conversation. . . .
> Be not morose or surly.
> . . . Avoid rude expressions. . . .
> Be not dark or mysterious. . . .
> Swear not in any form. . . .
> Few jokes will bear repeating.
> Debate not for victory but truth.
> Be not clamorous in dispute; but
> Dispute with good humor. . . .
> Display not your learning on all occasions.

In contrast, these are the book's "Instructions Peculiarly Adapted to Young Women":

> *Be scrupulously modest.*
> Never be afraid of blushing.

Do not talk or laugh loud in company.
Refrain from talking much.
Do not even *hear* a double-entendre.
Avoid lightness of carriage.
Be discreet.
Affect no languishing.
Be not too free.
Dread becoming cheap.
Be not too often seen in public.
Avoid gaming.
Be modest and moderate in dress.
Shun the idea of a vain woman.
Shun satire.
Avoid envy.
Cultivate benevolence.[6]

Some writers expressed doubts that women's minds were even capable of responsibly examining serious subjects. According to Charles Butler, an intrinsic "fault in the mind" of women, compounded by inadequate education, would certainly unfit them for forensic activities:

> [It] leads lively women often to pronounce on a question, without examining it: on any given point they seldomer doubt than men; not because they are more clear-sighted, but because they have not been accustomed to look into a subject long enough to discover its depths and its intricacies; and not discerning its difficulties, they conclude that it had none. Is it a contradiction to say, that they seem at once to be quick-sighted and short-sighted? What they see at all, they commonly see at once; a little difficulty discourages them; and, having caught a hasty glimpse of a subject, they rush to this conclusion, that either there is not more to be seen, or that what is behind will not pay them for the trouble of searching.

Not all commentators disparaged women's minds, however. William A. Alcott, an innovator in education, urged young women not to underestimate their power, but he begged the question of whether women were men's intellectual equals: "It is sufficient, perhaps, to know, that every young woman is capable of a much higher degree of improvement than she has yet attained, and to urge her forward to do all she can for herself, and to do it with all her might."[7]

Conduct books made clear the dilemma posed by women's intelligence and, implicitly, by their increasing interest in public affairs. On the one hand, women were cautioned against stereotyped flaws such as vanity, affectation, empty babbling, frivolousness, and love of scandal; on the other, they were told that too much evidence of intelligence would frighten away potential husbands. "The faculty termed *wit*, is commonly looked upon with a suspicious eye, as a two-edged sword, from which not even the sacredness of friendship can secure. It is especially, I think, dreaded in women." Of course, these genteel principles were prescriptive, not descriptive; many women were ardently pursuing mental improvement. Popular literature sometimes ridiculed women's endeavors toward self-culture. "The Reign of Petticoats," an 1856 sketch, caricatures a woman who goes out every evening to a different improvement society or lecture, leaving the baby to her husband and the family home in desperate chaos. Her crowning misdeed: on Saturday nights she attends the Married Women's Debating Society.[8]

Some nineteenth-century writers did encourage women to improve their minds—in an appropriate fashion. By the middle of the century, women's advice books were prescribing systematic courses of reading and self-study. Authors who urged their male readers to establish debating societies sometimes recommended that women create "more suitable" types of self-improvement, such as forming social reading clubs.[9] Contrast the vigor of Charles Morley's preface "To Young Men" in *A Guide to Forming and Conducting Lyceums*—

> Dear Friends—We live in an age of invention, enterprise and improvement; the watch-word is Onward; let it be yours, and inscribed on the tablet of your hearts.

—with the passivity he recommends "To Ladies":

> You, too, can and ought to form societies for mutual
> improvement; you might meet on a stated day and read
> essays and discuss subjects that you feel interested in;
> or one might read extracts from some interesting book,
> and then make the subject read a topic of conversation
> and remark.[10]

Women's reading and study clubs did multiply exponentially during the latter part of the nineteenth century.[11] But such sex-specific activities flourished most among women of elite or middling classes in towns and cities. Lacking daytime leisure and often living on widely scattered farmsteads, women in outlying villages and hamlets were much more likely to seek mental improvement by participating in the mixed company of the village lyceum on winter evenings than they were to form separate women's groups.[12]

Though we may doubt that many New England farmwomen read treatises on education or fashionable conduct, they were familiar with those principles, which were well represented in the periodicals and gift books they and their families did read. As William Gilmore has pointed out, the flood of printed books and newspapers into rural New England enabled women to move far beyond their initial rationale for reading—their duty as republican mothers raising virtuous citizens—and to become active as early as the 1820s in the cultural life of the region. Sarah Josepha Hale pointed out that the advent of mass printing brought "a blessed era for women" because it "destroyed that monopoly of knowledge which men would engross. . . . The female mind received a new impulse." Much of what rural New Englanders encountered in newspapers, magazines, and novels put them into contact with the nineteenth century's earnest cultural disputes about women's education and women's rights.[13]

The ideas of urban America filtered readily into the countryside and were echoed—and sometimes decisively modified and even resisted—in the lyceum papers. Probably as a response to the Seneca Falls Convention, a popular poetic theme emerged in 1849 in a poem by Mrs. E. Little:

> WHAT ARE THE RIGHTS OF WOMAN?
> "The rights of woman"—what are they?
> The right to labor and to pray,
> The right to watch while others sleep,
> The right o'er others' woes to weep;
> . . . .
> Such woman's rights, and God will bless
> And crown their champions with success.

This paradigm for True Womanhood evidently caught the century's imagination; its format was imitated again in a poem published in Montreal in 1867:

> WHAT ARE WOMAN'S RIGHTS?
> The right to wake while others sleep;
> The right to watch, the right to weep;
> . . . .
> The right a happy home to make
> In any clime for Jesus' sake:
> Rights such as these are all we crave
> Until our last—a peaceful grave.[14]

That schema persisted long into the century. On February 26, 1880, lyceum editress Alma Harriman brought her issue of the *Gem of the Valley* (West Plymouth, NH) to a close with *"Womans Rights,"* a poem that built on this by-then traditional design, extended it with many details about women's responsibilities, and then came to an empowering conclusion, emphatically underscored, that accorded woman some entitlement to speak for herself:

> *All these are her rights: they'll number forty-four,*
> *So I will now mention only one more:*
> *'Tis her right to be firm when she knows she is right*
> *Despite every opposition, Now I'll bid you "Good Night."*[15]

Given its final rhyme and its position at the end of the issue, this poem was most likely composed by Harriman herself and used as a parting shot. Whatever its now-obscure story, the piece was timely in the village. A mere two weeks earlier the debate topic in the West Plymouth Lyceum had been "Resolved: that marriage does not increase the happiness of the sexes." ("Merits of arguments," reported the record book, "decided in favor of the negative.")[16]

As the century wore on, rural women were increasingly active in various aspects of the village lyceums. Their experience as schoolteachers paved the way. By 1860, 84 percent of common-school teachers in rural New England were female.[17] Communities became accustomed to seeing young women in these public and commanding roles. Given the high turnover rate of teachers, a very large number of young women, especially in the Northeast, became habituated to this public power. It has been estimated, for instance, that even before the Civil War one-fifth of all women in Massachusetts taught school at some point in their lives.[18] Because teaching was increasingly seen as an appropriate role for women, it is less surprising that, although they rarely took part in extemporaneous debating in the rural lyceums, women were frequently selected as judges responsible for the evaluation of the debates. Reviewing the early history of the East Cabot (VT) Debating Club in 1878, the editor of the lyceum paper celebrated the contributions of "the ladies": "*Our board of decision: This is a position that no one wishes to fill, but the ladies have nobly responded to the call of the Presidents and filled the board, and their decisions have been rendered according to the weight of the argument.*" All of the East Cabot debate judges were women, and in many other lyceums one or more of the (usually three) appointed judges tended to be female.

It is worth noting that when topics for discussion focused on women's rights, not all female judges were in agreement (though sometimes they were voting on the skill of the discussants' arguments rather than the topics of debate). After a

Bridgewater, Massachusetts, debate ("Resolved, That women are better qualified for physicians than men"), the three women judges disagreed, two voting for the affirmative, one for the negative. On the other hand, when, in March 1880, men in the West Plymouth Lyceum debated the resolution "That it would be degrading to society, and injurious to the country, to give women the same right of suffrage as the men," the three judges (including one married woman) decided unanimously for the negative. Like the women judges, female lyceum attendees did not always agree with the women's rights side of the decisions. In the Shirley, Massachusetts, lyceum on March 9, 1866, the resolution was "that in the selection and pursuit of business, whether professional or otherwise, and in our political econ-omy, Women should be allowed equal rights and privileges with men." "The vote of Gentlemen and Ladies was taken separately on this one," reported the Shirley secretary, "and both decided in the negative."[19]

In societies that maintained such offices, women also often took the role of lyceum critic, preparing and delivering written appraisals of the rhetorical accomplishments at each meeting. In this position they might not pull their punches. On January 20, 1872, the Williamsville, Vermont, correspondent to the *Aurora of the Valley* (Claremont, NH) reported that "At the lyceum of Jan. 4th, a 'sharp' criticism was read by Mrs. Alice Morse, followed by declamations." Not all women critics read their own reports, however: at the Greenfield (MA) Lyceum in January 1875, "B. S. Parker read Miss Brackett's criticism on the previous meeting, after which the discussion of the question was opened."[20]

Because village lyceums normally met in schoolhouses, women's positions as lyceum judges and critics could seem a natural extension of their teaching roles. The common-school connection also carried subtler and more wide-ranging mes-sages about women's intellectual equality. The rural common-school system taught girls and boys together, and by 1870 girls between the ages of ten and fourteen had outstripped boys of the same age in literacy. An 1866 article on "Female

Culture," published, significantly, in the *Vermont School Journal and Family Visitor*, argued that "wherever [woman's] power has been exerted for the right or for the wrong, she has shown that with the same opportunities for culture, she is in every department of life fully able to cope with the masculine mind." The author noted with approval the recent improvement in assumptions about women's education and asserted that women's minds should be cultivated thoroughly, concluding that "if not as *necessary* yet it *is* as *desirable* that our young women should receive as much mental training as our young men."[21]

In the rural lyceums gender issues were popular touch points throughout the century. In Duttonsville, Vermont, in the early 1840s debaters addressed these typical questions: "Is the influence of males on community equal to that of females?" "Is the mind of females susceptible of as great improvement as that of males?" "Would Society be benefited were women to enjoy equal advantages with men?"[22] By 1869 *Beadle's Dime Debater* was suggesting topics such as "Should women vote?" "Is celibate or married life preferable?" "Is man's and woman's equality in the eye of the law possible [or proper]?" and "Will not woman lose her influence over man if she enters the political arena?" Lyceums could advertise such debates in advance to draw increased audiences, as the Shattuckville, Massachusetts, society did before its February 14, 1882, meeting to discuss the topic "Resolved, that women exert more influence than men": "The question is one that has never been discussed here and ought to excite no little interest in its discussion. . . . Speakers from out of town are expected. All are cordially invited.[23] In short, lyceum debates about the influence, capacities, and rights of women echoed—and showed considerable familiarity with—the national conversation about gender roles.

Women's roles in the village lyceums took them far beyond sympathetic listening. As critics and judges, they were often in a position to evaluate the presentations of their male colleagues; as editresses of the papers (discussed in chapter 5), their responsibilities were both extensive and public. By midcentury, and increasingly in later decades, women might take part in lyceum debates, usually on topics concerning their sex. But even on topics relating to women, female debating was unusual. One woman in Landaff, New Hampshire, chose to write a piece for the village's lyceum paper rather than take part in the debate, and she opened with an explanation of her decision:

For the Emblem

Having had an invitation to write a piece for your paper, and thinking of no subject that will interest you more than the subject which is to be or has been discussed, I will take that. Were I accustomed to speak extemporaneously I would lay aside my pen, and when Friday night came, would rise up before you and attempt to say something in favor of Woman and her Influence; but should I do this a big heart would come up in my throat and throb so hard that my voice would tremble like a poplar leaf. So I must say what I have to say with my pen.

The writer praises woman's *"noble intellect"* and her influence on men as well as on schoolchildren and concludes with a conservative endorsement of the status quo, based on a scornful condemnation of the rude and ungenteel culture of men in public life:

It is true woman does not sway directly the sceptre of government, but her influence is the first great cause. And when we survey the vast empire over which it has been extended, we wonder that she should ever wish to have its boundaries enlarged, that she might control the political world as well as the social circles; and especially that this should be the case in our own country, where so many of the male sex make the political News Paper their Bible, and N[—] Songs their hymn book.[24]

Even when women engaged in the lyceum debates, they often did so via the more ladylike mode of writing and then reading their arguments.[25] In the South Acworth (NH) Public Lyceum on October 3, 1862, the male discussants presented their arguments extemporaneously, followed by "Essays on the question by Miss M. E. Watts and Mrs. M. J. Field," after which the members present decided the question by vote.[26] Later in the century a few more lyceums reported women debaters. On January 8, 1872, a correspondent to the Greenfield, Massachusetts, *Gazette and Courier* reported that the nearby village of Monroe "must certainly be the banner town in the State, for no town can boast of such lyceums as we have up here. The ladies debate as well as gentlemen. This is what makes it so interesting." In the Bridgewater (NH) Lyceum's 1880 debate on the question, "Resolved, That women are better qualified for physicians than men," the two disputants assigned to argue the affirmative were women; the negative speakers were men.[27] No other reports from Bridgewater in this season mention female discussants, which may suggest that women debaters were selected principally for topics relating to gender issues. Be that as it may, throughout the New England hill country in the 1880s women were taking more active roles in lyceums. In the Kenduskeag (ME) Literary Association women served not only as discussants in 1884 but also occasionally as officers.[28] In 1888 the West Randolph, Vermont, *Herald and News* mentioned that, in the Thetford Lyceum, "these discussions this year are far more interesting owing to the fact that the young ladies take part in them."[29] In the same year the Union Debating Club of West Deerfield, Massachusetts, conducted many debates in which women took part, even as principal speakers.

In small midwestern communities settled by emigrating New Englanders, some lyceums included women debaters even before the Civil War. In a letter Mrs. Jeannette Hulme Platt reported that in 1858 she had shared a hotel room in Zanesville, Ohio, with a young woman who had moved to an Iowa settlement with fewer than two hundred inhabitants.

> She gave a minute description of "our Lyceum," which meets every Wednesday night, in which women take part in debate and write essays. "Why," I said, "how many

women have you, out of the 200 men, women, and children, that are able to write essays?" "About five." "What do you do with your baby when you 'debate' and read your own 'essays'?" "Oh, I set her down, or hand her to somebody." "What kind of questions do you discuss? Give me a specimen, do." "Moral suasion; capital punishment; women's rights. We are all great women's rights folks."[30]

In the hill towns and hamlets of northern New England, as in the western settlements, sparse population may have encouraged women to move into what had traditionally been men's roles in the lyceums. Villagers were well aware of their declining numbers. The Bernardston correspondent to the Greenfield, Massachusetts, *Gazette and Courier* lamented on January 9, 1882, that "nearly every young man reared on the farm for the last ten years has left the farm to enter some of the professions or engage in some other occupation." Particularly after the Civil War, many neighborhoods were left with insufficient numbers of young men to sustain an active debating society. It is clear from the local columns in the regional press that even when a lyceum was felt to be desirable, it was not always possible to "get one up." In some villages with limited numbers of youth, only one major effort could be mounted each winter: one year, a debating society; the next, perhaps, a temperance lodge. The same names occur on the rosters of each. Women's participation was more necessary when population was low.

However, it was not only the paucity of available male participants that determined women's growing prominence in rural debates. Perhaps more influential was the dramatic increase in coeducation in higher education during the nineteenth century, which strongly challenged the earlier assumption that women's minds were inferior to men's. Since the late eighteenth century, coeducational academies and high schools had offered advanced education to both boys and girls. Oberlin College in Ohio began accepting women students in 1833, and another Ohio school, Antioch, followed suit twenty years later.

Normal schools, beginning with the founding of Westfield
State Normal School in Barre, Massachusetts, in 1839, were
coeducational and set a model for the intellectual mingling
of men and women. When the Normal School Improvement
Society was formed at Westfield in 1844, the entire student body
(twenty-eight men, forty-three women) was urged to join;
women took part in the debates, though usually by writing
and reading their arguments.[31] Thus, even before the Civil War,
some young women were gaining forensic experience in the
buffered environment of coeducational academies and normal
schools. Mary Swift's 1839–40 diary makes it clear that, in its
first year of existence, the Lexington (MA) Normal School,
founded in 1839, included coeducational debating among its
exercises.[32] At the Shawomet Lyceum, founded in 1860 at the
Old Warwick School in Rhode Island, both male and female
students participated in debates as appointed and voluntary
discussants.[33] In Wrightsville, Vermont, when the students of
Reverend Elisha Brown's school formed a lyceum in 1858, equal
numbers of male and female officers were named, though
the president was always male. In the Wrightsville debates
the assigned disputants were male, but women occasionally
spoke up as volunteers on the questions.[34]

Sometimes women refused to take part in school debates,
even when invited. The *Bridgton (ME) News* reported roguishly
that at the spring term's first meeting of the Bridgton High
School lyceum in April 1876, "the ladies were called upon to
give their views [in the debate], but declined to speak, probably
out of regard to the masculines, whom they hadn't the heart
to annihilate in cold blood."[35] Some academies had separate
societies for men and women, as at Wilbraham Academy in
Massachusetts, where the girls in the Athena Society held their
own debates.[36] When the *Milford (NH) Enterprise* on March 2,
1875, announced the closing exercises of Milford High School,
conducted by a Professor Blanpied, all of the students named
were female, including the participants in three debates, a temperance discussion, and selected readings. The only male mentioned was Ira Holt, who delivered "A Petition to the Selectmen

for a Fire Engine." Although relatively few women from small rural villages attended academies and normal schools, the school debating model was well known, and some women who participated in the public debates at the community lyceums certainly drew on their school experience, both for technique and for the empowering sense of entitlement.

Despite a growing respect for women's mental abilities, and despite their evolving significance in schools and colleges, women's leadership in the village lyceums remained limited. In 1882 a Charlemont, Massachusetts, correspondent to the Greenfield *Gazette and Courier* commented with wry amusement on women's new prominence in the local lyceum:

> The debate, upon the political interests which women have at stake, was very spirited and will be continued next week, although upon a somewhat different phase of the subject. The lyceum was then newly organized, and as a woman is to be president for the next four weeks and another woman to be treasurer, some fear that this favorite and popular institution is going to pieces, but we will hope for the best.[37]

Clearly women were understood to be the junior partners in the rural lyceums, and their entrance into traditionally male roles was scattered and infrequent. But if their participation in the central forensic activities was rare and tentative, if they frequently shared the majority view that women should not have the same roles in the world as men, they nonetheless achieved access to public authority in the lyceums that they had not experienced before. They achieved this prominence primarily by editing and reading the paper.

CHAPTER 5

"WHO WILL SUSTAIN THE PAPER?"

The Work of Editing

When the subject of starting a Lyceum was first broached the question was asked, who will take part in the debate: and who will sustain the paper, but the ladies came to the rescue and I think I speak the sentiments of the club in saying that there never was a paper so well sustained in this vacinity as the Monitor.

—*"Editorial," Monitor* (East Cabot, VT) 1, no. 11, February 27, 1878

Editing the paper entailed public prominence, responsibility, and vulnerability. The paper was essential; apart from the debate it was the only undertaking commonly specified in lyceum constitutions and bylaws. The evening began with the voice of the lyceum secretary—a man—delivering a businesslike reading of the preceding week's minutes; the evening often ended with the voice of the editor—usually a woman—performing a reading that contained and enacted the diverse characters, conversations, and concerns of the assembled neighbors. Lyceum members esteemed skilled reading and willingly allocated considerable time to the presentation of the paper. Thaddeus Perry Mason of Dublin, New Hampshire, noted in his diary the duration of these readings at lyceums he attended—from thirty minutes to more than an hour—and commented approvingly when the evening's paper was "quite lengthy."[1]

Both men and women, sometimes together, served as lyceum paper editors, but the majority were women. Judging from some sixty surviving papers whose editors' genders I know or can assign with some confidence, women were eligible to serve as sole editors of papers throughout the century. The East Andover (NH) Social Lyceum (later the Mountain Club) had single male editors in 1848 and 1849 and "editresses" thereafter. Some lyceums appointed a team of editors: a man and a woman (*Mystic Tie* [Carthage, ME], 1875; *Beans Corner Sunbeam* [Jay, ME], 1877–79; *Gem of the Valley* [West Plymouth, NH], from 1870–75, but just one editress thereafter). Others had two women (*Independent* [South Levant, ME], 1881) or a man and two women (*Emblem* [Landaff, NH], 1860; *Monitor* [East Cabot, VT], 1878; *Enterprise* [West Danville, VT], 1884). Women's participation in editing seems to have become more obligatory as the century wore on; I have found no papers after 1860 in which women were not involved as editors, either singly or in a team.

Although it is not clear how duties were allocated when papers were created by collaborating male and female editors, occasional hints suggest that the women bore most of the labor of production. A light-hearted spoof in the *Monitor* gives a glimpse into the distribution of work:

> *An afternoon in the Monitor Ofice*
> I had the pleasure of spending the afternoon with the Editor & Editeresses of the Monitor at their office on the corner of Glidden & High street, they being about their Daily work of preparing the moniter for the press. The Editor not being in when I arived at the office I sat down and began to take a "birds eye view" of the office. I had not sat long when I heard some one enter and on looking around I saw the Hon. gentleman himself and Miss Abbott one of the Editoresses of the spicy little Monitor. They looked as smiling as [a] "basket of chips." After passing the time of day with them, they sat down and began to write off the news. . . . I think the Editeresses must have bin out late the night before or something was the trouble with them, for they had not written but a short time before they began to scowl & sputter about the work, and to throw the wast paper into the wast basket, which means on

> *the floor under the table, and the way they went for the Editor*
> *is a caution to those wishing to get the office. But he took no*
> *notice of it however, but enjoyed himself by reading a dime*
> *novel and smoking a cigar and I guess he was all right. But I*
> *would warn the people to keep out of the office of the Monitor*
> *when the Editeresses are about their daily work.*[2]

In the only complete issue I have seen of Carthage's *Mystic Tie*
(c. 1875), edited (according to a note by the editors' son) by D.
Frank Holt and Betsey M. R. Bartlett of Weld, Maine, only the
opening editorial is in Frank's handwriting; the rest is written
in a female hand, probably Betsey's. (Possibly co-editing the
paper was a good courting activity; by 1880, Frank and Betsey
were married and had a two-year-old child.)

The editorial position usually rotated from meeting to
meeting. Minutes in the record books formally report the
program for the following lyceum: the topic of the next debate,
the disputants appointed to argue the affirmative and the negative, and the name(s) of the next editor(s) of the paper—all
of these assignments made by the president or by a designated
committee. Evidently it was important that the editorship be
distributed as widely as possible. In her opening editorial for
the *Veazie (ME) Light* Mrs. Katie Shaw's wry comment makes
this clear:

> *The editress would advise the secretary of the Lyceum Club to*
> *furnish the president with a list of the names in Alphabetical*
> *order of all the young ladies who attend their meeting so that*
> *each one "who has not" can have the privilege of acting serving*
> *as Editress, as she learns that some of them feel slighted at*
> *not receiving an invitation to do so.*[3]

Because the same editor rarely served twice in one season,
many local women were called upon. A poem in the *Gem of
the Valley* describing the West Plymouth Lyceum celebrated the
recent editresses but also made it clear that not all welcomed
the service:

> *Miss Helen M. Clark is here when 'tis fair,*
> *But always keeps out of the Editress Chair.*
> *Of others less fortunate, here we will name*
> *Mrs. Lizzie F. Morse, of literary fame,*
> *Mrs. C. S. Morrill, and Mrs. G. Payne,*
> *Whom we should be glad to hear from again.*
> *For Mary A. Sargent, and Mrs. E. Weeks,*
> *A good order of talent each paper bespeaks.*
> *With Sylvia Philbrick and A. Whittemore*
> *Miss Sadie Ash makes near half a score*
> *Of ladies who've served as Editress here*
> *And given us thoughts lifes pathway to cheer.*[4]

The editors and editresses of the papers were well-established members of their lyceums. In associations that had continued for several years, they generally had already taken part in other capacities—performing recitations or declamations, dialogues, music, judging debates, or even debating. They had finished school; some were already married and had children. Many had also served as teachers, so speaking to a gathering in the schoolhouse would have felt familiar. The age and status of editors in the West Plymouth Lyceum seems fairly typical for male and female editors across the century: of the twelve women named in the record book as editresses of the *Gem of the Valley* in 1879–80, half were married. Their ages ranged from seventeen to forty-seven, averaging thirty.

It was no wonder that editors tended to be older than many lyceum participants. The position called for diligence, maturity, and resourcefulness. Within a single week or fortnight the editor was responsible for creating and performing a complete paper. That involved encouraging potential authors and collecting submissions; evaluating, choosing, and arranging the submitted compositions; writing an editorial and often other pieces as well; making a fair copy of the whole; and presenting an engaging oral reading of the paper to an audience that ranged from schoolchildren to elders. It's no surprise that not all village women relished the job! Some simply refused to serve. Silvanus Hayward noted that when the Gilsum (NH)

Young People's Lyceum, founded in 1848, admitted women as active members, "an effort was made to secure their services in editing 'The Evening Star,' but only one number was read by ladies. This was by Christiana A. Spaulding (then teaching here) and Sarah E. Horton. All others, who were invited, declined the service, and the remaining editors were . . . [all men], making five numbers in all [before dissolution in 1849]."[5] The October 4, 1852, constitution of the Franklin Lyceum in Franklin Village, New Hampshire, called for the "reading of a paper," and the bylaws stipulated, "An Editress shall be chosen by the Lyceum once in four weeks. The paper shall be under her controll and read by her." However, when the chair attempted to appoint an editress on October 15, the records name three appointees who refused and concludes, "Appointment left with the Chair."[6]

Even the editor's first task, persuading the neighbors to write for the paper, was not easy. Facing public criticism could be daunting, as one essayist pointed out in the middle of a piece justifying a refusal to write: *"Some people will find fault no matter with how much care an article has been pened. This is too long, that too short, another too prosy, and still another has too much spice, too insipid, or something else, and so on in an endless catalogue of grievances."*[7] Contributors were often bashful about their abilities. *"If you like, insert it; if not, put it into the fire,"* wrote a Dublin, New Hampshire, contributor.[8] One Fryeburg, Maine, farmer attached a wry cover note to his submission:

> *Dear Miss Adams:—*
> *Herewith find something for [the paper] which I trust may be suitable. If you can't read it, send it back and I will hang it up in the corn field this summer to scare crows.*
>
> H. P. Pray

Some local writers made elaborate compositions about their writers' blocks, as in this poem from the *Meteor* (Kenduskeag, ME), probably published in January 1885.

A search after Something to write about.
What shall I write for the paper?
A question quite easy for some
To answer, for they know in a twinkling
And thought after thought will come.

But for me, oh dear! how plaguesome
For a subject I cannot find.
I have hunted and searched and hunted,
Till I'm nearly out of my mind.

I have looked in last year's Almanac,
I hunted the bible through,
And then I took the cook-book,
And scanned all its pages, too.

But not a single thing
Did I find in any of these,
That I thought would be just the thing
The friends of the Meteor to please.

I fling them away in disgust
And sat myself down to think
Then a thought came to me
As quick as a flash or a wink.

It was to tell you how I had hunted,
To find something about which to write,
So here, my friends, you have it
Right down in black and white.

How could the editors convince their neighbors to take up their pens? Believing passionately in the value of writing to improve the mind, some lyceum editors tried arguments. In his editorial on December 19, 1849, George E. Emery, editor of the *Kearsarge (NH) Fountain*, remarked on the relative virtues of debating and writing for the paper. "*The advantages accruing from discussions and literary compositions as exhibited in the*

*Fountain are nearly equal. No one will expose his ignorance enough
to deny it. By composing we learn to think—to think deeply—we
acquire a command of language and learn to express our thoughts."*[9]
Coming from farm families themselves, many editors knew
how to appeal to their neighbors in the language of farming:

> *The people who wish this good paper,*
> *With wisdom and instruction filled*
> *Will please remember an old saying—*
> *The brain won't yield until 'tis tilled.*

And they told their neighbors how to till the brain:

> *Thought engenders thought. Place one idea upon paper,*
> *another will follow it, and still another, until you have writ-*
> *ten a page. You cannot fathom your mind. There is a well of*
> *thought there which has no bottom. The more you draw from*
> *it the more clear and plentiful it will be. If you neglect to think*
> *yourself, and use other people's thoughts, giving them utterance*
> *only, you will never know of what you are capable. At first*
> *your ideas may come in lumps—homely and shapeless; but no*
> *matter—time and perseverance will arrange and refine them.*[10]

The lyceums stipulated—with limited success—that all
members were obligated to contribute to the paper. Some
papers stated the rule in the "Terms of Subscription" on their
cover sheets:

> *Terms: liberal communications to be paid invariably in advance.*
> (*Literary Banner* [Mont Vernon, NH] 1, no. 5,
> January 7, 1858)

> *Terms of Publication, A weekly contribution from each member*
> *of the society payable in advance.*
> (*Emblem* [Landaff, NH] 1, no. 3, January 20, 1860)

Terms of Subscription, a composition in advance.
(*Independent* [South Levant, ME] 1, no. 7,
March 23, 1881)

Despite such pronouncements, throughout the century editors struggled to overcome their neighbors' writing blocks. They wielded ingenious strategies, from parody—

Thousand dollars reward offered–
To one who'll invent a machine with a patent For the
sublime intent to furnish thoughts for the "Casket."
(*Casket* [Landaff, NH] 1, no. 7, February 10, 1855)[11]

to pastiche—

'Twas the night before Lyceum, when all through the house
Not a creature was stirring, not even a mouse;
An Editress sat all alone in her chair
In hopes that contributors soon would be there.
(*Gem of the Valley* [West Plymouth, NH] 3, no. 6,
January 22, 1880)

to irony—

Of the dozzen people asked to write, two single contributions
have been received. Were this paper an illustrated periodical
we should insert the photographs of both the authors and
underneath, these words: "Our Benefactors."
*   May all future editors and Editresses who have been asked*
to contribute to the present number, be blest with as many
manuscripts as has
*   The Present Editor*
(*Miscellany* [Dublin, NH] 3, no. 3,
December 3, 1886)

to sarcastic characterizations—

There are quite a number belonging to this society, who gen-
erally write for this paper. Why not more than one piece for
our last. One says really I do not see as I can write this week.
It takes all the time I can possibly get to learn my lessons, as I
attend school; besides I have to write for the school every other
week, and this is my week to write. I think there are others
who can write better than I can. There is Miss S. and B. and
some others who do not attend school I should think they might
write. Another says I should be very happy to write for your
paper, but we have so much work to do this week, that I do not
see as I can write possibly. I intended to have written this week
but as it is I think I must be excused. If I only attended school
I would write. A third says I have never written but a very
little, therefore I cannot write any thing decent for a paper: If
I could I would certainly. Another says to her self I generally
write, but I guess I will not this week. I think the others will
about all of them "hand in pieces," so there will be enough
for a paper if I do not write. Such are the excuses generally
made, and very good ones, too. . . . Now if this is the course
to be taken, what will become of our paper?

(*Ladies' Miscellany* [Dublin, NH] 5, no. 4,

November 1, 1842)

Once the editors collected the submissions, they decided
which would be included in the paper. Sometimes they had
just what they wanted. Mary E. Batchelder, editress of the
Kearsarge Fountain, was able to close one week's issue by assur-
ing her listeners that *"Every article which has been forwarded*
for publication has been coppied and read this evening there being
nothing which in our opinion was unsuitable for our columns" (East
Andover, NH, c. 1850). William and Laura Glidden, editors of
the *Enterprise*, announced their criteria somewhat defensively:
"If in making up this paper any articles have bin omitted, which
you had reason to suppose would appear, we can only say we done
what we thought best, and only omited those which were verry long"
(West Danville, VT, January 24, 1884). Editorial decisions could
affect the self-esteem of the contributors. In Sophie May's

1871 novel *The Doctor's Daughter*, set in fictitious Quinnebasset, Maine, young Marian's friend Judith tremulously submits an acrostic poem to the lyceum paper—her first venture—and is crestfallen to discover at the meeting that it has not been selected for the *Aurora*.[12]

Mediating between contributors and listeners placed editors in a situation of power—but also of vulnerability and dependence. They were empowered not only because they could choose among submissions but also because they alone knew the contributors' identities. Most editors made a fair copy of the final paper in their own handwriting. This certainly made it easier for them to read the text aloud, but it also preserved the anonymity that local authors desired. Contributors were not named and might be able to escape criticism of their work, but editors could not. Their editorials, in which they spoke in their own voices on behalf of the paper, the lyceum, and even the community, were almost the only pieces whose authorship was obvious to all—a significant public exposure, especially, though not only, for women. Editorials were often laced with apologies. *"We . . . beg your forbearance while we lay before you our ill-developped sheet,"* chorused the editresses of the *Emblem* (Landaff, NH, 1860). D. Frank Holt opened the first issue of the *Mystic Tie* (Carthage, ME, c. 1875) with more elaborate contrition:

> *Again the duty devolves upon us of wielding the Editorial pen but we find our Editorial ability is yet to be acquired and it is with a great degree of modesty and diffidence that we assume the responsibility of editing a sheet which is contributed by so many able correspondents as we hope this to be.*

Charles Howe, Mrs. Laura Glidden, and Mrs. Steffi Howe, editors of the January 9, 1878, issue of the *Monitor* (East Cabot, VT), pushed the limits of fulsome contrition:

> *In presenting its readers with this number of the Monitor we feel our utter incapacity for writing any thing in the line of an editorial that will add to its usefulnes or extend its circulation.*

*But beging your indulgence in this our first attempt as editor,
and knowing that the abundance of other good reading this
number contains will more than compensate for what may be
lacking in the editorial, we will do the best we can.*

Underlining the ritual status of editorial excuses, the editor of
the *Kearsarge Fountain* (East Andover, NH, February 14, 1849)
penned a striking aporia:

Ladies & Gentlemen

    *Omitting the stereotyped apoligies for ignorance inexper-
iance inability want of time and of seasonable contributors
here, you will find all these out in the course of the reading
of the paper.*

A team of Landaff, New Hampshire, editors defended themselves with a parable:

Editors Corner.

*We once read of an old lady who was famous for cooking good
dinners and also for apoligies to her guests that she had nothing
better for them to eat. On one occasion a gentleman was eating
who was unacquainted with the old lady's peculiarities, and
who was at a loss to know how to regard her many excuses. At
last came her favorite dish, the pride of her cookery, the dish
which of all others she considered the most excellent, and at
the same time she commenced to pile on the apoligies—really
she didn't know as he could eat it—was sorry she had nothing
better for him, etc The guest tasted, looked at her, and tasted
again, and finally said, well I have seen better and I have seen
worse. "You lie," says she, "you never saw better in your life."*

    *We have related this little anecdote by way of giving our
hearers a gentle hint that we have our own ideas in regard
to the present number of our paper and that those ideas are
unchangebly fixed and if any one should venture to speak
lightly or disrespectly of it perhaps we should be disposed to
quarrel with them as quickly as did the old lady in the story
just related.*

The team's editorial closes with scorn for reluctant writers, calling attention to the burden they placed on editors:

> To those who have kindly contributed to our columns we render our sincere thanks. To those who have obstinately refused to aid in our work, we will say that we hope you at some future time, may have the pleasure of occupying the place which we now willingly vacate—that you may know from experience the exquisite pleasure of constructing an acceptable literary paper out of nothing.[13]

Indeed, editors did not always gather sufficient local submissions. William A. Bachelder of East Andover, New Hampshire, detailed his problem in the *Kearsarge Fountain* (February 14, 1849):

> Each article written expressly and originally for the present number.
>> Number of pages in this number twenty eight
>> Number of writers for this number four!!
>> Number of pages received from Correspondents nine!!

If only nine of twenty-eight pages came from contributors, and "*each article*" was "*written expressly and originally for the present number,*" then the editor himself was claiming to have composed nineteen pages of original literature within the week! As far as I can tell, he did so, for none of the contents of this issue appears to have been copied from a commercial publication.

Not all editors were so industrious. When submissions were lacking, some refused to create a paper. Writing about the previous week's lyceum, a *Toll Bridge Journal* author commented, "*Our journal was omitted on account of the negligence of some of our contributors*" (Fryeburg, ME, March 12, 1870). Some editors mined past journal issues. In 1878 Mrs. Laura Glidden was among the editors of three issues of the *Monitor*, the paper of the East Cabot (VT) Debating Club. Evidently she kept them, because six years later she and her husband William copied three pieces from the *Monitor* as they edited the first issue of the *Enterprise*, the paper of the neighboring West Danville Debating Club.[14] Other undersupplied editors abandoned the criterion of originality in order to fill up their pages and copied or adapted articles, stories, jokes, and poems from commercial sources such as gift books, almanacs, and the weekly family newspapers whose rural circulation blossomed after the Civil War. One week when young Emily Harriman was drafted after *"the Editress chosen refused to serve,"* she expostulated and apologized at the same time:

> Many thanks are due the brave <u>one</u> who ventured to contribute to this paper and I hope no fault will be found if it is not as interesting as previous copies have been and to the faultfinding ones I would say "write a piece." People think they <u>cant</u> write <u>one</u> piece, but an Editress can write a long interesting paper, full of wit and Common Sense, which is lacking a great deal in this copy.

For that issue of *Gem of the Valley* (West Plymouth, NH, January 22, 1880), Emily created several pieces herself. She probably wrote the *"'Twas the night before Lyceum"* pastiche quoted earlier in this chapter and might also have conjured up local mock advertisements, word play for teasing courting couples (*"Is it because our hall is so warm that Chas. Quincy always brings a Fan?"*), and the like. But at least six of her paper's fourteen pages came from published sources, including several filler jokes and a long comic sketch, *"How a Man Helps His Wife,"* describing a hapless husband's struggle to bring in frozen washing from the winter clothesline.[15] She did sometimes alter the pieces she copied. Her issue included a popular anecdote beginning *"In Sweden a bride has her pockets filled with bread."* This line appeared as part of a human-interest item in numerous periodicals in the United States, the United Kingdom, and Australia at this period, always followed by the explanation, "It is supposed that every piece she gives to the poor on her way to church averts misfortune." This second sentence is not in the *Gem*. Instead, Emily's Yankee love of word play triumphed: she wrote, *"Then she is better bread than many brides in our own country."*

Although transcribing and adapting items from commercial sources certainly became more common later in the century, the practice occurred even before the Civil War. Article 10 of the 1858 "Constitution of the South Acworth [NH] Public Lyceum" shows a significant bit of editing: "The paper shall ~~consist of articles strictly original, and shall~~ be conducted and read by two editresses to be appointed each week by the Board of Directors." The deleted words are covered by unequivocal penciled *X*s in the original record book. Unfortunately, none of the South Acworth papers seems to have survived, so it is impossible to check the originality of their contents, but copied items—particularly poems—occur in several surviving antebellum papers.[16] Editors had complete discretion in determining the contents of their papers; some drew more material from commercial sources than others did, but originality was the ideal and original pieces predominated in the papers throughout the century.

After the Civil War, as newspapers and other periodicals circulated more freely to remote rural areas, lyceum papers included more previously published content, some chosen by editors and some submitted by other lyceum members. The way published items were included seems significant. Editors did not simply cut and paste clippings, scrapbook-like, into their papers; instead, they chose to incorporate the commercial pieces in the same way they copied original submissions from the neighbors: in their own handwriting and without attributing authorship or origin. In borrowed items the commercial was frequently made local by the insertion of neighborhood names and places, even in popular jokes, as in these typical pieces from the *Bow Lake Journal* (Strafford, NH), where local boys' names are grafted onto frequently published witticisms:

> *Arlin thinks young ladies ought to have rifles and guns so they can get accustomed to having arms around them.*

*Knowlton says the cheapest thing in the world to ride is a
hobby—It eats no oats, wants no groom, breaks no traces,
and wants no shoeing.[17]*

Whatever sources they drew upon, homegrown or commercial,
the editors were responsible for creating a paper that reflected
the concerns, characters, and values of their community. What
they accomplished for their villages seems analogous to what
individuals throughout the century undertook for themselves
privately as they copied favorite texts into personal commonplace books. Perhaps we could imagine the lyceum editors
creating a weekly community commonplace book by bringing
together meaningful, interesting, and amusing pieces to suit
the collective mind of the neighborhood.

Creating and copying the paper, however, was not the
end of the editor's responsibility. The paper's culmination—
often the final event of the evening—was oral performance.
Nowadays, its name may evoke images of silent reading, but
the paper was always read aloud by the editor or editress. When
Maria Gordon's neighbor Sam Frye missed the February 12,
1870, Toll Bridge meeting for which she had edited the *Journal,*
she noted in her diary, "I read my paper to him." She did not
hand him the fair copy for his silent perusal. Even in a private
visit in the parlor, the paper was meant for listening.

Particularly in rural areas, print and oral cultures remained
entwined for much of the nineteenth century, and reading
was still regarded primarily as an oral activity. "Learning to
read," as an author wrote in the *Common-School Journal* in 1839,
"is, in fact, something like learning to sing. . . . As it is good
music only that can delight the ear, so it is good reading only
that can afford instruction and entertainment to the hearer."[18]
Common-school education was founded on memorizing, recit-
ing, and reading aloud—a continuity from the eighteenth
century's literacy-learning practices.[19] William Gilmore has
pointed out that oral transmission of information remained
the dominant mode of education in the upper Connecticut
River Valley well into the 1820s and that in the antebellum years

newspapers were commonly read aloud in post offices, general stores, and taverns.[20] Reading aloud was understood to be an important intellectual exercise. In an 1856 essay George William Curtis compared reading to oratory, portraying the activities as "two movements" working "side by side . . . and tending alike to the elevation of the masses."[21] A much-reprinted article from the *North American Review* contended that reading aloud could itself promote mental development: "It requires a constant exercise of mind. It demands continual and close reflection and thought, and the finest discrimination of thought."[22]

Reading was keyed as a particularly suitable female activity in nineteenth-century America.[23] Educators encouraged women to see the intellectual challenges in reading and to regard as comparable the improvement to be gained from reading and from oratory. "There may be eloquent readers, as well as eloquent speakers," wrote Anna Russell in *The Young Ladies' Elocutionary Reader* (1845). But reading aloud, for women, was generally a private, domestic activity—very different from standing in public before a mixed crowd of men and women, old and young, and reading the lyceum paper. Yet because most lyceum papers were edited by women, it was most often a woman who stood before the audience to read. How was this possible? From one angle of vision, the options for participation in the lyceum that were usually offered to or chosen by women kept them within—or near—socially acceptable bounds and protected them from accusations of unseemly display. Girls' lyceum recitations could call to mind the academic exhibitions of the common school, the sanctioned juvenile coeducational training space where girls learned to speak well so that they might benefit their future families.[24] Reading aloud could also evoke a school context, as did many of the compositions (some of them retouched school or academy essays) that found their way into the lyceum either as individual essays to be read aloud or as pieces for the paper. However, under cover of these sanctioned activities village women extended their local domain. Having been schooled to write, young women could push themselves to write for the wider audience of the village; this may have encouraged them to take their own mental development and opinions more seriously, as well as their skill in writing. Having been accepted as readers in the domestic circle and the school and as teachers to the young, they could push themselves to extend this context to include the gathered neighbors at the lyceum.

Nonetheless, performing the paper in front of the lyceum could be daunting. Although in some neighborhoods joint editors shared the reading of the paper, most often it was presented by a single reader, who would have held the floor longer and more continuously than any debater, declaimer, or reciter. Taught the fine points of reading even in the common schools, listeners often critiqued the skill of readers. Reflecting in 1866 on a neighbor's rendition of the *Club Museum*, the paper of her North Waterford, Maine, lyceum, Mary Frances Hodsdon wrote in her diary, "Mrs. J. B. Rand presented the paper, it was not very well read but there were some good articles in it." Three weeks later Mrs. Hodsdon assessed her own initial performance of the paper: "I didn't break down but failed to satisfy myself in reading."[25] Local columnists reported on their village lyceums in the regional press, rating not only the debaters but also the caliber of the paper and its readers. In the *Aurora of the Valley* (Claremont, NH), the Quechee, Vermont, correspondent commented that the season's first lyceum paper "was very beautifully read by its accomplished editresses, Misses Bragg and Simmons." One submission to the *Literary Banner* (Mont Vernon, NH) chronicled in quasi-biblical style the events of the previous lyceum meeting and exulted,

> The ladies of the tribe who are always forward in all good works, not deeming it proper to dispute in public with their lordly masters, did write both wise and witty sayings which one of their number did read to the people in a tone and style, so captivating, that the whole crowd did listen, and wonder, that one so beautiful, and unassuming, could read in such a natural, and forcible manner, word[s] so well befiting these subjects and the place.[26]

Although the gender politics of oratory kept most women from debating, their voices rang out in the lyceums in other ways. Building on their daytime experience as pupils and teachers, they delivered recitations, judgments, and criticisms. What is more, in their primary responsibility, editing the paper, they took control of one of the central events of the lyceum evening, molding the varied expressions of their neighbors into a compelling and lengthy performance. Producing the paper called for an impressive range of literary skills as the editress created an engaging text featuring disparate modes and genres.

CHAPTER 6

"EFFULGENT IN WISDOM AND SPARKLING WITH WIT"

Exploring the Papers

The Quechee Star—a brilliant luminary of the literary Heavens—also made its appearance, and its well rounded columns sparkled with an abundance of goodly things both of the sentimental and humorous.

—*Aurora of the Valley* (Claremont, NH), October 26, 1872,
reporting on the opening lyceum of the season
in Quechee, Vermont

The "abundance of goodly things" in each lyceum paper provides ample evidence of the flourishing literacy of nineteenth-century northern New England. Dozens of literary genres provided models for the pieces submitted to the lyceum editors, testifying to the depth and energy of rural reading. William Gilmore asserts that, as early as the 1820s, New England was entering an Age of Reading, "an era marked by the emergence of mass literacy and a mass culture in which print and written forms of expression joined oral and visual forms as dominant modes of cultural understanding." Texts experienced from early childhood entered readers' minds as tools of thought and expression. As Ronald Zboray and Mary Zboray comment, New England writers "could not help but think in a literary manner. Literature was embedded deeply enough in their consciousness as to structure it."[1] Children grew up with common nursery rhymes, word games and verbal puzzles, school readers, youth magazines, gift books and chapbooks, songs, poetry, and, of course, the Bible. Adults read almanacs, farming treatises, histories and travel writings, novels, legal documents, sermons and biblical commentaries, scientific accounts, political tracts, and, increasingly, newspapers.[2] All of these sources provided models and inspiration for lyceum pieces—a situation dramatized by the complaint of a Kenduskeag, Maine, author seeking inspiration to write for the paper:

> *I have looked in last year's Almanac,*
> *I hunted the bible through,*
> *And then I took the cook-book,*
> *And scanned all its pages, too.*[3]

Writing—letters, diaries, essays, poems—was practiced from childhood onward.[4] Young scholars' first composition models were the school readers whose selections they read aloud, reread, parsed, and memorized every day.

> When we look back upon our school days, and think of the Readers we then used; when we recall the rules that were taught us; when we recollect (as who cannot, almost verbatim?) the pieces we read; when we consider carefully their impress upon us, we are disposed to rank the influence of the School Reader upon childhood and youth, as second only to that of the Bible. Every sentence is dwelt upon, every sentiment expressed is pondered, until it is indelibly stamped upon the mind, while those books which are only once read, make but a slight impression which soon fades away.[5]

Taking their readers as models, schoolchildren were encouraged to address ambitious topics. Laying out eight rules for student writers of compositions, a Vermont educator promised that "if the student follows such a course, he will not only improve in composition, but in all his intellectual powers." Among the precepts:

> II. Reason upon your chosen theme, and make the broadest assertion truth will admit of, and the very broadest you dare attempt to prove;—for you, like the pleasure-voyager, are out for adventure, and should lay your cruise as far as your bread and water will allow. . . .

VI. Be content with no little theme. Seek something that demands labor—that admits argument. Let your efforts have a good head, and hold their size proportionately to the end. Exert your mind to the utmost. Use the most sure mental labor you are capable of.[6]

Such early injunctions laid the groundwork for the weighty topics of essays found in almost every lyceum paper: ruminations about virtue, proper behavior, the acceptance of death and the brevity of life, family responsibilities, the beauty of nature. Although many essays submitted to the papers seem to be mature compositions, older scholars often attended the neighborhood lyceums and probably submitted actual school essays to the lyceum paper's editor.[7] They had early experience of public performance of their work. Children presented their compositions at frequent school exhibitions, when parents and neighbors were invited into the schoolhouse to witness the scholars' achievements. Some schoolteachers created lyceum-style papers for their students, incorporating select student compositions and even the teacher's original contributions.[8] The Young People's Society for Mutual Improvement in Dublin, New Hampshire, actually included in its weekly proceedings the local schoolteacher's reading of a paper, the *Scrap Gatherer*, made up of such student compositions.

Because the lyceum almost always met in the schoolhouse where most of the lyceum participants had been—or, in some cases, were still—scholars, even the physical setting could suggest dense possibilities of allusion. In addition to inspiring serious poems and essays, school lessons provided templates for teasing and humor.

Parsing Lesson

John Staples is a common noun third person singular number masculine gender and the subject of Jessie Brown. . . .

George Dunning is a pronoun and agrees with Carrie Newman.

> George Staples is an adjective and belongs to Cora
> Brown. . . .
> Everett Newman is an adverb and modifies Ada Holt.[9]

> Berdell Pratt is a regular transitive verb future tense and shall
> or will have Ella May Libby.

> Transitive verbs require an object to complete the sense.[10]

As might be expected in a group dominated by young, single adults, most of the teasing was about courting, although in the longer pastiches, such as the popular alphabetical poems parodying the reading lessons of early childhood, other issues entered.

> ### Alphabetical poetry
> A stands for Albertie who is very smart
> and always ready to do his part.
> B is for Bean whose other name is Nellie
> To change it to Ranger would serve her quite well.
> C is for Cora who loves the fine art
> And often with Harvey is seen to depart.
> . . .
> O is for Opinion which people will express
> Sometimes upon our appearance and then upon our dress.
> . . .
> U is for Union which we must maintain
> Or all we can do will only be in vain.
> V is for Virtue which all may embrace
> Who'll drink nought but water and seek true grace.
> . . .
> Z is for Zenith of goodness and truth
> Which all may attain who start right in youth.[11]

For some writers, persisting all the way to Z was a challenge.

> W is for Wise—Wisdom and Wider
> X is cross and will not rhyme

Y is left to another time
Z is tired and so am I
So will bid you all good bye.[12]

The most popular schoolbook parodies were playful similes.

Ratios

As pearls are to diamonds,
So is Mary Hutchings to Sam Simonds. . . .
As a candle to the dark,
So is Fred Noyes to Jane Clark.[13]

Sometimes the rhyming comparisons suggest startling relationships:

As the book is to the cover,
So is Lena Getchel without a lover.
As the bark is to the birch,
so is Lizzie Berry to Mel Merch.
As the quilt is to the bed
So is Celia S. to Holts Fred. . . .
As the fire is to the coal
So is Almon to Ellen Towle.

And even . . .

As the fine comb is to lice
So is Hatty Gilman to Walace Tice.[14]

But not everyone was teased for romance:

As the water to the brook
So is Henry to his book.[15]

Childhood and family pastimes provided another set of literary models. Some papers presented word puzzles and provided answers in the following week's issue.

Charade
By "Joel Snap"
My first is the time when wild witches roam;
My second, plus N, is the travelers home;
My third rolls the ocean billows and foam.
Read forward, I'm all that is sweetest to hear,
But backwards I chill every sailor with fear.
Answer Next Week.[16]

Some included lists of local people's initials and "interpreted" their characters and habits by expanding the initials.

Abbreviations
L. B. C.	*Loves Beautiful Curls.*
M. H. C.	*Much Knowledge Carrys.*
W. E. C.	*Wants Every Cent.*
B. C.	*Beautiful Child.*
J. B. N.	*Just Before Night*
O. H. G.	*Oh! How Genteel.*[17]

Rhyming "Echo" couplets poked fun at courting couples and at wishful admirers.

Echoes
Who does Hattie Bean think fears to be alone.
Echo answers—John Holmes

Whose love would Willie Taylor like to gain
Echo answers—Josie Paine.

When does Floriman think Nellie is splendid
Echo answers—when their days work is ended.[18]

Regional delight in punning and other word play runs throughout the papers. Literalization of metaphors gave particular delight.

A Notorious eavesdropper. Rain.
Difficult lock to pick. One from a bald head.

Why is a prudent man like a pin. Because his head prevents him from going to far.[19]

In multiple genres local authors made puns on neighbors' names. Most common were teasing conundrums.

Why is a certain young man of this Lyceum like an Old Toper when going up to the bar to take a drink?

    Answer. Becaus he is bound to have a little Whit-More.

(Whittemore)[20]

Some writers extended the challenge. In an address marking the centennial of the town of Sweden, Maine, Wellington H. Eastman recalled a memorable item in an early lyceum paper:

It was made up of ingenious puns on the names of the residents, some of whom were exceedingly Smart, while others were extremely Poor. At one time in its past history, we are told, there was a Knight on one side of the road and a Day on the other, but at the time the article was written the Knight was perpetual. Yet notwithstanding the long Knights (I believe one was six feet two) had hard Frosts, they had Berrys the year round.[21]

The influence of prayer meetings and church sermons, and especially of lifelong reading of the Bible, shines through the essays and poetry, the pastiches and parodies. Heard again and again, the language and rhythms of the Bible gave neighborhood writers a powerful model for playful contributions.

My Wife's Commandments

Thou shalt have no other wife but me, nor shalt thou in thy sleep dream of other women. . . .

Thou shalt not get drunk, nor go to bed with thy boots on.

Thou shalt not say nice words to other ladies in my pre[se]nce nor praise them in my privacy. Remember I am a jealous wife.

Thou shalt not stay out after nine o'clock at night or snore at my side, or kick in thy sleep.[22]

Village authors occasionally submitted mock proverbs and pro-
phetic epistles (such as the jeremiad about hogs in the *Toll Bridge
Journal* quoted in chapter 1). They particularly enjoyed mimicking
biblical prose and images in longer narrative pieces. Generally
given the title "Chronicles," these pieces often describe the
founding of a particular lyceum or the events of the previous
meeting, layering local happenings with a mischievous overtone
of sacred history.[23] In 1849 an East Andover, New Hampshire,
author in the *Kearsarge Fountain* found the arch "Chronicle" style
useful for narrating the effects of the Gold Rush:

Chronicles Chapt. 5

*And it came to pass toward the latter part of the reign of Jared
king of the realm of N. Hamp. even the granite country, that
Jerico, called also Andover, and the whole valley of Jehosaphat
went away after strange idols. Inasmuch as all the people fell
down in their hearts and worshipped the golden calf which had
been set up before them. Certain men of the tribe of "Uncle Sam"
who dwelt beyond Egypt and the banks of Jordan, even in the
land of California or Gopher told certain marvelous words to
the people, which put a burning fire into their hearts; even a con-
suming flame of avarice. For verily it was spoken throughout the
whole land, that gold, yea very fine gold, like that in Solomon's
temple, was scattered in all the dust of the distant rivers.*[24]

This might have been the same author who penned for the
Fountain the following year a roguish chronicle about a temperance lecture so dull that young men fell asleep: *"their eyes
were heavy with watching on the night before."*[25]

Legal language also provided the stuff of humor. Sometime
in the 1870s a writer in East Bethel, Maine, came up with a set of
"Blue Laws" for Kimball Hill, the local neighborhood of most
of the paper's contributors, with such Sunday prohibitions as

*It shant be lawful for Etta Bartlett to be courted Sunday night
unless her mother sits in the room and takes notes. . . .
It shant be lawful for Jim Bartlett to kiss Etta more than three
times a day unless by her request in writing. . . .*

It shant be lawful for Mell Howe to court Grace in the school house unless Henry is present.[26]

Parody wills were also opportunities for teasing and laughter—though their points are often obscure to us outsiders. The "will" of Orlando Garvin in the *Emblem* (Landaff, NH) draws in much of the village.

A Will.

I, Orlando W. Garvin being weak in body but sound and perfect in mind, do make and publish this my last will and testament, in manner and form following.

First I give and bequeath to my beloved wife Lizzie all my personal property and real estate. I do also give and bequeath to my eldest son Benj. Morrill my best pair of thin boots. I do also give and bequeath to my two younger sons R. H. Noyes and R. T. Gordon my old hats to be divided equaly between them. I do also give & bequeath to my eldest daughter Laura G. Sherman one square foot of ground on which to raise beans for her especial benefit. I do also give and bequeath to my intended son-in-law Wm. H. Webber my new coat hoping he will make good use of it. I do also give and bequeath to my remaining daughter Martha Taylor the only brass kettle the family ever posesed. I do also give and bequeath to my great-uncle Foster Hall my iron bowed spectacles. I to also give and bequeath to my great grandfather Alson Little my new pair of cow hide boots. . . .[27]

The alleged testator, Orlando W. Garvin, was twenty-one years old and unmarried when this paper was created in 1860. His *"eldest son,"* Benjamin Morrill, was a forty-eight-year-old farmer, and his *"younger sons"* were likewise adults: Rufus H. Noyes, a local merchant, and Russell T. Gordon, a neighboring farmer, both thirty-five years old. Extending the joking inversion of ages, Garvin's *"great grandfather"* Alson Little was a fifteen-year-old schoolboy at the time and his *"great-uncle"* Foster Hall was sixteen. The bequests are likewise obvious jests, though we have little hope of recovering their community resonance. Other lyceum authors created versified wills whose rhyming couplets teased local courting couples. An 1877 issue of the *Bean's Corner Sunbeam* (Jay, ME) carried *"Aunt Jemima's Will,"* which begins:

> My will I've made, now free and clear
> I will all my things to my Children dear.
> . . .
> To Ossian Ripley and his Nellie
> I will give my Apple Jelly.
> . . .
> To Emma Niles and Grover Frank
> I give my dog that is so lank.
> . . .
> To Albertie Bean and Mamie T
> I give five cents to go on a spree.

It ends:

> This closes the list of all my wares
> to be given to my Children who live in pairs
> and any whom I've left behind
> may get all the dollars they can find.[28]

Adept as the lyceum authors were at versifying teasing couplets, they also composed a great deal of substantial poetry with more complicated prosody. Poetry was always a significant component of the lyceum papers. From their earliest childhood, community members had experienced poetry as a spoken social ritual, recited or read in the family home or the schoolhouse. Villagers knew, enjoyed, and could imitate poetic styles; they had a repertoire of stock poetic phrases and images to draw upon. All but six of some seventy lyceum papers I have read included poetry (as distinguished from casual taunting verses), with an average of three poems per issue. Though ballad stanzas and other quatrains are the most common form, some lyceum poets experimented with more complex prosody.

> Spring is coming making happy
> Ev'ry creature;
> Spreading joy and gladness only
> In every bosom sad and lonely
> While sweetest pleasure's ruddy bloom
> On each feature
> Assumes the place of sorrow's gloom.[29]

And—

> Fair Lizzie with such lovely hair
> And graceful form and queenly air
> And features so divinley fair
> That now they fill
> My mind with dreaming's that shall ne'er
> Within my heart be still.[30]

Prose fiction occurs only rarely in the papers I have seen. Particularly in the earlier decades lyceum stories echoed the modes and themes of popular published fiction. *"It was not all a dream"* narrates the sad history of a beaming country boy, "the darling of his mother," who went off seeking broader opportunities in the city, met bad companions, *"fell before temptation,"* and wound up in a grog shop in Canada, where he *"died a drunkard,"* leaving his poor mother with only her Christian faith to support her in old age.[31] Abolitionist sentiments spawned the horrors of *"A Picture,"* which presents *"a little group of happy children"* playing at nightfall *"on the seacoast of Africa,"* then captured by *"ruffianlike men"* from a lurking slave ship, to be free again only in heaven.[32] *"Lovers Island—A Legend of Loon Pond"* serializes through several issues of the *Kearsarge Fountain* a romantic local legend of star-crossed Indian lovers. Occasionally authors experimented with science fiction or fantasy.[33]

Lyceum authors' chosen topics ranged even more widely than the genres in which they wrote. A commentator on the papers of Pawlet, Vermont, remarked, "Contributions are furnished by members of the lyceum of volunteers, on almost every conceivable subject. This is the most attractive feature of the lyceum, and taxes the wit and wisdom of the contributors to their fullest extent."[34] The word "almost" is significant: although they accommodated occasional disagreements on other topics, lyceum papers deliberately avoided political and religious partisanship that could magnify rifts in the community. In 1841 editor Levi W. Leonard opened the new season of the *Rural Repository*, the paper of the Dublin (NH) Lyceum, with words that spoke to enduring practice:

> The principles laid down for its direction in past years, it is thought best to adhere to in future. . . . Sectarianism in religion and party politics, will be seen at once to be improper subjects for its columns. A paper thus conducted may not be so immediately interesting, as one in which, personal conflicts & the contest of parties are prominent. But there are subjects enough deeply interesting to well regulated minds, & highly useful for discussion, which are free from all objection; and many of the exciting topics of the day, if treated in a spirit of kindness and candor, might be profitably introduced.[35]

This editorial principle extended throughout the century. In 1859 the South Freeport, Maine, editor of the *Cruiser* complained about the difficulty of finding a topic for his editorial. "*We often feel that if ours was a political sheet, that if we could launch into the stormy waters of Politics, . . . it would be a comparatively easy task. But we know that 'Far removed from party turmoil / Ours a peaceful way must be.*"[36] The January 16, 1877, editorial in the *Bean's Corner Sunbeam* of Jay, Maine, offered a righteous justification, promising that the paper would be *"leaving out the political issues of the day and confining our selvs to the advancement and promotion of moral and social virtues."* Political commentary was rare and, when it appeared, was buffered by humor: "*Mr.*

Fred Farrington while in Saco recently was mistaken for a member of the last Legislature and arrested. He was charged with burglary, conspiracy, embezzlement, sedition, and false pretenses."[37]

Although the lyceum papers consciously avoided partisanship, their well-informed writers discussed some of the most challenging issues of the day: the value of farming, the wisdom of migration to the West, women's rights, temperance, the evils of slavery, the eviction of the Cherokees, the Gold Rush. The papers amply demonstrated Hal Barron's observation that the rural Northeast "was cross-hatched by competing visions deriving from a variety of sources including class, ethnicity, gender, and age."[38] The January 24, 1849, issue of the *Kearsarge Fountain* contains six pieces of varying styles and opinions relating to the Gold Rush, beginning with the arch biblical parody quoted earlier in this chapter describing the discovery of gold in California (*"Gopher"*), the subsequent worship of *"the golden calf,"* and the transmission of *"this unholy longing"* to East Andover, New Hampshire—where, however, the temptation was resisted: *"The father of the Mountain Club, even Wm. Fessenden, and Wilder the fox hunter, and the honest grinder of grists, with Ephraim the sower, the son of Jacob, and Joseph the black smith and Joseph of Aramathea, the shoemaker, all spoke wonderful words, and marvelous wonders, yea, verily, they set their faces towards Gopher, but not their feet."* However, "The Gold Fever," the essay immediately following, seems to argue in favor of joining the rush:

> *Why should men who can go remain here with the fact staring them full in the face that with all their persevering industry and close economy, they must remain barely "above board" through life. There are eight chances out of ten for a steady, sober industrious persevering man to go and load himself with riches enough for the wants and necessities of his future life. It is no wild scheme.*

On the other hand, a letter to the editor (*"Correspondence, From California. San Francisco. Jan. 1, '49"*) ostensibly provides a report from an East Andover man at the end of his first successful week in the gold fields, warning others not to come yet because of the dense swarm of diggers: *"You can't strike a pick down between the men who crowd the whole valley of the Sacramento. . . . A man in the crowd hasn't room enough to stoop down!"* The humorous thread is extended by a spoof advertisement (*"Notice: Ho! For California!!"*) seeking passengers for *"The new aerial 'semiballoons' steam propeller 'Forked Lightning'"* that will set off for California via the moon and *"the East branch of the Milky Way."* Cracker-barrel humor has its day in a letter to *"Mister Eddytur"* that seems a humorous parallel to *"The Gold Fever"* essay: *"I've got 'the fever,' it's a goin to sweep me off, I'm fraid, to anuther world, that is, to Californy. Its ragin in this place like the cholera."* The writer offers *"the follerin meloncolly fusion,"* eleven tetrameter stanzas that he wrote while deciding to start for the gold fields:

> *'Tain't no use to be discurridged:*
> *Men like me must earn their porridge,*
> *If they're poor and growin old*
> *They ought to go, and get some gold,*
> > *By Gracious.*
> *It shan't be said of Obed Grout,*
> *"He started once and then backed out";*
> *I think too much of my good name*
> *To play so weak a woman's game,*
> > *By Gracious.*
> *Come, rig yer tackle, fix yer strings!*
> *Histe them blankets up for wings!*
> *We'll plough the waves like fields of corn*
> *And cross cut goin round Cape Horn,*
> > *By Gracious.*

The final piece in the issue, a serious *"Penny Sermon"* on the dangers of relying on deceptive outward appearances, urges hearers to seek out the genuine *"solid substance, the reality and not the shadow."* Wittily written, the essay touches on the Gold

Rush: "*Sisters, if you can get your fingers upon a likely chap keep him as you would money—against the time of need! Don't let him dodge to California. If he don't now esteem you better than gold, you can bring him over and he will sometime!*"

In matters of faith as well as politics, lyceum members steered clear of disputes. Lyceums stayed rigorously apart from the century's intense competition among Congregationalists, Methodists, Free Will Baptists, Calvinistic Baptists, Universalists, and others. "*Sectarianism in religion,*" as Dublin's Levi Leonard put it, was strictly excluded from the papers, as it was from the community lyceums as a whole. Even if a neighborhood church building could have accommodated a lyceum meeting, members typically avoided the very appearance of sectarian affiliation, choosing to gather instead in the neutral space of the local school. Christian faith pervades the lyceum papers, but only on matters beyond controversy. Authors of all ages wrote repeatedly of the consolations of faith in times of sickness and death and of God's immanence in sunsets and rainbows, in the nearby landscape, and in the vastness of the ocean. They revisited perpetual, profoundly troubling issues—the brevity of our lives, the longing for loved ones who have passed away, the fear of losing those we love. Of the eight pieces by schoolchildren presented in the *Scrap Gatherer* at the November 8, 1854, meeting of the Young People's Society in Dublin, fully half focused on death, and the opening essay stated the conviction that lay behind the serious writings of young and old lyceum authors throughout the century: "*We are led to see . . . that the God of nature has some design in creating us, and placing us in this world. Let us then endeavor to meet the design for which we were created and placed here but for a few short years.*"[39]

"Eugene," the pseudonymous author of "*Footprints in the Snow*" in the *Kearsarge Fountain* of December 19, 1849, was evidently influenced by the rhythms of Edgar Allan Poe's "The Raven."

> *'Twas snowing snowing snowing*
> *And the wind was blowing*

When a stranger passed our door:
We bade him tarry through the storm
But his heart was stout and warm
And we saw him never more.

The snow kept falling falling
He passed beyond our calling
For the winds did fiercely blow:
All his record of the past
Were the footprints that he cast—
Were his footprints in the snow.

. . .

Thus, our names from earth will fade
Like the tracks the trav'ler made
When we leave these scenes below.
Thus shall vanish honors name
Thus man's glory, thus his fame
Like the footprints in the snow!

Overwhelmingly, the poets asserted the importance and the consolation of religious faith. Some of their poems urge faith directly.

Lines to a Doubting Brother
By Milo

Brother at the wayside doubting,
Why this sadness! why delay
Hear ye not the ransomed shouting
Those who trod this lonly way? . . .

If today your bark is driven
Among the rocks and surges roar
And you rest your hop[e]s in heaven
Then how soon the storm is o'er.

Oh! then press on in faith believing
Heaven will light your darksome way,

Cease forever all your grieving,
Aim for glory—launch away.[40]

Epideictic poems praising natural beauty conclude with gratitude to its creator.

The Rainbow
. . . O glorious emblem! with religious sensation
I view the[e] a token of God unto man,
My mind is filled with this sweet consolation
As I pensively view thy measureless span.[41]

Natural disasters and terrors likewise bespeak God's power, as in *"The Earthquake,"* whose tremors and passions *"All, all but tell us of a God / Who ruleth Heaven and earth."*[42] Human disabilities are, in the long view, temporary: *"The Blind Girl"* laments her darkness on earth but knows she will see glories in heaven.[43] A Dublin writer's poem in praise of books concludes that the greatest lesson they offer is to *"teach the tired spirit above earth to rise, / And soar to the mansions of rest in the skies."*[44]

Despite occasional differences of opinion, the lyceum writers shared and celebrated common ethical convictions. Authors submitted and audiences willingly listened to serious moral essays reflecting homogeneous values: "Men's Vanity," "The Duties of Youth," "The Influence of Bad Habits, "Politeness." Much lyceum poetry urged good behavior: do not waste time, never gossip, avoid the temptation of drink, persevere.

When once you've resolved to aim
At virtue's pure and lovely mark,
You surely will press on, obtain
The fair laurels of a pure and lovely heart.[45]

Writers applauded self-culture (the lyceums' stated mission), as in the Dublin paean to books:

Ye are friends to the young, ye are friends to the old,
Your pages are light, they myst'ries unfold.

> *Ye are solace in trouble, ye gladden our way,*
> *And make the dark night resplendent as day.*

Authors criticized misconduct—drinking, smoking, flirting, gossiping, and heedlessly joining the Gold Rush. Signing himself "A Friend," a Carthage, Maine, author directed a piece "*To our Boys at the Mills*," exhorting them to cease "*profane swearing*."[46] Writers employed humor as well as sober injunctions. Courting was one of the most popular topics in these papers—but propriety had to be observed or ribbing was sure to follow: "*Norris Kenerson and Rose Goodwin are giving free lessons in modern courtships at all our public entertainments. Come to our Lyceums and learn how to court by the improved method.*"[47] Writers acclaimed friendship and married love, prescribed the best way to seek a wife, lamented the failings and miseries of bachelors and "old maids," but sometimes applauded the freedom of single life. Occasionally editors juxtaposed items reflecting divergent views. The Landaff, New Hampshire, editors of the *Emblem* included "*The Wife That Meets One at the Door*," a popular, often-published paean to the joys of married life (prefaced by the explanation that "*A married man sends the following for the profit of the young gentlemen present*"); however, they followed it immediately with a locally composed poem, "*The Bachelor*":

> *Oh give me a life that's devoid of strife*
> *That never takes heed for the morrow*
> *With no woman to please, & no children to tease*
> *For their's no other fountain of sorrow.*[48]

However artfully deployed, some of the raillery in the papers seems rather ruthless to an outsider's modern ears. A wag in East Cabot, Vermont, composed seventeen stanzas of sharp tittle-tattle, building on the familiar what-shall-I-write-for-the-paper trope:

> *Poetry*
> *Write for the paper.*
> *What shall I write about*

Some silly caper
> *That's nearly played out.*

Or shall it be something
> *You all are familliar with*
The party at Durgans
> *Or Badgers last journeyings.*

Or better than that
> *Shall I tell you so sly*
Of the ride in the moonlight
> *And how they got high. . . .*

And theres Henry Jackson
> *So handsome and pert*
He's known to you all as
> *A heartless old flirt.*

He's been cutting up lately
> *Some way or some how*
With the kindly affections
> *Of Mrs. Nancy G. Howe.*[49]

Marital infidelity was fodder for badinage. Several papers tease married men ostensibly caught in compromising situations. The most extensive and entertaining narrative, headlined *"A Startling Incident,"* reports *"an unsuccessful attempt of a prominent citizen to elope with a married lady."* Mr. Abbott's unusual behavior had given his wife premonitions. Once, she reported, he actually hung up his hat when he entered the house, *"a thing he had never before been known to do."* Finally the wicked man left home as if for a committee meeting, but actually met one Mrs. Goodwin and set off with her in his wagon:

> *When half-way to Bethel Hill, however, the horse became frightened at something by the roadside and Mr. Abbott being unable to restrain him (having only one hand not engaged)*

*they were both thrown violently from the wagon and the horse
freeing himself from the shafts ran home. A passerby soon
noticed the mishap and set about to release the unfortunate
couple who were struggling to regain their equilibrium but
were unsuccessful as the wagon and its contents were top-most.*

*Upon finding herself free the lady took to her heels leaving
only one thing that betrayed her identity. This was a dental
plate set with two teeth in front which were thrown from her
mouth, at the time of the disaster.*

*Mr. Abbott was injured about the skull and has slowly
been recovering his senses ever since much to the satisfaction
of his wife.*

*It is stated upon good authority that as there was a box
of eggs in the wagon the unhappy pair presented a striking
symphony in yellow at the time of rescue. This is the second
mishap Mr. A. has experienced in trying to manage the horse
with his dexter hand. Moral:—don't try to do two things
at once.[50]*

This delicious episode seems to be a spoof directed at two
South Bethel, Maine, residents, Joshua Gayton Abbott and
Electia L. Goodwin, both of whom had married their respective spouses three years earlier. But as with so many pieces
in lyceum papers, there seems no way now to reconstruct
the background or the dynamics of the joke. Had the two,
perhaps, been courting each other before their engagements
to other partners? Had a recent wagon accident provided the
foundation of the elopement spoof? Who in the audience
found this funny, who found it offensive, and why? Everyone
in that schoolhouse understood; but barring the appearance
of extensive new evidence, we never will.

Despite their obvious enjoyment of gossip and teasing,
village authors idealized their communities. A Fryeburg poem,
"The Loggers," portrayed the skills of forest workers and celebrated their importance to the larger world, whose manufac-
tures depended on Maine lumber. The *Milford (NH) Enterprise*,
January 8, 1877, praised a recent paper read at the Wilton

Lyceum as "excellent and original, one of the pieces bringing in all of the places of business in town, in a very mirthful and pleasing manner. It was enthusiastically and loudly cheered." A New Hampshire writer celebrated East Andover, where

> No Lawyers office e'er was seen
> Within our village fair—
> Nor ever yet hath Sheriff been
> To find the guilty there—
>
> In this dear valley all are friends
> With no discords to jar;
> And chests and doors have never need
> Of lock or bolt or bar.[51]

Writers also commended their own lyceums as epitomes of friendship and virtue. This graceful salute to the members of the Landaff lyceum opens the January 20, 1860, issue of the *Emblem*:

> *Prelude*
> Hail social band, of friends most dear
> With joy replete I meet you here
> To join our friendly hearts sincere
> In sweet association.
> The joys of friendship none can guess
> Unless this jewel she possess
> For tis a source of happiness
> That we can meet in this retreat
> And feel our hearts in union beat
> Nor fear dissimulation.
>
> But destitute of discipline
> No land can long in splendor shine
> Nor actions e'er become divine
> Attaining to perfection.
> If through forgetfulness or pride

Any should be left to turn aside
May you in friendship gently chide
Or them suspend, till they amend
And walk by circumspection

Thus blest are we in pure delight
Secluded from the scoffers sight
In friendship sweet we here unite
In this association.
When cares or trouble us annoy
Or weariness doth mar our joy
[Or] ills or aught our bliss destroy
We'll here repair, forget our care
Instructions rich we e'er will share
Worthy of institution.[52]

Other lyceum eulogists were no less enthusiastic, though often less graceful:

Verses for the Sunbeam
Come one and all both old and young
Come for the good, if not for fun
For we have here a lyceum good
Which all may enjoy if they only would.

We have a question with a long debate,
And a declamation hard to be beat.
Then a recess, which the young like so well
So they can play and scream and yell.

After recess a nice paper is read. . . .[53]

Throughout the century, about a third of the poetry in the lyceum papers was intensely local—"folk poetry," in Pauline Greenhill's definition, "indigenous verse directed to a group or community of peers," tending to be "timely rather than timeless."[54] As the lyceum audience listened to these poems, to "chronicles" of their activities, even to rhymes and spoofs, perhaps they could see themselves as subjects of literature, elevated by prosodic translation into a realm like that of books or newspapers, made significant in the community by the authority of literature.

Because the surviving sample of lyceum papers is disappointingly random, scattered unevenly across the region and the century and representing the work of very few of the many editors and authors, it is impossible to know with certainty how the contents of the lyceum papers changed over time. Extant papers from earlier decades do include larger numbers of epideictic and expository essays, on a wider range of topics, compared with those later in the century. In January 1858, editress Sarah E. Batchelder of Mont Vernon, New Hampshire, included six essays in one issue of the *Literary Banner*: a lengthy description of the *"joyous and glad"* beauty of a summer's day, an angry essay contrasting America's boasts of liberty to its guilt in slaveholding, a short piece on the essential value of water, an article on the importance of using money properly, a piece (perhaps by a schoolchild) on the beauty of nature, and a final essay urging the cultivation of a contented mind. In later decades papers contained fewer and usually shorter essays on such topics, some drawn from published sources. The December 16, 1879, issue of the Fremont (NH) Literary Society's *Poplin Herald* included two derivative edifying essays: a virtually unchanged piece, *"Improvement of Time,"* that had been published and republished in school readers since the 1820s; and *"Other People's Spectacles,"* taken from a much longer 1872 original in *Harper's Bazaar* and pared down to statements relevant to village experience and assumptions.[55] The same issue also contained some extensive original pieces, including a history of Fremont attributed to a sixty-four-year-old local man and an unsigned tongue-in-cheek *"Chronicle"* account (quoted in chapter 2) of the founding of the local lyceum. In other lyceum papers, as in the *Poplin Herald*, original expository prose tended to be more locally focused as the century wore on.

Similarly, original poems composed for the papers in later decades tended primarily to be verses teasing neighbors, descriptions of the village or lyceum, or injunctions to write for the paper. Before the Civil War, local lyceum authors had composed much original poetry on general topics such as proper social behavior, the compensations of religious faith, relations between the sexes, rural life, and the value of friendship. But later, as commercial publications became more abundant in the countryside, editors and contributors often copied poems on these subjects from print sources—principally from newspapers but also from gift books, magazines, and other collections. Practice varied among editors. As early as March 1859, the editor of the first issue of the *Cruiser*, paper of the South Freeport (ME) Mutual Improvement Society, presented an editorial that seemed to suggest that he intended to include previously published poems: *"Besides the original matter, the Paper will contain the current news of the day, Poetry, a shipping list as well as all other matter of interest usually found in similar publications."*[56] The *Cruiser* contains a higher proportion of copied poetry than any other antebellum paper I have found. In contrast, in the surviving four 1858–59 issues of the *Literary Banner* of the Mont Vernon (NH) Young Men's Literary Club, I can identify only one of fourteen poems as derivative.[57]

Whether copied from print publications or composed by local authors, lyceum poems were easily understood by the listening audience, restating and validating feelings and opinions they already held. Such poems were generally constructed from familiar and durable stock images. In January 1859, for example, a local Mont Vernon author submitted an apparently original composition, *"How to seek a wife,"* to the *Literary Banner*:

> Look to the heart, and you will surely find
> If there are gems within its centre shrined.
> If you would choose a faithful friend for life
> Remember then 'tis the heart that makes the wife.[58]

Such conceits dwelt in the air for decades. In 1880 Alma Harriman, editress of the West Plymouth (NH) Lyceum's *Gem of the Valley*, chose to copy into her paper a widely published popular poem, *"The Wife,"* with very similar sturdy concepts and images:

> For that full heart in her dear breast
> If rightly prized, eternal rest
> Is not with blissful sweets more rife
> Than that pure heart—a loving wife.[59]

It may be no coincidence that the editress opened her paper with an editorial thanking *"the few contributors."* It was her responsibility to present a complete paper, and she could not be expected to compose it all herself. She was, however, expected to uphold positive community ethics and aesthetics in her paper, as another poem in the issue makes clear. In this locally written piece, the author (possibly Alma Harriman) celebrated by name many of the lyceum's editors, thanking the *"ladies who've served as Editress here, / and given us thoughts life's pathway to cheer."* Apart from this poem, only the editorial and one teasing couplet are certainly original in the issue. Harriman, and possibly some of her *"few contributors,"* drew on printed sources for *"The Wife"* poem, for a portion of an essay on *"Keeping Secrets,"* for a humorous sketch of a man who mistakenly put his head into the kitchen cupboard at night to check the weather, and for multiple short jokes (*"What is the oldest Woman's Club? Ans. The broomstick."*).

Some of the derivative pieces in this issue of the *Gem of the Valley* demonstrate another aspect of the relationship between lyceum papers and commercial content: local writers felt free to alter and adapt the pieces they borrowed. *"The Wise and Foolish Man,"* a comic piece widely published from Maine to California in 1879, usually began "The foolish man payeth six dollars a year for his daily newspaper. The wise man standeth and readeth from the bulletin board and obtaineth his information for nothing." In the *Gem of the Valley*, however, the piece was brought home to West Plymouth: *"The foolish man payeth a dollar a year for the Grafton County Journal. The wise man cometh to our Lyceum, & obtaineth his information for nothing."*

Popular culture often provided lyceum authors with a takeoff point for comic parodies. The author of *"Serenade by Peter,"* which appears in an 1848 issue of the *Kearsarge Fountain*, adopts the meter and refrain of a contemporary popular song, "Wake, Lady, Wake":

> Wake, lady, wake, and list to me,
> While I my love unfold to thee,
> The silver moon looks smiling down
> And sheds her mellow rays around
> And flow'rets gemmed with pearly dew
> The glowing landscape wide bestrew,
> Wake, wake, lady, wake.[60]

but invents original words that tweak the nose of the sentimental favorite:

> *Wake, lady, wake,*
> *Your dad is now a snoarin',*
> *So lift the window, rosy gal,*
> *And hear the song I'm pourin',*
> *So, wake, lady, wake!*[61]

Given the delight that lyceum authors and audiences found in witty teasing, it is not surprising that they appropriated published pieces for this purpose. A Maine contributor, for instance, made free with verses originally from the Harvard *Crimson*:

> *Riding in a sleigh*
> *on a winter night*
> *Sat a Weld youth* [in the original, "a Harvard Junior"]
> *with a maiden bright.*[62]

A contributor to the *Enterprise* of West Danville, Vermont, adapted the popular poem "The Old Maid's Prayer" as *"Frantie's Prayer,"* substituting the local name "Frantie" for the generic "old maid," and naming "Will Walker"—a thirteen-year-old!—as Frantie's intended.[63] In the *Monitor* of East Cabot, Vermont, a writer slyly substituted the names of Frank Chandler and Mae Howe, a local courting couple, for the stock names in the much-reprinted "Popping Corn." The violation of the rhyme scheme in the altered first quatrain attests to the fact that the social benefits of the substitution were more important than technical quality.

> And there they sat a poping corn,
> F. Chandler and Mae Howe. [in the original, "John Styles
>   and Susan Cutter"]
> Frank as fat as any ox,
> And Mae as fat as butter.
>
> And there they sat and shelled the corn,
> And raked and stirred the fire,
> And talked of different kinds of corn,
> And hitched their chairs up nigher.
> . . .
> And Frank he ate and Mae she thought,
> The corn did pop and patter,
> Till Frank cried out, The corn's afire!
> Why Mae, what's the matter?
>
> Cried she, Frank C—it's one o'clock
> You'll die of indigestion!
> I'm sick of all this popping corn—
> Why don't you pop the question?[64]

We can imagine the general laughter in the schoolhouse at the couple's reaction to the final stanza.

The range of literary styles and topics in the lyceum papers is extensive, and their miscellany was deliberate, as Webster, New Hampshire, editor Detta Goodhue acknowledged in her opening editorial for her lyceum's paper, the *Scrap Book*. Playing with the title, she began, *"Our lives are mostly made up of scraps,"* and after comparing lives of happiness and affliction to different kinds of scrapbooks, she concluded by describing *"those that are a mixture of smiles and tears, a little of every thing that help the world to be better by the variety of thier talents. . . . The scrap book that I offer you tonight is of that type."*

Despite my modern literary tastes, which would skim past many pieces no longer in fashion, and despite my inability to reconstruct the weekly events and quotidian lives that made so many of the pieces meaningful to their original listeners, I take seriously the lyceum writers' conviction that their papers could improve the mind and the world. George E. Emery's concluding editorial for the Mountain Club's *Kearsarge Fountain* makes a strong claim.

> *The Kearsarge Fountain should be supported even at the expense of all our other exercises aside from our discussions [i.e., debates]. The advantages accruing from discussions and literary compositions as exhibited in the Fountain are nearly equal. No one will expose his ignorance enough to deny it. By composing we learn to think—to think deeply—we acquire a command of language and learn to express our thoughts. We enlarge the mind and cultivate the imagination. New channels of thought are opened to the mind. Ideas that glow with beauty—thoughts that burn with the fire of feeling flash like new created constellations of stars across the once dark and unenlightened sky of the mind and we may go on to higher and higher attainments until the light of knowledge shall beam upon us like the glory of the meridian sun. Let us not scorn the privilege that the pages of the Fountain afford us for improvement. Let each member of this club feel that this paper is not calculated only for amusement and the enjoyment of the hour but for a Fountain of unfailing good.*[65]

Emery's purple rhetoric blossoms from a profound conviction of the value of every aspect of the paper.

The papers proclaimed and maintained the community's shared identity and aspirations. Playful and serious by turns, they spoke to the neighbors' joy in social occasions, their pleasure in literature, and their earnest devotion to mental improvement. It is little wonder that, apart from the debates, they were the only activity specifically called for in lyceum constitutions. In many ways the two undertakings were complementary: the debates primarily controlled by men, the papers by women; the debates focused on single topics, the papers deliberately miscellaneous; debate participants appointed and identified, paper authors voluntary and anonymous; the debates agonistic, the papers convivial. Together they brought people face to face to renew their commitment to both individual education and the collective good.

CHAPTER 7

"READ BY SO MANY EAGER SUBSCRIBERS"

The Press as Model

We are happy to offer the Kearsarge Fountain to the public, as the most valuable double, compressed, royal mammoth octavo sheet, ever issued from the American press; and it will ever be the aim of its Editors, to render it the most acceptable and popular paper ever taken by the citizens of this "great and growing" city.

—Kearsarge Fountain (East Andover, NH) 2, no. 1, December 6, 1848

Although rural lyceum authors had no shortage of models for their creativity, their literary efforts were most obviously inspired, shaped, named, and framed by those vigorous and generative nineteenth-century publications: newspapers. Yet on first acquaintance, lyceum productions bear little resemblance to newspapers. They were handwritten, never printed. They were not formatted like newspapers; their articles were simply written onto copybook or ledger pages that were then folded, pinned, or sewn together or tied with ribbon or yarn. They could not circulate like newspapers because each issue existed in only one copy. They were intended not for mass distribution or private reading but for public performance to a community group. And their editors, being predominantly female, did not fit the masculine norm of the American newspaper editor. In their production, material appearance, gender associations, and presentation, the lyceum papers communicated intimacy, neighborliness, and sociability; they might seem to be the antithesis of the commercial newspapers of their era.

Nonetheless, their creators and their audiences called these little manuscript documents "papers," and lyceum members chose to emulate newspapers even though other models were available for the incorporation of literature into their meetings. Members' compositions could simply have been read aloud individually, as they were in some college literary societies. Had the lyceums wished to adapt a different form of literary compendium to contain their compositions, they could have modeled their production on commonplace books, albums, or scrapbooks, all of which were readily available. Instead, the village lyceum tradition fashioned papers whose very names evoked the contemporary press: *Wednesday Evening Post, Literary Banner, Toll Bridge Journal, Bean's Corner Sunbeam, Veazie Light, Monitor, Poplin Herald, Gem of the Valley, Enterprise.* Beyond their titles, lyceum papers emulated the popular press in other obvious ways. Occasionally a paper sported a hand-decorated banner, with graphics or elaborate calligraphy, although much more frequently the cover was plain written. Elaborate or not, the cover usually included some of the kinds of information

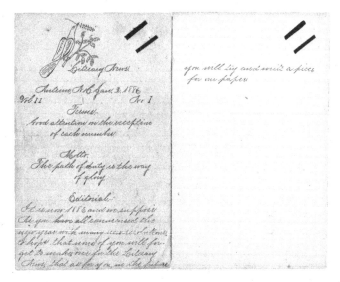

FIGURE 8. An unusually decorative lyceum paper cover: *Literary News* (Antrim, NH) 2, no. 1, January 2, 1886. Courtesy of the New Hampshire Historical Society, Concord.

found on a printed paper's banner and masthead: the number of the volume and issue, the date, the place of publication and perhaps the name of the sponsoring organization, the names of the editors, a motto, and the terms of "subscription." The language of this standard information ("*published by . . .*") and the naming of the producers as editors and editresses evoked the organization of the publishing world. On the cover page of the *Independent* (South Levant, ME), March 23, 1881, the two editresses even list themselves as "Publishers."

It is not surprising that residents even of the smallest villages of northern New England were thoroughly familiar with the commercial press. "No people are equal to Americans in their appreciation of newspapers," wrote George P. Rowell, the editor of the first directory of newspapers in the United States,

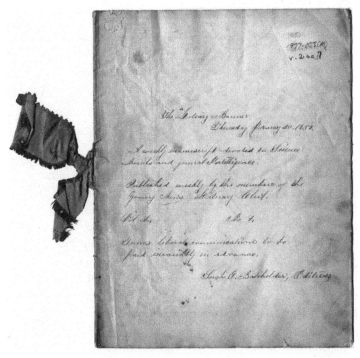

FIGURE 9. Cover page, *Literary Banner* (Mont Vernon, NH) 2, no. 7, January 20, 1859. Courtesy of the New Hampshire Historical Society, Concord.

in 1873.[1] The nineteenth century saw astronomical increase in the publication of newspapers. By one tally, ninety-two were published in the United States in 1790; fifty years later, the number was 1,404—a growth that was more than three times faster than that of the U.S. population. Circulation to private citizens increased accordingly: at the beginning of this period, perhaps 10 to 12 percent of American households subscribed to newspapers; by the end, at least two-thirds held subscriptions.[2] Rowell claimed that, by 1885, 13,494 papers were being published.[3] Looking back through his lifetime to his 1790s childhood in Ridgefield, Connecticut, the author and publisher Samuel Goodrich remembered, "Even the young approached a book with reverence, and a newspaper with awe. How the world has changed!"[4] Small wonder that M. F. Sweetser, contributing to a volume of *Hints for Home Reading* in 1880, saw newspapers as a threat to the reading of actual books:

> When to the city dailies we add the rural weeklies, the
> story papers, the agricultural and specialist organs, and
> the great host of religious papers, the wonder rises how
> America can find time to attend to such a mass of ephem-
> eral prints, and it seems that the larger part of our reading
> must be done outside of books.[5]

A local correspondent reported in the *Grafton County Journal* on a debate held at the Bridgewater (NH) Lyceum in the same year: "There was a full attendance, over 90 being present. . . . Question: Resolved, That newspapers exert more influence than books. . . . Decided by judges in the affirmative."[6]

This explosion in newspaper publishing fostered widespread popular imitation of the commercial press. Beginning in the 1830s, and increasingly as professional journalism expanded, not only lyceum members but also hobbyists, associations, social groups, and even families were inspired to produce a variety of private newspapers. The postbellum national amateur newspaper movement was particularly visible. Especially in urban areas, middle-class teenage boys (and a very few girls) flocked

toward what was termed *amateurdom*, printing small papers
that mimicked the physical format of commercial newspapers
and often gave priority to professional form over content.[7]
The movement blossomed in the 1870s and after as aspiring
amateur editors set their own type, printed, and circulated
their little papers nationally, chiefly in exchanges with editors
of other papers in "The Dom," as its devotees called it.[8] Jessica
Isaac suggests that the rise of amateurdom in America was
connected with the evolution of the idea of adolescence, when
"middle-class teenagers were being increasingly infantilized
by the growing length of the 'idle' years of dependence" and
wished to demonstrate their own independence and readiness
for adulthood. Indeed, for many youths, publishing amateur
papers was the preface to a journalistic career.[9]

Locally focused and less conspicuous than the more durable
productions of the amateur movement was the century's flow-
ering of local manuscript newspapers. Even children produced
handwritten domestic newspapers. Probably the most famous
was *The Pickwick Portfolio*, created in the garret on rainy days
by the sister members of the Pickwick Club in Louisa May
Alcott's *Little Women* (1867). Authors of books on children's
amusements recommended making an impromptu newspaper
as an absorbing and improving family activity. Aunt Carrie's
Popular Pastimes for Field and Fireside gives typical instructions
for a "Family Newspaper," showing that some of the conventions of lyceum papers were common in other handwritten
papers as well:

> This is an excellent pastime for a large family, or several
> families can unite in it. Choose the most ready writer, and
> the person of the best judgment among your number, for
> the editor. He must also be a good penman. Your paper
> can be a weekly or a monthly journal as you please. Every
> member of the family must contribute one or more arti-
> cles for the paper, either serious, laughable, instructive,
> or absurd pieces, and give to the editor in season for him
> to arrange his paper, and publish it at the appointed time.

> Such as wish to conceal their authorship must notify the
> editor, and he is bound in honor not to reveal the name of
> any writer without his permission. . . . The paper can then
> be read aloud to the family, or each can read it separately.

In the family, as in the larger community, the production and performance of a manuscript paper could promote sociability. "The family paper," Aunt Carrie added, "will be found to add another link to the home chain."[10]

Community-focused manuscript newspapers were a welcome literary addition to many kinds of gatherings. In addition to the rural lyceums, they were created for and read aloud at Sunday schools and other church groups, village temperance societies, Civil War army camps and military prisons, common schools, extracurricular student debating societies in secondary schools and colleges, women's literary clubs, and more. Special occasions could inspire a group to create a paper; young people gathering for a Christmas party in Chatham, New Hampshire, for example, produced a very full compendium.[11] In her 1875 diary Emily Luther McKenney of Bethel, Maine, reported: "T 2/23 Went up to the spelling school at the school-house this evening and had a rather good time. The boys spoke pieces and Sybil read a Candle Lecture, and I read "The Echo" Volume 1st, No. 3. There was quite a crowd out."

In the autumn of 1856, Bristol, New Hampshire, teenagers Annie D. Green and Annie P. Bartlett created *Bristol Wild Flowers*, a manuscript journal of prose and poetry with covers featuring elegant calligraphy.[12] A neighborhood circle in Sweden, Maine, produced *The Ladie's Enterprise*, "An Elegant Literary Journal," "Edited and published by females."[13] The writers of the *Hampton Budget* of October 20, 1847, perhaps boys at Hampton (NH) Academy, used its pages to take enthusiastic aim against evident rivals in the neighboring town of Epping.[14] Local temperance lodges, generally energized and supported by the same young adults as were active in the lyceums, often included papers in their meetings, adapting popular genres to the cause:

> A is for alcohol, that wicked king
> When he is dead we'll rejoice and sing.
> B is for beer, some think it a thing small,
> But those who indulge are liable to fall.
> C is for cider, 'tis made on the farm,
> When it is freely used it causes much harm. . . .[15]

Individuals who loved to make papers tended to produce them for diverse occasions.[16] Ada Berry of Carthage, Maine, who edited the temperance paper just cited, had also been involved with Carthage's lyceum paper a few years earlier.[17] In addition to editing the *Scrap Book*, a lyceum paper, Gavuetta "Detta" Goodhue of Webster, New Hampshire, edited the *League Scrap Basket* for the Methodist ladies of her Epworth League; the *Golden Harvester* for the Daniel Webster Grange; and numerous papers for the children she taught in various local schools. She also encouraged a group of local children in the "Fun Club" of Webster to produce the *Corser Hill Journal*.[18] Thaddeus P. Mason of Dublin, New Hampshire, created many papers for his common-school pupils in the 1840s. When Mason initiated the *Scholars' Gazette* for his pupils in Dublin, he explained its purposes in a lyceum-style prospectus that argues with ponderous wit for the educational importance of such journals:

> To meet any objections that may be urged against the
> propriety of adding another to the almost infinite host
> of newspaper periodicals, the editor would say, that not-
> withstanding the vast amount of newspaper wares with
> which the country is literally flooded, still a publication
> of this kind is absolutely needed to meet the pressing
> wants of the community; and further, that the paper has
> for its object the improvement, intellectual and moral,
> of its supporters, and particularly their improvement in
> English composition.[19]

Like the lyceum papers, these other manuscript papers were ephemeral, each issue existing in only one copy and intended to be read aloud to a group. Compared to the village lyceums, however, their audiences were less diverse in age and interests, and perhaps this is why their papers tended to be less miscellaneous in their contents. Most focused on single purposes (temperance, religion, training in composition), made fewer local allusions, and avoided the pointedly teasing humor of the lyceum compendia. Although the non-lyceum manuscript papers adopted some of the external trappings of commercial newspapers—titles, masthead information—the lyceum papers engaged far more thoroughly with the conventions and intentions of contemporary journalism.

Lyceum editors probably modeled the contents of their papers on the typical nineteenth-century weekly newspaper that circulated to rural households. In the words of *Haney's Guide to Authorship* (1867), such papers differed from the dailies "not only in giving more space to local news, announcements, and interesting specialities, but in sharing [their] pages with general literature, having stories, poems, sketches." The commercial rural newspaper in particular, *Haney's Guide* observed, had a necessary formula: "A little of everything, and everything in little, will make a journal that must win favor."[20] The handwritten lyceum papers proclaimed their eclectic approach even in their mottoes: "*Devoted to Science, Morals, and general Intelligence*" (*Literary Banner* [Mont Vernon, NH], 1858–59); "*Devoted to Amusement & Instruction*" (*Meteor* [Kenduskeag, ME], 1884). As we have seen, the editors of lyceum papers sometimes supplemented local material with pieces copied from printed sources. The popular press, too, routinely reproduced pieces from other papers, with or without attribution. *Haney's Guide* explicitly advised rural editors how to do this: "The literary portion of the paper may be easily made fresh, and so of miscellaneous matter. Instead of reprinting a story from some second-class American magazine or from some old book and clipping labored wit from exchanges, not always the freshest, it is best for the country editor to steal from the same sources as his city neighbors."[21] Although the lyceum journals were primarily dependent on their readers (their local audience) for their content, even in this they had some kinship with the contemporary press, which allocated large sections to readers' correspondence, some of which amounted to full articles.[22]

In the public-spirited missions they proclaimed for their papers, the lyceum editors compared themselves to the publishers of contemporary family papers. *"Advancement in morals"* was the motto of Carthage, Maine's, paper, *Mystic Tie*, one that matches the portrait it paints in its idealistic piece on *"The Value of the Press"*:

> The press exerts great influence on the minds of the people: our characters are formed from what we read. . . . The press is always on the side of justice and humanity; it is the first to censure the corrupt management of our congressmen, it is first to demand the punishment of all crimes. . . . There is nothing else in the country that tends to improve the morals of the people as much as the press.[23]

Like the village lyceum productions, commercial papers aimed to engage and serve a diverse community. In 1860, preparing to defend the virtues of the *New York Ledger* for a public debate in Barre, Vermont, nineteen-year-old Rufus Fowler (who had for more than two years been an active member of a rural lyceum that also produced a paper) argued that the *Ledger* served all readers:

> The N.Y. Ledger seeks to present something which shall be suited to all classes and conditions in life, something which shall cheer the lone hours of gloom and despair which sometimes do hover around the family fireside, to give advice to such as need counsel in the tumultuous journey of life, to afford a means of recreation to the student, the professional man and the man of toil as he seeks to cool his heated brow by a moment's respite from a day of noble industry.

Indeed, Fowler concluded, the *Ledger*'s "mesmeric influence" on its wide readership created national unity: "The *Ledger* is today the exponent of ideas which course alike through the veins of all its patrons binding its millions of readers together in one united brotherhood with bonds stronger than the fickle ties of interest or of friendship."[24]

Some of the contents of the lyceum papers seem well designed to match the high goals their editors felt they shared with the weekly press. Authors contributed serious essays on moral topics; they produced sentimental poetry and fiction reflecting domestic and community life and an appreciation of natural beauty; they wrote letters to the editor and thoughtful pieces on contemporary events. However, most of the obvious allusions to the commercial press were tongue-in-cheek, as in this 1878 editorial in the *Monitor* (East Cabot, VT): *"Though it has bin but a short time since* [the *Monitor's*] *first appearance before the public, its large and still increasing circulation tells how well it has been received by the people."* Business and personal notices, advertisements and solicitations for ads, lost-and-found announcements, letters to the editor, news items, farming and domestic advice, weather reports, police records, recipes, announcements of auctions, marriage and obituary notices, shipping news— these characteristic newspaper genres, often mimicked in the lyceum papers, were almost always manipulated as jokes. From the *Gem of the Valley* (West Plymouth, NH), January 22, 1880:

West Plymouth Market

Yeast cakes are rising.
Liquors of all kinds have a downward tendency.
The demand for certain young ladies is good. Market price one to every two young gents.
Belles are still in great demand.

The *Monitor* carried the following report on February 27, 1878:

We have often urged upon our patrons the necesity of advertising in the Monitor, and a few have patronized our advertising columns, and always with good results. We publish but one instance. In our issue of last week Miss Lizzie Abbott, who is sorely afflicted with corns, advertised for a remedy. The next

> *morning bright and early a pedd[l]er called with a plaster*
> *warented to pull them out by the roots every time. You can all*
> *see the value of advertising in our paper.*

Like every other lyceum paper, the *Monitor* never contained an actual "advertising column."

Many of the journalistic pastiches play with the local courting aspirations and disasters that bulked so large in the lives of the lyceums' young adult members.

Lost

A verry small pastboard box containing a pinch of ashes. This being all that remains of a true heart, devoured by the flame of love, kindled by that false-hearted lass, Hatty Gilman. Any person finding the same will please return it to its owner, Will Abbott.

> (*Monitor* [East Cabot, VT] 1, no. 3, January 9, 1878)

Marriages

The upright notorious Frank Morse and the surpassingly beautiful Florence Field were united in the holy bonds of Door Lock. The poor fellow had to walk home in the rain saying it was the first time she ever turned the key on him; she would never have a chance to do it again.

> (*Gem of the Valley* [West Plymouth, NH], vol.
> unknown, issue 1, November 30, 1878)

In the case of the frequent lyceum paper pieces entitled "*Marine News*" or "*Shipping News*," there was an immediate wink, because almost invariably the lyceums were located in inland villages with no access to the coast and no shipping business whatsoever. Instead, these pieces were always a sly tease about the fortunes and activities of courting couples:

Marine News

The fast sailing schooner Amasa Snow in company with the big Minnie Wing, sailed from Wilson's harbor Tuesday morning

March 15th with a fine breeze from the northeast! They passed the great war vessels Walker and Eldridge, and were hailed by them, but as they had such an amount of canvas spread they did not hear them! They were going eighty knots a minute. They arrived safe in port somewhere between the time they started and the next day.

All of the "ships" named are actually young people of South Levant, Maine. The Walker and Eldridge vessels evidently were not sailing together permanently, given this business notice in the same issue:

Dissolution

The copartnership hitherto existing under the name of Walker and Eldridge is hereby dissolved and after this date will be known as Griffin and Eldridge.

Signed Daniel Walker
Carrie Eldridge

And the fast-sailing "big Minnie Wing" was in for even more teasing in this piece of the weather report: *"Minnie Wing says the snow is getting soft, and she ought to know."*[25]

The teasing targeted much more than romance. "Journalistic" notices played with many areas of rural life. A *"Sheriff's Sale"* announcement in 1858 promised *"one good sled minus the runners,"* and *"Household Furniture, such as a feather bed and pillows, minus the feathers"* and even *"an Old Cat with five kittens."*[26] A *"Runaway"* notice sought *"a valuable pig . . . so large that he made his exit through the spout from which he received his daily food."*[27] In a piece ostensibly presenting theater reviews, the *Kearsarge Fountain* of December 19, 1849, included this account of the local common school's end-of-term exhibition: *"The season closed with magnificent tableaux and the favorite Local Drama entitled 'Winter School Is Over' before a house crowded almost to suffocation."* Three of the *Toll Bridge Journal* writers' responses to an unwise hog purchase by some leading citizens (discussed in chapter 1) took the form of journalistic parodies: a brief "news" item, headlined *"No Certainty in Hogs,"* a notice of a forthcoming *"scientific lecture upon the subject of hogology,"* and a deadpan recipe for soapmaking, detailing the false economy of buying a sick pig solely for its lard.

The lyceum papers echoed and burlesqued the commercial press not only in specific journalistic genres but also in the content of local news reports. In 1867 *Haney's Guide* presented rather condescending guidelines for rural newspaper reporting:

> A good rural paper should . . . aim at chronicling every-
> thing of interest that occurs in its neighborhood; and its
> editor should bear in mind that scarcely anything can
> occur in a rural district, from a fight at a rustic gathering
> to an extraordinary crop of corn, that has not interest. . . .
> Where occurrences of the week are not exciting, things
> of less wonderful nature are proper, as they are the only
> substitutes.[28]

Local news columns in the weekly press typically reported a variety of everyday or seasonal occurrences such as social or family gatherings, school activities, and public meetings and events, but they also seized upon any phenomena at all peculiar, from crimes, accidents, and natural disasters to remarkable accomplishments, bizarre creatures, and agricultural abnor-malities.[29] Playing with these conventions, the lyceum authors gleefully created pieces of *"Home News"* not for information but for tongue-in-cheek commentary. According to the *Independent* of South Levant, Maine, *"The oldest inhabitant of this village is Mellie Shaw who is 105 yrs of age. He has a keen recollection of some war incidents, can even remember kissing Minnie Booker to the party last Sat. night."*[30] In a similar vein, the *Gazette* of South Bethel, Maine, included a "report" about an unusual local farmer:

A Great Curiosity
There is a great curiosity at South Bethel which attracts
everyone far and near (especially the ladies). This is a living
encyclopedia the only specimen found in this country. 'Tis an
ungainly-looking object somewhat resembling a gorilla but
possessing the organs of a human being.

> *The amount of food it consumes is most extraordinary. It has been known to eat with great gusto 9 qts. of baked beans, 5 lbs. of pork, 4 loaves of brown bread, 29½ doughnuts and 7 pumpkin pies at one meal, but what surprises everyone most is its ability to answer the most difficult questions thus manifesting remarkable brain power. It can tell the definition and pronunciation of every word in the Eng. language, explain the Bible from first to last, in fact as far as wisdom goes Solomon has to take a back seat on account of this strange biped whose common name is Columbus Kimball.* [31]

Lyceum writers poked fun at the humdrum non-events of the winter season and at the fact that there was no news in the village that was not common knowledge: *"People not aware of the fact will be pleased to hear that we have had a storm beginning March 2nd ending March 6th."* [32] Editors were well aware that the bar was low for the newsworthy. *"It don't do to tip over when you go sleighing, and to tell the truth its dangerous to be safe, for if you do or if you don't, you will be sure to see an item in the Monitor. But then it makes the Editor good natured, he is verry glad to get the news, no matter who the victim may be."* [33]

Clearly, newspapers were so common in rural New England villages that they provided an available code, a ready cultural language of allusion and metaphor, ripe for the verbal joking that Yankees have so long delighted in. This journalistic humor in the lyceums can be interpreted in several ways. One of the most obvious qualities in the jokes is self-deprecation: rueful, ironic acknowledgment that, although its natives read the city papers, the rural hamlet is not the city. Nothing of note happens here to report. (It snowed a lot in March.) We may not be proficient businessmen. (Courting couples are our "shipping" business; our auctions feature broken-down paraphernalia.) Our artistic accomplishments are humble. (The school exhibition is our "Local Drama.") Even our prominent farmers can blunder. (They invest in moribund hogs.) Unlike the weeklies we read, our lyceum paper is not a major marketing tool. (At best, our ads can lure a peddler to bring corn plasters.) We are not publishers of major newspapers. (*"This paper is young,"* wrote the editors of the *Emden (ME) Center Times* in 1893, *"but if nourished, will be one of the leading papers of Emden."* At that time no papers at all were published in the tiny village.) The first issue of the *Cruiser* (South Freeport, Maine, 1859) opens with an editorial that makes a moue at the world of commercial journalism: *"Not being in a situation to pay large amounts for Prize Stories, Prize Essays, Mount Vernon Papers, etc, we shall not try to compete with the New York Ledger at present, in these respects. We shall have to depend principally on common sense articles from the common sense community of South Freeport, and we feel assured that in so doing our devil will never want for copy."*

On the one hand, therefore, the lyceum papers' journalistic jokes acknowledged that the village lacked the advantages of the city. On the other hand, they can be seen to claim that the city lacked the advantages of the village. In their journalistic humor, the villagers simultaneously acknowledged their handicaps in the modern commercial world and challenged how that world was impinging on the rural life they valued. Sigmund Freud has taught us that jokes can express resistance to control. In this case, they gave a minority—and the villagers *knew* they represented a minority—a satisfying way of subverting the structures that controlled it.

What were the lyceum authors subverting? One clue lies in their many parody newspaper items relating directly to the sale of papers and the commercial uses of the popular press: terms of subscription, ads and solicitations for ads, business notices, auction announcements, shipping news. The nineteenth century saw the first major move toward commercialization of the news, as small-circulation party publications yielded to the dominance of the penny press and readers, in the eyes of publishers, changed from voters to consumers. "A newspaper is a thing made for sale," proclaimed *Haney's Guide*. "It is as much a marketable matter as a pair of shoes, or a coat. It must be made to suit the views and wishes of its customers."[34] In their tongue-in-cheek allusions to their "subscribers" or to the "terms" of subscription, the lyceum editors, masters of irony, called attention to the fact that *their* papers were not commodities; they could not be bought. In an announcement typical among rural lyceum papers, the cover of the *Literary Banner* (Mont Vernon, NH, 1858) proclaimed its price: *"Terms: liberal communications to be paid invariably in advance."* That is, this paper was "purchased"—supported—not by cash but by the pieces its contributors wrote. Lyceum commerce was not in money but in communication and personal participation.

This message was reinforced by the physical production of the lyceum papers, which were invariably handwritten. It is true that rural hamlets had little access to commercial printing presses, but this does not fully account for their exclusively chirographic papers. Although affordable presses for hobbyists were available and well advertised after the Civil War, these were never used by village lyceums. Instead, the editors copied pieces carefully onto whatever paper came to hand—copybook or ledger pages, miscellaneous stationery—in a process more akin to private letter writing than to commercial publication. Consciously or not, lyceum members made a significant choice to avoid mechanical printing. "It was print," writes Tamara Thornton, "that endowed handwriting with its own, new set of symbolic possibilities; script emerged as a medium of the self in contradistinction to print, defined as characteristically impersonal and disassociated from the writer. Handwriting thus became a level of meaning in itself, quite apart from the sense of the text."[35] As the lyceum editress copied her neighbors' contributions, one at a time, strategically arranged, in her own handwriting, she could envision a personal connection to each writer and think, perhaps, about what the piece had meant to its author, about how she would perform it, about how the familiar crowd of listeners was likely to respond. Making the fair copy maintained authorial anonymity by concealing the writers' distinctive scripts; as she wrote, therefore, the editress's private knowledge of the authors reinforced her individual connections. As lyceum editors held and read aloud their handwritten papers, they simultaneously invoked popular journalism and symbolically distanced themselves from much of its cultural message, asserting the virtues of the intimate village community against the mercantile, urban, and depersonalized nation. Through the national press, they knew that cosmopolitan world; but as they invoked and parodied the press in their own handwriting and among their neighbors, they also claimed covert control over it.

The first printed issue of the student paper of the Bridgewater (MA) Normal School, the *Normal Offering* (January 1870), provides an interesting and explicit contrast between the local intimacy of handwritten papers and the more impersonal quality of printed ones. After decades of producing and reading manuscript papers at their lyceum meetings, the students decided to print their newspaper, which could then be distributed to a wider readership. The paper's oral heritage is conspicuous in the notice on its cover page: "Read monthly before the Bridgewater Normal Lyceum." The editorial, however, makes plain the coming change in the paper's relation to its audience:

> The Normal Offering, having lived through seventy-four volumes of manuscript, makes its first appearance in print with the present number. . . . The articles are those which were written for the Offerings of the term, to be read before the Lyceum, and not for print. Hence, many things will seem meaningless to the general reader, which are of the deepest interest to the members of the Lyceum. There has been no time for new articles.[36]

The "general reader," unconcerned with locally focused pieces that would have been read aloud to the close group at the school lyceum, will require "new articles."

I suggest that one primary effect of the lyceums' burlesque of journalistic forms was to chip away at the increasing dominance of public commerce and to assert the value of an older, more personal style of community interdependence. "If [a joke] devalues social structure," writes Mary Douglas, "perhaps it celebrates something else instead. It could be saying something about the value of individuals as against the value of the social relations in which they are organised. Or it could be saying something about different levels of social structure; the irrelevance of one obvious level and the relevance of a submerged and unappreciated one." Douglas suggests, however, that such resistant humor may be ephemeral and insubstantial: "The joke merely affords opportunity for realising that an accepted pattern has no necessity. Its excitement lies in the suggestion that any particular ordering of experience may be arbitrary and subjective. It is frivolous in that it produces no real alternative, only an exhilarating sense of freedom from form in general."[37]

Seen apart from their immediate context, detached from the drama of the entire lyceum evening and from the realities of villagers' lives, the lyceum papers' journalistic parodies might indeed seem to be frivolous but exhilarating jabs at an evolving national economy that was beyond the reach of hill-town residents. But this would oversimplify the situation. It is useful to revisit the most basic inference we can make from the village authors' easy familiarity with journalistic conventions: that rural northern New Englanders in the nineteenth century read the commercial press regularly, attentively, even avidly. Silvanus Hayward enumerated the periodicals taken by households in the little village of Gilsum, New Hampshire, in 1879: "Three dailies, two semi-weeklies, two hundred and thirty-five weeklies, sixty-four monthlies, and seven quarterlies"—this, according to him, in a population of 611 living in 161 dwellings![38] John Greenleaf Whittier's poem "Snow-Bound" (1866), which nostalgically recounts a week of isolation in rural Massachusetts during a blizzard in his childhood, describes the family's joy when the postman finally delivers the newspaper:

> At last the floundering carrier bore
> The village paper to our door.
> Lo! broadening outward as we read,
> To warmer zones the horizon spread

In panoramic length unrolled
We saw the marvels that it told.
. . .

Welcome to us its week-old news,
Its corner for the rustic Muse,
Its monthly gauge of snow and rain,
Its record, mingling in a breath
The wedding bell and dirge of death:
Jest, anecdote, and love-lorn tale,
The latest culprit sent to jail;
Its hue and cry of stolen and lost,
Its vendue sales and goods at cost,
And traffic calling loud for gain.
We felt the stir of hall and street,
The pulse of life that round us beat;
The chill embargo of the snow
Was melted in the genial glow;
Wide swung again our ice-locked door,
And all the world was ours once more!

"All the world was ours once more!" Through the newspaper, rural readers felt they could become citizens of the world,
participating in the cosmopolitan identity of newspaper readers
everywhere: they shared urban sophistication, business acumen, broad knowledge, contact with the exotic. With a printed
work, Michael Warner says, the reader "incorporates *into the
meaning of the printed object* an awareness of the potentially
limitless others who may also be reading. For that reason, it
becomes possible to imagine oneself, in the act of reading,
becoming part of an arena of the national people that cannot
be realized except through such mediating imaginings."[39] In
Scribner's Monthly in 1873 Gilbert Hamerton described this sensation vividly: "The journalist is to future historians what the
African traveler is to the map-makers. His work . . . enables
us to become ourselves spectators of the mighty drama of
the world."[40] It was incumbent upon rural as well as urban

citizens to stay abreast of the news. As the *Piscataquis (ME) Observer* declared in 1865, *"The Maine Farmer* says truly: The man who takes no newspaper at the present day is shut out from the great family of man as outcast. He is a representative of the past rather than the present age." Consider the broad (and smug) humor of this midcentury sketch in *Beadle's Dime Humorous Speaker* (1866):

THE FAMILY THAT DON'T TAKE NEWSPAPERS

> The man that don't take newspapers was in town the other day. He brought his family in an ox wagon. He still believed that Millard Fillmore was President, and wanted to know if the "Kamschatkians" had taken Cuba, and if so, where they had taken it. He had sold his pork for six cents, when he might have got ten. One of his boys went to a blacksmith shop to be measured for a pair of shoes, and another mistook the market-house for a church. He hung his hat on a meat-hook, and patiently waited one hour for "meeting" to begin. One of the girls took a lot of "seed onions" to the post-office to trade off for a letter. She had a baby which she carried in a "sugar trough," stopping occasionally to rock it on the sidewalk; when it dried she filled its mouth with a cotton handkerchief, and sung "Barbara Allen." The oldest boy had sold two "coon skins," and was on a bust. When last seen, he had called for "sody and water," and stood soaking gingerbread in it, and making wry faces. The shopkeeper, mistaking his meaning, had given him a mixture of sal soda and water, and it tasted strongly of soap. But he'd "hearn tell of sody water," and was bound to give it a fair trial, "puke or no puke." . . . We told the old fellow he ought to read the papers, but he would not listen to it. He was opposed to "internal improvements," and he thought "larnin" was a wicked invention.[41]

Despite their backcountry homes, the northern New England lyceum members felt that, thanks to the press, they belonged fully to the modern, changing world. Sometimes they said so outright, as in this Fryeburg, Maine, editorial for New Year's, 1871:

> We look back a twelvelth month over the writen pages of the world [i.e., the newspapers], and we are filled with wonder and amazement at the great physical political and social changes that have been taking place. Our own country, throwing off the gloom that spread like a pall over us, after the terrible shock of arms, the loss of kindred, and waste of means, [has] bounded forward in prosperity, enterprise and perseverance, showing its handiwork all over our native land.[42]

The editress went on to celebrate many *"outward gladsome changes that are taking place around us"*: the arrival of *"tens of thousands"* of immigrant families to settle the nation, the extension of the railroad to Fryeburg, the completion of the transcontinental railway *"so that one can leave his home in Maine and in a single week walk the streets of San Francisco."* Delineating the modernization of knowledge in the nineteenth century, William Gilmore points to the "decline of localism as the dominant perceptual environment," "replaced by an integrative perspective combining local, state, regional, national, and international contexts." He proposes that rural northeastern America "was the first society in the Western world where the vast majority of residents—all but the poorest families, and a few of those, and females as well as males—strove to accommodate the integration of local and distant worlds."[43] The lyceum papers were major expressions of this integration in the small—and, indeed, shrinking—hill towns of northern New England. The lyceum audiences listened to the reading of the paper with complex awareness, valuing both the importance of intimacy with a small village of known neighbors and the sophistication of membership in a large national cultural web. Embodied in a deliberately homegrown and local medium, the manuscript papers' wide-ranging contents, deliberate formal allusions, and exuberant emulation and pastiche of mass-produced commercial journalism expressed, in Steven Feld's phrase, the villagers' "dialectic of accommodation and resistance" to modernity.[44]

CHAPTER 8

"THE SPEAKING EYE
AND THE LISTENING EAR"

Performing the Papers

*We are social beings. We need the speaking eye and the listening
ear to enable us to go on with success. We meet on a cold &
bleak spot. But if there is warmth & resolution in our hearts,
our meetings here will not be thin, nor in vain. We shall be able
to say, with conviction, at the close of the season, "The time
spent here had not been wasted." Let us then do what we can,
not only for Lyceums, but for schools, for friends and families,
& for the public welfare. Amen.*

—Dublin (NH) Rural Repository, 4, no. 1,
November 10, 1841

Touting the freedom of the penny press in 1837, the publisher
James Gordon Bennett famously declared that the *New York
Herald*, which was sold to the "man in the street" rather than
by subscription, was "entirely ignorant who are its readers and
who are not."[1] This radical disconnection between producer
and consumer could not have been more unlike the situation
of the lyceum papers, so profoundly embedded in the life of
their neighborhoods. Lyceum editors and authors knew their
audiences intimately and produced their work specifically for
the evening's performance—for the "speaking eye" as well
as the "listening ear." As they wrote, they could imagine the
exquisite modulations of individual response around the small
schoolroom, the attendees seated on benches, listening, laughing, perhaps blushing, clapping, nodding, scanning faces across
the room for reactions.

How can we begin to recapture this lively scene? By the
time we read a lyceum paper today, it serves as only frail

FIGURE 10. Interior of the Toll Bridge schoolhouse, Fryeburg, Maine, during the nineteenth century. Courtesy of the Fryeburg Historical Society.

evidence of a distant event. The dynamic performance of the paper was a highlight of the evening's ritual, but the few papers that have survived come to us in the twenty-first century as words on a page, not as oratorical experiences. We can apply critical tools to those words—noting the genres of the papers' component pieces, their relationship to other contemporary literature, their various aesthetic properties, and so forth— but to understand them more fully, we must also seek clues as to how they may have functioned in the village and in the lyceum's social drama. The physical papers were not meant to stand alone as documents. Created for one specific moment in the life of a particular community, they were not even meant to survive. They were so closely tied to their group and to the moment of their performance that they were inevitably ephemeral. Most papers were probably discarded soon after their one-time use.

Significantly, what the lyceums kept systematically were their record books, listing the proceedings of each meeting and the names of the people who had taken prominent part. Just the facts. Nothing in writing could document the social power of such a high-context event as the reading of the paper, doubtless accompanied by outcries from listeners, laughter, cross-talk, restless fidgeting by schoolchildren, private glances, and signaling. I have found no information about how the editors performed individual papers, though I have seen a few hints that editors made side comments about what they were reading. In the *Kearsarge Fountain* of East Andover, New Hampshire, editor George Emery wrote personal remarks at the bottom of the page following certain pieces. Below a very sentimental essay, *"Night,"* he scrawled an astringent note: *"The author of the above we presume forgot to state that night is the time for cutting apples, sly courting, husking frolicks, lightning bugs to shine, and rats to scamper above the plastering! (Ed)."*[2]

Even regarding the papers as scripts for a community drama does not open up the enormous breadth of their evanescent context: personal, familial, local, regional, national. But if we cannot recapture all of the circumstances that gave rise to any particular paper, we can reconstruct the general social dynamics of production. Village writers drew on their varied literary experience to express hopes, test relationships, chastise wrongdoing, comment on local and national events, glory in the natural beauty around them, and fathom profound questions of faith and mortality. As they composed their pieces to submit to the editor, village authors—unlike reporters for the commercial press—would have been thoroughly mindful of their audience. They knew the identities of their first reader (the editor) and of the listeners (the lyceum attendees).

From their past experience in the lyceum meetings they could imagine how their work would be received, and from their membership in the close community of the village they could imagine (and even strategically evoke) individual reactions and responses: who would laugh, who would blush, who would nod approvingly, who would dismiss.

Writing for the paper was a social act. Just as a boy's first assigned role in a debate constituted a rite of passage, a signal that he was deemed ready to take part in adult deliberations, so, too, a writer's first accepted submission to the lyceum paper changed that person's relationship to the community. Even anonymous "publication" moved the writer into a public position. If the submission were an essay on moral values or proper behavior, the author implicitly joined those who claimed wisdom or conserved social propriety. Submissions relating to village matters such as farming, roads, or emigration established the writer as a concerned and responsible citizen. Descriptive poetry and prose enabled contributors to see themselves in the ranks of literary artists. Even teasing verses and clever wordplay about neighbors were instruments of local power, likely inspiring embarrassment and chuckles at the time and (if sufficiently memorable) recitation and laughter later on.

At every stage of production, from choosing submissions to making a final fair copy, the lyceum editor, too, was mindful of the paper as a performance—and one that had to appeal to an audience diverse in age, gender, marital status, and civic stature. Reading to such listeners presented a special challenge. Performed aloud, the papers were phenomena in time. Every word of every author's piece was to be spoken. No skimming, no selective reading according to personal taste, was possible. The editor made crucial decisions not only about what pieces to include but also about how to arrange them to satisfy the hearers. The organization of a lyceum paper had nothing in common with commercial newspapers—no columns, no household or ladies' sections, no advertising pages or clusters of international, national, and local news. Instead, miscellany ruled. Apart from a cover page or a small banner at the top

of the first sheet, the contents of each lyceum paper followed
no predictable order. Tone, topic, and genre varied from one
piece to the next. Rapturous poetry comparing the dying year
to the frailty of human life might be surrounded by punning
conundrums poking fun at local courting couples. Take, for
instance, the contents of one issue of the *Emblem*, read at the
Landaff (NH) Lyceum on February 25, 1860 (see appendix C
for the full text). A plain cover sheet announces the title, the
date, the issue (vol. 1, no. 8), a motto (*"Devoted to every thing
good"*), and an epigraph expanding on the *"every thing good"*
hoped for from the paper:

> *A type of truth may it ever appear*
> *Of friendship and joy and kindly cheer*
> *To honor and virtue be its pages given*
> *Moving our spirits nearer to Heaven.*

As in most of the papers I have seen, the issue opens with an
editorial, this one stating the paper's intention *"to improve the
mind in all the various duties in which it is called to act."* An essay
following the editorial, *"Tis infamy to die and not be missed,"*
carries forward this serious tone, taking its title from Reverend
Carlos Wilcox's monumental poem "The Religion of Taste"
and urging hearers to live their lives so as to hasten *"the ransomed earth . . . toward its final glorious completion and perfection."*[3]
Immediately after this sober injunction come four lighthearted
miscellaneous *"Conundrums,"* ranging from generic wordplay
(*"Why are the* [railroad] *cars the most durable things in the world?
Because you can brake them without damage."*) to punning comments on a local shopkeeper's inventory and an unnamed
member's habits of dress, to a reprimand to attendees who
never participate in lyceum activities. Tone changes again with
a passionate poetic plea against the stigma of the term *"old
maid,"* fear of which might drive young women to marry too
hastily and unwisely. This is signed (or teasingly attributed to?)
"M. J. Noyes"—that is, Martha Noyes, a twenty-four-year-old
local teacher who, in fact, never did marry. Then comes *"A*

Will," a spoof list of impossible bequests (discussed in chapter 6) attributed to Orlando W. Garvin, a local young man, followed by what seems to be a factual announcement of a local wedding, and then a *bon mot* possibly copied from a recently published popular miscellany:

> *Our latest Wish*
> *That gold dollars like scandal*
> *might grow big by circulation.*[4]

Another copied item follows, the lyrics to a school song, *"The Car of Education,"* portraying education as a railway train on which all ages *"claim a seat"* and work *"to keep the car in motion."*[5] The paper closes with its longest—and perhaps, for the contemporary audience, funniest—piece, *"Forty Years Ago,"* a letter ostensibly written forty years in the future by an unnamed old woman reporting on what had "happened" in the lives of the young people in the 1859–60 Landaff Lyceum: who married whom, who went insane from a woman's rejection, who chose bachelorhood, who fled from his wife, who failed as a lawyer and became a Mormon saint.

What a jumble! But this seeming confusion was a lyceum paper convention and was obviously deliberate. Given that editors changed with every issue and that they were free to select and organize the pieces in their papers as they wished, it is striking how similar the papers were, from issue to issue, from village to village, from decade to decade, in their very hodgepodge. In a poetic editorial, a Landaff editress personified her paper as a generous innkeeper of the intellect:

> *From your sumptuous bill of fare*
> *Any one can suit his taste. . . .*
> *Everything the reader wishes*
> *Is upon your table placed*
> *Where there are a score of dishes*
> *Every one can suit his taste.*
> *Whether he is seeking after*

Essays or domestic news
Or a tale exciting laughter
To relieve him of the "Blues."
Folks of liberal education
Who possess a jolly mind
Wish for general information
Which they here are sure to find.[6]

In their motto and epigraphic quatrain, the editors of the *Emblem* proclaimed that their paper's varied contents served *"every thing good"* and that the *"type of truth"* the paper embodied included *"friendship," "joy," "kindly cheer," "honor and virtue"*; their editorial mentioned the goal of cultivating *"our intellectual, social, and moral faculties."* Indeed, the contents of the issue could fulfill all of these goals for the close village community: an essay and a poem urging right living and lifelong pursuit of education; a poetic exhortation for kind and considerate behavior toward single women; an announcement of a local event (a wedding); several items based on clever wordplay; and two long original prose items, the spoof will and the retrospective letter, that name a great many members of the lyceum and tease them for qualities that were obviously well known to the audience.

Taken together, these typical paper contents provided balanced literary sustenance for the attendees, yet that sustenance was presented in deliberate disarray.[7] Editors seem to have been responding to a powerful community aesthetic—and to a performance imperative. The mélange was not as random as it seems to today's reader. Each editor created a crazy quilt of available literary materials, an intentional arrangement of the different voices of the village, structured strategically to engage an audience that included older common-school pupils of both sexes, young adults (most of them unmarried and thus situationally interested in the topic of courting), and older adults who had responsibility not only for their families but also for farms and businesses and for the government and welfare of the village. If listeners did not enjoy the current piece, they could expect that the next one would be different.

In juxtaposing news items, philosophical reflections, teasing rhymes, sentimental poetry, conundrums, and more—the general and the local, the epideictic and the argumentative, the solemn and the comic—the editor tried to ensure that every few minutes the interests of a different segment of the audience would be engaged. It was probably the miscellany of the papers, as well as their convention of naming some of the attendees, that enabled these diverse people to listen tolerantly to what were often very lengthy productions. On January 11, 1843, Thaddeus Mason of Dublin, New Hampshire, observed that the paper "took an hour longer than I had expected" but that the audience had listened to the reading with "a good degree of attention." On a few occasions in Dublin the reading of papers even crowded out the evening's planned debate.[8]

For such a disparate audience, however, editorial success was not always assured. *"It is not to be expected that all will be pleased,"* complained George Emery, editor of the *Kearsarge Fountain*: *"Some would have no paper at all; others would have one and wish it to be long, while many would prefer to have it 'short and sweet.' Many complain that our papers contain too much nonsense; some that they are too sober—not spicy enough; and almost every person will find some fault."*[9] Editorial fears notwithstanding, lyceum audiences often received the papers with delight. Correspondents to regional weeklies reported that papers were "enthusiastically and loudly cheered" or greeted with "tremendous applause."[10]

Editors made fair copies of their papers for ease of reading, but copying also prevented audience members from identifying contributors from their handwriting. Authorial anonymity was surely incomplete in a small neighborhood, but it was an important fiction. It gave writers a protected place from which to tease, to express tendentious opinions, to adopt experimental personae, or to attempt sundry writing styles. It even permitted a kind of literary cross-dressing: women could write argumentative or robustly humorous pieces; men could rhapsodize about natural beauty.

An unusual trove of materials from Dublin, New Hampshire, offers evidence that this masquerade actually took place. In that town the Young People's Society for Mutual Improvement simultaneously sustained a women's paper, the *Ladies' Miscellany*, and a men's paper, the *Wednesday Evening Post*. Members of both sexes were expected to contribute to each other's papers. In January 1845, a young man attached the following explanation to a piece he offered to the editress of the *Ladies' Miscellany*: "As . . . you was so good as to write for mine [i.e., the paper I edited] I cannot conscienciously neglect to fulfill the requisition." Apparently others *did* neglect that duty: in November 1842 Eliza Gleason, editress of the *Ladies' Miscellany*, complained that only one man had furnished a piece for her paper. Some reciprocal contributions might have had more than literary motives. In 1841 Thaddeus Mason offered a laudatory poem about an unnamed woman's beauty and "gen'rous, feeling heart" to editress Fidelia Piper's *Ladies' Miscellany*, prefaced by a graceful note: "Miss Piper, If you deem the following lines worthy of a place in your paper they are at your disposal"; in May, 1843, Thaddeus and Fidelia were married.

When men and women in Dublin did write for their counterparts' papers, they shaped their submissions to fit the papers' separate gendered conventions. Regardless of the sex of their authors, pieces in the *Ladies' Miscellany* tended toward the romantic and sentimental, mirroring the interests urged on young women in the etiquette books and newspaper columns of the era: health, music, landscape, religion, appreciation of the beautiful. The *Wednesday Evening Post*, on the other hand, featured a pointed and teasing sort of humor that alternated with argumentative rhetoric; its pieces included youthful interests such as dancing schools and courting.

The separate, gendered Dublin papers were the exception, but they offer insight into the rule. Lyceums in other villages typically produced only one paper, which combined these gendered styles and thus offered to their diverse anonymous contributors the same possibility of literary masquerade. Although we do not know the authorship of specific pieces, we may assume that the great majority of lyceum writers were women. (In Dublin, Thaddeus Mason's histories of the Young People's Society mention explicitly that women wrote more prolifically for the papers than men did.) Tacitly, the lyceum members colluded both in women's wishes to move beyond the domestic, sentimental, and devotional borders of their conventional intellectual sphere and in men's wishes to write within those boundaries. Women could take advantage of the anonymity of authorship to write as they pleased, to step beyond the limits of the ladylike and to adopt masks that were more generally appropriate to young men (argument, humorous criticism) or to older men (discourses on national affairs, appraisal of local issues, wry comments on foibles). As avid consumers of the popular press, rural women were aware of a wide world of information and discussion, and they used the lyceum papers to extend their voices.[11] We can infer that this social and intellectual stretch was important to them from the fact that women were usually the ones who kept the papers going.

Whether male or female, the editor was required to speak more continuously than any other lyceum participant and was responsible for performing a dynamic community conversation. "Good reading is not a *receptive*, but a *communicative* state," commented William Russell in 1843 "—not a *passive*, but an *active* condition. . . . The true position of a reader, is that of a person engaged in earnest, animated conversation, actuated by *a vivid feeling*, which he is *desirous to express*."[12] To fulfill community expectations, the editor or editress needed to capture and communicate the different feelings animating each of the varied voices in the paper, imaginatively stretching to embody multiple characters and attitudes.

Lyceum members treated the papers as conversational and responded from week to week to each other's contributions. In 1882, explaining that it was *"sent in in reply to an article in the last number of the 'Scrap Book,'"* a lyceum author in Webster, New Hampshire, submitted a poem about his mustache. An author submitted a letter to the editor of the *Cruiser* (South Freeport, ME, 1859) in response to critics who had objected to his arch piece about *"loafers"* in an earlier issue.[13] Editors encouraged these exchanges as the best way to deal with literary provocation:

> *After recess a nice paper is read*
> *But ah me, I here it said*
> *That some are mad at the contents there in*
> *Pray tell me what can it have been.*

> *For we do not intend to plague any one*
> *But we do want a little fun,*
> *So if you get hit a little in that*
> *Just write for the next paper tit for tat.*[14]

The papers were certainly livelier vehicles of community communication than we can now verify from the bare texts of surviving issues. If we had any complete season's run of a lyceum's paper—and someday one may be found—we would be better able to evaluate the papers' role in village conversation. But we would still be far from understanding their essential nuances. Why were some neighbors teased sharply and repeatedly and others given a pass? What were the risks of submitting particular pieces for the paper? When was authorial anonymity completely preserved, and when was it intended to be a tantalizing screen? We have no way of tracing the consequences of the editor's reading of the paper. Did a certain conundrum propel a couple together? Was a particular man shamed into marital fidelity by the journal's teasing? Did any of the mill boys in Carthage, Maine, stop swearing because of the protesting essay in the *Mystic Tie*? Did an editor's pleas result in more plentiful contributions to the paper? Some allusions are so esoteric that I am unsure if authors were teasing or censuring or if audiences would have found allusions to local behavior hilarious or offensive (or both). The *Monitor*, for instance, included a piece attributed to a local East Cabot, Vermont, merchant, N. K. Abbott, describing his wife growing hugely fat, week by week, until her children do not recognize her. Abbott (allegedly) concluded, *"My neighbors think I had*

better put her on exhibition." I assume that he did not actually
compose the piece; given that authorship was traditionally
concealed in the papers, any ostensible signature is suspect.
Certainly some sort of irony is at work in this piece, but without knowing more about the family (was Mrs. Abbott, perhaps,
as thin as a rail?) I cannot begin to guess what was funny or
why Mr. Abbott was said to have written the report.[15]

However precarious, the convention of anonymity gave
writers a protected place from which to joke. In Sophie May's
1871 novel *The Doctor's Daughter* two young friends compose
and anonymously submit to the *Aurora* an injudicious verse
taunting a local couple. When read in the lyceum, the verse
ends the courtship and teaches the remorseful girls a severe
lesson in social responsibility; questioned later, however, they
protest their innocence and vigorously deny knowledge of the
authorship of the verses.[16] Aware of the pungent possibilities
of anonymous teasing in lyceum papers, Thaddeus Mason
of Dublin, New Hampshire, deplored "the introduction of
personalities" that would lead listeners "to give their attention
to a spirited, vituperative article in the paper where the charm
of curiosity is endeavored to be presented by enveloping the
authorship in a shade of mystery."[17] But he was in the minority;
even in the 1840s and, increasingly, later in the century, most
papers included local joking. Anonymity created opportunities
for speculation and secrecy. "Fred Young wrote the piece in the
paper about Bemis and Eva Heath," Emily Luther McKenney
of Bethel, Maine, confided to her diary in 1875. Lyceum audiences, as active listeners, responded heartily to the performance
of the paper—especially to local references—as one South
Levant, Maine, author pointed out:

> As we've listened to some sharp bit
> Of pointed scorn or youthful wit
> We've laughed to see the faces change,
> And shrink behind our visions range.
> But when they joked us in our turn
> With silent rage our face would burn.

People listened, in part, because they might hear allusions to themselves. The same South Levant poet depicted the swirling emotions of a courting couple going home after the lyceum:

> And when 'twas finished and all was o'er
> We've lingered bashfully around the door
> And when that one of all the rest
> Had kindly granted our request
> Then up the horseback chill and bleak,
> We quickly turned our willing feet,
>
> Or past the shop beyond the mill,
> And wished the way was longer still.
> We smiled to think we should not fear,
> If all the world should know and hear.
> And when at last with sweet goodnight
> We're left alone in the silent night,
>
> In some mysterious way we find
> We've left our courage all behind
> We know they'll rhyme or prose about it
> And well we'll wish we hadn't done it.
> And so through all our life it goes,
> Our joys are mingled with our woes.[18]

Only occasionally were the papers' wit and raillery declared to be transgressive. Although most lyceum members did not share Mason's utter disparagement of personal teasing, some called for moderation. "*He that cannot take a jest should not make one,*" runs the statement of "*terms*" on the cover of one issue of the *Firefly* (Fayette, ME). A correspondent for the *Enterprise and Vermonter* (Vergennes, VT), reporting on the paper read at the Vergennes Lyceum, commented:

> The Vergennes Miscellany was read by Miss Fanny Tudor and Miss Alice Nichols. It contained several excellent articles. . . . While the last half of the paper was as a whole,

highly creditable to the editor, we could but regret that the first half was so marred by offensive personalities. If the Lyceum is to continue, as was remarked by a very excellent gentleman, the evil should be nipped in the bud, or it will lead to results by no means pleasant.—We presume the object was more to make sport than to vent petty spite, and so we must look more to the intention than the act. (March 21, 1862)

A letter to the editor of the *Bean's Corner Sunbeam* (Jay, ME) protested that visitors should be exempt from banter:

> *You say in your Lyceum papers, that you do not wish to hurt any ones feelings. That you do not intend to be too personal, you only intend a little fun. Yet you who write the fun, forget people are by nature sensitive; and do not enjoy so much sport at their expense. And yet, hardly a paper is read but what some ones feelings are hurt. I think we should all try and remember, the Golden Rule do unto others as you would that they should do to you. Now I enjoy fun, and a good time. But I do think it does not show respect to strangers, to use their names, quite as freely, as has been done, it neither shows wit nor wisdom. Words used in jest may be misconstrued and do harm. Therefore I would say in defense of those who have lately been in your midst spending a few weeks, are in their respective homes, much esteemed, and beloved by all who know them. . . . I hope all who write things for fun hereafter, will let it be confined to those whom we personally know about Town.*[19]

Local residents had durable social and kin networks; outsiders lacked this protection.[20] Despite such splutters, the lyceum papers continued to delight and irritate by tweaking local noses, as the editors presented their compilations to an audience of authors—and victims.

Performance of the papers suggests elements of the carnivalesque. Much as carnival "brings together, unifies, weds, and combines the sacred with the profane, the lofty with the low, the great with the insignificant, the wise with the stupid," so, too, the papers deliberately jumbled together disparate literary genres and registers.[21] More significantly, the papers' admixture of teasing and the license provided by anonymity linked them to carnival. Like carnival participants, whose identities are often concealed (sometimes only partially) by masks, the lyceum authors were disguised (sometimes only partially) by anonymity. Disguise enabled suspension of the normal rules of hierarchy and appropriate behavior. Women could write (or speak) like men and men like women. Respected community members could be playfully accused of folly, as were the Toll Bridge farmers who injudiciously purchased diseased hogs in 1870. Intimate secrets and gossip could be proclaimed in a transgressive inversion of public and private. In 1871 the *Toll Bridge Journal* included a prank forgery: an elaborately detailed week ostensibly from the diary of bachelor Hiram Kelsey Hobbs, poking fun at his failures at courting (he proposes to a different woman, and is rejected, each evening) and mocking his meager farm and business acumen.

> *Thurs. Pleasant. Went to Cold River today, to see if such a great change had been wrought in Hannah's feelings as in others in the short space of two months. I told her of my broad acres and my princely mansions on old Saco's banks, and my expectations of realizing an immense fortune from my renowned Hair Renewer (the ingredients of which were discovered near her homestead). I had nearly gained her consent to return with me as my wife, as I thought, when lo! a former admirer of hers appeared with plenty of money at his disposal, and my hopes were again blasted. She turned from me coldly, and said Adieu. For a bird in the hand is worth two in the bush.*[22]

Such japes brought laughter but not shame or ostracism; Kelsey was well liked and on at least one occasion was elected president of the Toll Bridge Lyceum. Indeed, to be teased in artful words could have been a positive marker of community membership. Carnival blurs the distinction between delight and ridicule. Like carnival costumes and masks, authorial anonymity in the papers could permit momentary violation of propriety and release tensions. Yet at the same time it blunted the effects of those violations, paradoxically helping to preserve the social order it so playfully violated.

It thus seems appropriate that in the customary order of many and perhaps most lyceums, performance of the paper was the last event on the evening's program, the inclusive envoi that served to celebrate and validate the community and, through humor, release its tensions and buffer the antagonism intrinsic to debating. In presenting the paper to the assembled lyceum, the editor revolved its spotlight, regularly illuminating and engaging different people. The papers' performative aesthetic demanded variety, discontinuity, a deliberate *dis*order that paradoxically promoted social order (or at least quiet-enough attention), a miscellany that enacted and betokened a larger social unity.

In their debates, declamations, recitations, lectures, dialogues, and papers, the New England rural lyceums presented a spectrum of public speaking from spontaneous argument to rehearsed reading. They constituted one of the last whole-hearted expressions of the golden age of American oratory.[23] Oratorical occasions have a particular ritual magic: they foster a sense of community—an awareness of shared expectations, values, history, and place.[24] Within the village lyceums the papers intensified this sense. They presented the literary productions of many village authors, all mediated through the reading editor, whose "community voice" gave back to the lyceum as a whole an aural image of itself, multiple yet united. Fledgling authors and practiced essayists, lawyers and wheelwrights, apprentices and farm girls: all had significance in the performance of the paper. As the editors mustered their elocutionary skills to express the tone and feelings of each writer in turn—to perform the diverse villagers' written conversation—they were creating and echoing back to their community its ideal democratic self: a model for the nation, writ small.

CHAPTER 9

"HOW SHALL WE WIN BACK LOST GROUND?"

The End of an Era

Today few will give up their life for the glory that will live after them. We want our rewards as we go along, and are angry if we do not get them. The love of literature, the cultivation of the taste for the beautiful, art and science, are not common among us. How shall we begin to win back lost ground, how awaken the languishing interest, and stir the smouldering ruins to living flame, bring out the power lying dormant within us?

Toll Bridge Graphic (Fryeburg, ME), c. 1886

Lyceum members read the national press. They were aware that the prevalent image of rural New England was shifting, as the century wore on, from a democratic utopia—"the republic's republic," the epitome of ethical, religious, industrious, and intellectual community—to a region of dissipation, depopulation, and despair.[1] Nineteenth-century artworks often presented an archetypal portrait of Old New England: a land of small, changeless, pre-industrial villages populated by pastoral, hardworking, pious, neighborly people. Eastman Johnson, who spent his first twenty-one years (1824–45) in the village of Lovell, Maine, painted his classic *Sunday Morning* in 1866, depicting a family of three generations sitting in an old-fashioned cottage kitchen, dressed formally and listening attentively to the grandfather reading from the Bible by the hearth—a quintessential presentation of the New England myth. *Sunday Morning* expressed an expatriate New Englander's nostalgia, but Johnson's vision was poised at the tipping point of the national view of rural New England. Just two or three years earlier Johnson (in collaboration with Worthington

Whittredge) had created a very different portrait of the region, *Sunday Morning, New England*, which under nearly the same title presents "just two old people in a hauntingly empty room."[2] Magazine authors and popular fiction writers projected to the nation a pessimistic image of moral and economic decay in the rural Northeast. Youth, growth, and excitement belonged to the frontier and to the new industrial cities; it became a commonplace that rural New England—especially the farm villages of Maine, New Hampshire, and Vermont— had become a dispirited backwater. "Now there is nothing but the ghosts of things, / No life, no love, no children, and no men" became the national lament, crystallized in Edwin Arlington Robinson's 1896 sonnet, "The Dead Village."[3]

Familiar as they were with these trends in the nation at large, the lyceum writers persisted in their optimism. Established and reestablished in northern New England even as the nation altered profoundly, the rural lyceums reflected the determined conservatism of their small villages. Sometimes the villagers seem to have strained to sustain their meetings. In late 1886 the editor of the *Miscellany*, the paper of the Dublin (NH) Literary and Social Union, commented, *"Some doubt was expressed at the commencement of the season concerning the advisability of a reorganization this winter, on account of the scarcity of young people in town; but experience has clearly proven that the lyceums can be made just as interesting and profitable this season as last."* Those who chose to remain in the hill towns defied negative stereotypes with energy and wry wit. If they echoed the gloomy external view of their villages, it was often to mock or disprove it. Witness the cheerful chuckle in the South Bethel, Maine, lyceum paper in November 1889 as the editor named the neighbors *"the people of Poverty Hollow,"* undaunted by the *"forbidding landscape"* of winter *"for there are the Lyceums and Circles, the dances and the 'Stormy Day Association' held in the blacksmith shop to call us out even if there were no other attractions to keep us from taking a four months nap."*[4] Villagers might call themselves *"the people of Poverty Hollow"* in jest (in a moue that Tad Tuleja would name a "parodic parry"), but they maintained strong positive images of their communities.[5] A Webster, New Hampshire, writer composed a lengthy poem chronicling the dwellings and inhabitants of *"this quiet little hamlet"* in the distinctive prosody of Henry Wadsworth Longfellow's "The Song of Hiawatha"—a choice that, by its unmistakable allusion, cast an epic glow over the village:

> At the eastward, toward the valley liveth Colby,
> Colby, builder of our dwellings,
> Workman he of good repute,
> Liveth eastward toward the valley.[6]

As the century wore on, lyceum writers looked increasingly to the future and imagined how they, their neighbors, and their villages would evolve. *"It has been some ten years since I saw you"* began a letter signed *"Eugene Barrett"* to the editor of the *Mystic Tie,* the lyceum paper of Berry's Mills in Carthage, Maine, in January 1875. Pretending to be reporting back to his lyceum friends from the vantage point of 1885, Barrett continued with breathless enthusiasm: *"Great has been the change at Berry's Mills since then. The place has grown. . . . We now have three Churches two school houses and an Accadamy, several Factorys and other large buildings to numerous to mention here."*[7] Barrett, a twenty-one-year-old sawmill worker who may or may not have been the actual author of the letter, was writing in a genre increasingly common in lyceum papers toward the end of the century. I have seen eight such retrospective spoofs, each professing to depict the fortunes of a lyceum's village and its current younger generation from a standpoint ten to forty years in the future. In these reports the prospects for the villages look rosy. By 1897, twenty years ahead of the current moment, East Bethel's meeting house is said to have become an *"elegant granite structure"* to match a new *"large hotel"* and a *"large seminary for ladies."*[8] In the most exaggerated forecast of all, two decades after 1882, Webster, New Hampshire, is said to have become *"a bustling city"* with its own train depot, *"college for Young Ladies,"* textile factory, paper mill, resort hotel, and

"several fine mansions."[9] Although these playful local prophecies
ring with confidence about the villages' long-term viability,
they were, of course, far from the evolving reality. Today
Carthage is still a tiny town with a population barely greater
than it had in 1875, the East Bethel meetinghouse remains a
one-story wooden structure, and neither railroad nor industry
has ever made its way to Webster. By the time of the Civil War,
the populations of most of the small towns of northern New
England were already declining.[10]

However inaccurate their predictions, the lyceum authors
anticipated that their village and their values would endure.
They asserted the ideals of self-reliance and neighborliness that
undergirded the farming communities. Villagers did not see
themselves simply as remnants—"those who stayed behind,"
in Hal Barron's words.[11] They could write confidently, fond
of their stability but also feeling fully involved in the exciting
postbellum nation. They did not give up their long-established
commitment to improvement—mental, civic, or material. "A
general spirit of improvement prevails," wrote the columnist for the village of Wilton, New Hampshire, in the *Milford
Enterprise*, November 17, 1874. Scattered among the column's
general notes are testaments to the town's improving spirit,
encompassing farming, education, commerce, the lyceum,
and transportation:

> The school-houses in Wilton are valued at $10,000.
> Wilton has an area of 10,391 acres of improved land. . . .
> The Western Union Telegraph is doing a good business
> since it opened to the public.
> With the exception of Bedford, Wilton exceeds every
> other town in the State in the sale of milk. . . .
> There are but few towns in the State that can show more
> intellectual enterprise than Wilton.
> The Lyceum is a credit to any town. . . .
> The Wilton railroad is doing a good thing by putting in
> elegant waiting rooms at the depot.
> The workmen have been engaged on the work for nearly
> three weeks. . . .

Confidence did not, of course, signal uniformity of opinion in the villages. Even the few surviving lyceum papers testify to a multivocal conversation about rural identity and about the nineteenth-century challenges to village life that would eventually overwhelm the lyceums and forever change their communities. They discussed competition from western agriculture abetted by improved transportation, outmigration by New Englanders who saw little hope for the old hardscrabble farms, and large-scale manufacturing that would displace home industries. Individuals argued one way or another. One author might lament the farmer's lot, while another might salute it. The tone of the discussions changed through the century. In 1840 a piece in Dublin's *Rural Repository* encouraged farmers "*of ordinary means*" not to be discouraged when they compared their farms to those of "*an establishment of a wealthy and extensive farmer*" or when they considered improvements prescribed by "*agricultural books and papers.*" Rather, such farmers should use their "*Yankee ingenuity*" to figure out how to apply new information to their own particular circumstances; their discoveries would be of general use.[12] The following year an essay in the *Rural Repository* offered sober praise of the farmer's way of life, despite his lack of luxuries. Self-sufficiency was paramount. After the midcentury, however, as midwestern agricultural products increasingly dominated the market, the reliability of New England farming—and even, occasionally, the effectiveness of Yankee ingenuity—came into question. An 1885 Antrim, New Hampshire, lyceum author claimed to have "*listened to an article in the 'Literary News' at our last meeting*" arguing that farming was profitable and healthful and, in response, commented that the writer was "*a little off his base.*" The author poured forth a litany of the risks of a farming life, declaring that the only successful farmers are men with "*incomes from other sources which keep the farms alive.*" "*Writer of the last months article,*" the author requested, "*please write again.*"[13] Villagers sometimes managed to deny the writing on the wall. A decade earlier, in January 1874, the debate topic at the West Plymouth (NH) Literary Association had been "Resolved that railroads have a tendency to injure the farming interests in N.H." The record book reported, "Merits of the question and argument decided in favor of the Negative."

Outmigration was also a matter of discussion and literary creativity. The week after the railroad debate, the topic in West Plymouth was "Resolved that the New England states are superior to the western states." In the lyceum papers, one author might praise the success of outmigrants as evidence of the viability of village education and sophistication, another might create a scenario that demonstrated the probable failure of outmigration, and yet another might point to the effect on the home village of so many departures. A writer for the South Levant, Maine, High School *Centennial Gazette* argued in 1876 "that a man can do as well in the state of Maine as in the Western states, providing he works as hard, and plans the same as if he was living in a dugout, as they call it." A poignant 1859 poem, *"Lines dedicated to the absent members of The Literary Banner,"* pointed out the emotional costs of emigration, expressed in the words of neighbors who had moved away:

> *Are we remembered? those friends that are gone,*
> *To grapple with lifes fierce embrace.*
> *Say loved ones dear! in this school house here*
> *Do you oft remember the absent face?*
>
> *Are we remembered? though the praries wide*
> *And mountains high divide us twain,*
> *Can distance the immortal soul divide*
> *And sever fondest friendships chain?*

Just a page later comes a letter from an *"old contributor"* celebrating the Yankee influence on *"western manners and western life"* as *"settlers from the north . . . are fast leaving there northern and eastern homes, and planting the seeds of industry, and instilling the principles of early education."* This earnest writer cannot sufficiently praise the West as a prospect for northeastern settlers:

> *It is impossible to enumerate the resources of this great val-*
> *ley, or contemplate its future progress. The elements of its*
> *prosperity are imbeded within its bowels, its mighty rivers*
> *afford a sufficient outlet, which with the innumerable iron*
> *tracks that span it o'er, afford the most perfect system of inter-*
> *nal intercourse and foreign communication that a wise and*
> *benificent providence could possibly have bestowed on this*
> *mundane sphere.*[14]

The spoof retrospective letters of the 1870s and 1880s often "report" the outmigrations of their current lyceum colleagues, both men and women, across the nation and the world. According to these letters, women generally have left the village in order to marry; one is said to have wed a Boston merchant, another a college professor in the West, another a *"celebrated lawyer in Chicago,"* another a wealthy planter in Havana. Some have traveled with their husbands for missionary work or for teaching *"out West"* or in Africa. Men's alleged fortunes abroad were supposedly more mixed. Some were said to have succeeded (their successes reflecting well on the self-education made possible by the lyceums): as a minister in Bangor, a broker in New York, a dentist in Boston, a member of Congress, a hotelier in Canada. Others were given more tongue-in-cheek fortunes. One man fled his wife to teach school in China; another was shipped in a barrel to Calcutta. Complementing the papers' general advocacy of local marriage, men who left the village to marry strangers are often said to have met with misfortune. In one report, Ossian D. Ripley left Beans Corner and, after a mere two months' courtship, married a widow reputed to have a fortune—only to discover that her "wealth" consisted of nine dependent children.[15] The West offered varied marital hazards, reflecting the period's common prejudices. Fred Noyes from Landaff, New Hampshire, failed in his law career and *"at last account was a saint among the mormons with 16 wives and 50 children."*[16] In a racist construction typical of the times, the writer of a retrospective letter home to Veazie, Maine, snickered that Charley Rollins, said to have gone to California twenty years earlier, *"was so well pleased with life in the western wilds that he wooed and won a young Modoc maid, and is now living very happily with her as queen of his wigwam surrounded by a little army of half Modoc braves."*[17]

The general tone of these outmigration fantasies is positive and jocular. The spoof writers did not portray their towns as diminished by those who had moved away. But perhaps they were whistling in the dark. Despite his joking "memories" of his lyceum friends' fortunes, a Jay, Maine, author commented twice that in his (fictitious) old age he saw his 1877 lyceum friends *"not as a happy united band but scattered in every land."* In an earnest piece in the same paper, a contemporary older woman recollecting her actual school days *"twelve to fifteen years ago"* lamented that even in 1877 *"we can hardly realize the great change there has been since then, so many are gone, some to their long homes others to the far west, others to the South, and to the East, the most of them are scattered, not hardly one are left here now, that enjoyed those days."*[18] Many of the lyceum pieces later in the century maintain a negative image of outmigration. Merten Cheney of East Cabot, Vermont, wrote in 1879, *"I had a brother who tried it away from home, but before he had been gon[e] a great while he was glad to come back again, and I think there are many others that do not wish to stay at home with their parents and so go away. But they are pretty sure to come back after trying it a short time."*[19] "Hayward" in 1886 reported back from Chicago that *"the girls out here are all Dutch, and think a great deal, of their sour crout, and beer. I long to see the Antrim girls again."*[20]

The desire to keep residents in the village and conserve their traditional ways of life runs as a thematic thread through the lyceum papers. An 1877 author in Maine offered *"A little plain advice to Veazie girls,"* criticizing their devotion to urban ideals of fashion and luxury: *"the Church, the schoolroom, the dancing hall, the streets . . . embellished with crinoline silks, velvets, furs, & dry goods generally."* Village girls should not expect their mothers to do all the housework

> *while you are simpering or playing the fool to some brainless*
> *mustached fox in the parlor or stitching away upon a useless*
> *piece of embroidery or thumping your fingers off on the piano*
> *keys. Is that the way to become energetic women prudent wives*
> *or consoling mothers. Is that bewhiskered "feller" your idea*
> *of a husband? Better set your cap for that young farmer or*
> *river driver at whom you have nearly died a laughing so many*
> *times. . . . Go to work, and be no longer the contempt of all the*
> *smart active, go ahead marriageable young men in Veazie.*[21]

Marry local men, maintain local values, do practical labor, preserve the community as it has been.

These themes blend with prognostication in an extraordinary composition, honoring the centennial of the United States, that concludes the *Bean's Corner Sunbeam* (Jay, ME) of January 16, 1877. In *"The Three Centuries,"* three female figures are conversing, each representing one American century: 1776, 1876, and 1976 (see appendix D for the full text). 1776, as the oldest, begins, describing old-fashioned kitchens and women's chores. 1876 interrupts: *"You do not mean that your Daughters worked in those days! Why, our daughters only learn the fine arts."* 1776 confirms that *"our Daughters were a great help in all the household affairs"* so that *"our houses were clothed with the industry of our hands."* 1876 begins her own account, boasting of her century's improvements in transportation. Unperturbed, 1776 counters that *"if a stagecoach was slower than the modern steam cars or steam boats, it was pretty safe."* 1876 persists with *"exultant pride,"* flaunting *"all our improvements in agriculture, all our sewing machines, our machines of all kinds for farming; and the advances in science: our telegraphs."* Finally it is the turn of 1976, *"a lady of great talent seeming much younger than the others,"* to speak of *"the improved age in which she lived."*

> *It seemed a great effort to speak as all of their work was done*
> *by machinery, also all their Education was done by that pro-*
> *cess. "We do not learn any thing. We have only to look at our*

wonderfull machine—it gives us a look into the future. It tells us the result of our inquiries and realy leaves us nothing to do but to enjoy or amuse ourselves as we think best. Our music is all arranged and by changeing a little we have whatever tune we desire. I think our wonderful moniters of war would quell any rebellion of the land without sending our friends to battle. Of course we need directors to that and it gives more dignity to have a government, but a look into these machines tells us just who to Vote for and what their political life will be, so that saves the trouble of sending orators to rouse the public spirit, and stump speeches are out of place here."

"But don't you think Women begin to have their rights more than before?"

"Why, nearly all the Ladies scarcely know their own Children, they spend so much of their time abroad, and with their friends. But we know just when our friends are coming and all is arranged on such a perfect plan you can but see we realy live in a wonderful age. We scarcely need the improvements of the last century."

She seemed exhausted with the effort and the others feeling a little behind the times kindly invited her to sit down.

When I first read this piece, I was stunned by its uncanny foreshadowing of technology—not of 1976 specifically but of the early twenty-first century, with its computers and smartphones, Roombas, Google, Spotify, drone warfare, social media, Zoom, and more. It took some effort to pull back and imagine what was essential in this historical sequence from the point of view of the 1877 lyceum author. For that writer, "improvements" and modern inventions were certainly not an unequivocal benefit and, if carried to their logical conclusion, could result in a nightmarish *"improved age."* Farming seems to have vanished: despite the nineteenth century's *"improvements in agriculture,"* 1976 makes no mention of husbandry—perhaps a reminder that for the thin rocky soils and small hilly fields of northern New England, many of the labor-saving new *"machines of all kinds for farming"* were proving useless.

Increasingly, even the Northeast was being fed by produce from the Midwest. In the twentieth century self-education—a primary civic responsibility for the lyceum members—has disappeared: *"We do not learn anything. We have only to look at our wonderful machine."* "Orators" will no longer be needed; face-to-face public speaking, the crucial means of self-education embodied in the lyceum, will be gone, and this loss may even be adumbrated in 1876's celebration of *"advances in science: our telegraphs,"* which replace speech with dot-dash-dot buzzes, personal communication with impersonal information. In a world run by machines, civic responsibility is unnecessary and governments merely decorative. When music comes from a machine, there is no need for communal gatherings for song and dance. Family life itself, centering on the roles of women, is already on the decline in 1876 because of women's *"rights,"* as daughters learn only the *"fine arts"*; it will fade away entirely in another century when *"Ladies scarcely know their own Children, they spend so much of their time abroad."* Representing in her languor the inanition of her age, 1976 is exhausted by speaking even a few words and must sit down.

As this perspicacious dialogue makes clear, the villagers' conservative values coexisted in precarious balance with the "spirit of improvement." Lyceum authors were wary in their assessment of the nation's direction. *"To glorify modern civilization, to boast of its achievements is an easy matter,"* wrote one. *"True wisdom will strive to ascertain its deficiencies and provide a remedy against them."*[22] The cautious villagers were pushing back against increasing pressures. In the final months of 1887, the *Cold River Journal* of Alstead, New Hampshire, published a series of five articles headed "What is to Become of the Hill Farms of New Hampshire?" In the beginning the writer laid out the major threats to rural life in the region: depopulation in towns far from railroads and manufacturing centers, the "very rapid development of the western states," and the crushing competition from sales of western grain, livestock, and wool. Chiding the traditionalism of the hill towns as counterproductive, the author lamented that rural young people "look around them and see everything so extremely conservative that any new departure in thought or business is talked about and is often treated as little better than a crime itself." The writer proposed a very Yankee remedy. Instead of whining, "we may as well look the matter squarely in the face" and develop local solutions for local markets.[23]

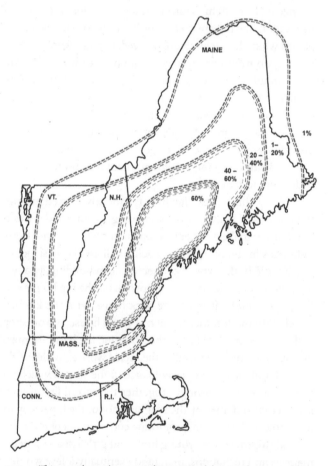

MAP 2. This map shows the geographic range and density of connected farm buildings in New England. Percentages within zones denote the relationship of connected farmsteads to all other detached house and barn arrangements. From Thomas C. Hubka, *Big House, Little House, Back House, Barn: The Connected Farm Buildings of New England* (1984; reprint, Waltham, MA: Brandeis University Press, 2004). Reprinted courtesy of the author.

In their own way and according to their own values, those rural northern families had been developing local solutions throughout the century. Conservatism buffered by ingenuity was a guiding principle of their lives, in their lyceums, and even in the farmsteads they inhabited. It is striking that the geographic area of New England where the village lyceums flourished coincides almost perfectly with the distribution of connected farm architecture as studied by Thomas C. Hubka. In addition, the time period of the lyceums corresponds to the period when this architecture evolved: beginning in the 1830s, picking up momentum in subsequent decades, and tailing off in about 1890. Both phenomena proceeded from a powerful love of the traditional rural way of life: mixed farming combined with woods work and home industries; a strong focus on neighborly relations within a small community that provided support through cooperation. Both shared the prevailing devotion to improvement, mental or material, and a dedication to practicality.

During this period, farmers frequently moved existing structures and built new ones, creating a connected series of buildings to make it easier to supplement farming with home industries in the off-months. Each small and large structure had its role in the typical connected farm building, promoting family cooperation and improvement: the big house with the parlor and bedrooms; the back house with the kitchen; the ell with the summer kitchen, a wood house, a workshop, and a milk room; and finally the privy and the barn. Farmers' ingenuity in bringing together the mixed work activities of the whole family had some resemblance to the way in which the lyceum supporters brought together the mixed literary and intellectual activities of the neighborhood. Each participant had a role in the lyceum, promoting community cohesion and mental improvement: young boys and girls speaking declamations and recitations, men (and eventually a few women) arguing in the debates, respected elders delivering lectures, various community members presenting music and prepared dialogues, everyone composing pieces for the paper, and editors and editresses presenting to the assembly the village's collective conversation.

The practical motives that drove lyceums and farm renovations did not exclude aesthetic considerations. Hubka points out that farmers' desire to create beauty can be seen in their new impulse to arrange and decorate the outsides of their connected buildings harmoniously (at least on the sides facing the road), with barn details often echoing the trim of the house. We also hear an aesthetic ambition in the *Toll Bridge Graphic* editor's complaint that *"as the world grows richer and advanced, it at the same time lowers its standard of dignity, elegance, art and literature. How shall we begin to win back lost ground . . . ?"* The remedy was clear: join a *"literary circle,"* spend your *"lesure hours in study,"* and *"write a piece for the paper."* Beauty, in the eyes both of the renovating farmers and the studying, writing, and speaking lyceum participants, had distinct classical connections. Hubka notes that New England farmers tended to adopt details from Greek Revival architecture, a style that was already common in houses in towns and cities. Likewise, it is no coincidence that the rural New Englanders chose to call their winter gatherings lyceums, invoking the ancient academy. *"Where are the great men of Athens?"* cried that *Toll Bridge Graphic* editor.

FIGURE 11. The Merrill-Dunlea Farm, Lovell, Maine, typifies the features of a nineteenth-century connected farmstead. (The garage doors on the barn are a modern addition.) Photograph by the author.

The aesthetics of connected farm buildings did not aim
for perfect symmetry. Farm families created individual, non-
symmetrical, offset arrangements of structures, no two alike,
in a spirit that Hubka associates with "a certain amount of
individuality, zealousness, even bravado" and perhaps "a
degree of anti-city formality or an individual pride in breaking
formal rules." I think of the lyceum papers, each arranged
somewhat differently by its editor, each in explicit and implicit
ways resisting the commercial imperatives of urban America,
the components of each strategically jumbled to hold the
attention of those present. As the disparate units of the farm
building, connected ingeniously, bespoke the family's resolve
to use all of its available means to perpetuate the farm, so,
too, the miscellaneous order of the lyceum paper—rocking
back and forth from hilarity, to sentimentality, to philosophical
reflection, to mockery, to religious meditation; constantly dis-
locating expectation as it was read aloud; embracing divergent
opinions—proclaimed and promoted neighborhood cohesion.
Lyceums and farmstead architecture both testified to northern
farmers' determination to stay and succeed.

Yet so many aspects of life in northern New England were
not destined to endure. Hubka points out that New England
farmers tended to stop keeping detailed journals in the last decade of the nineteenth century—just about the same time that
the "sustaining spirit of optimism, perfectibility, and progress"
finally wore out in rural New England. People had "diminish-
ing expectations for the future."[24] The writing was on the wall
for the lyceums, not only because national economic developments were outstripping the villages' traditional capabilities
but also because of a prevailing shift in ideas about learning. By
the end of the century it was no longer assumed that an educated person was a generalist skilled through self-education.
As distinct disciplines emerged in the academy, professional
subcultures were increasing. As law schools evolved, appren-
ticeships ceased to be the path to the legal profession. Medical
schools were developing uniform standards and requirements.
As English departments absorbed the function of teaching

writing and rhetoric, college literary societies waned. Joseph Kett speculates that mutual improvement societies were collapsing by the 1880s "because their clients no longer saw cultural acquisition as important to their careers."[25]

By the mid-1890s, northern New England's village lyceums had all but ceased to meet. Rarely were they noted in the village columns of newspapers.[26] I have found no surviving lyceum papers from the 1890s (although such an absence is not conclusive, given the general sparsity of the remaining papers).[27] By 1900, mention of village lyceums in regional newspapers was largely retrospective and nostalgic, and most were described as "old-fashioned" or "old-time."[28] The tradition lingered in memory. In 1908 the *Deerfield Valley Times* of Wilmington, Vermont, published a substantial article, "The Lyceums of Yore." The writer located the "old-fashioned Lyceums" in a far-off era: "These, like everything else, had their day, and their day was before the advent of the daily paper or the era of Telegraphs, Telephones, and Phonographs, when rural life was in its native, its primitive glory." He sketched vividly "the peerless debaters and arguerers [*sic*] of their respective neighborhoods. . . . The flashes of wit, the blazes of oratory and the array of facts marshalled on both sides, was at once the admiration and envy of all spectators and listeners, especially the impressible young." The debates taught crucial skills: "Participators and listeners, the young and the old, learned thereby the worthlessness of opinions not founded upon facts, beliefs that would not bear the light of discussion, theories that failed to stand the test of reason or submit themselves to the abatriment [*sic*] of well-informed and critical judgment." And finally "came what was a pleasing adjunct of the evening's entertainment, the reading of a 'Paper' gotten up and read by the ladies, filled to the brim with local hits, spicy items and literary tidbits well calculated to soothe and beguile the rancor of debate and leave all in the best of humor." The writer concluded, with a rhetorical flourish, "A fig then for the many alluring pastimes and amusements of today!"[29] Lyceums were so far gone that they could even be presented as historical reenactments. In February 1909, residents of the little village of Randolph Center, Vermont, put on an "old-fashioned lyceum" as an entertainment, re-creating the various typical exercises, including a debate, a declamation, selected readings, a paper, and music. (One of the activities was "a brief history of the old lyceum.") "All performed their parts well," commented the reporter. Attendees were charged ten cents admission; the proceeds went to support the Young People's Society of Christian Endeavor.[30]

For farm families, the evolving local Grange organizations might have in some ways replaced village lyceums. After the Civil War, the Order of Patrons of Husbandry, or the Grange, was founded to improve methods of agriculture and promote the social and economic needs of American farmers. As the movement took hold in northern New England in the last quarter of the century, many of the farm families who had supported the village lyceums joined the Patrons of Husbandry, and for a time the two institutions existed simultaneously in some neighborhoods. In Fayette, Maine, the Starling Grange was organized in 1875. Then, in December 1881, Albion Watson and others who were also active in the Grange "organize[d] anew" the North Fayette Lyceum, which held its meetings on Fridays in the Grange hall.[31] Like the lyceums, rural New England Grange meetings provided regular occasions for sociability and education and invited women's participation. Some of the public positions designated for women were more ceremonial than functional (Ceres, Pomona, Flora, and Lady Assistant Steward), but the Grange also gave women access to leadership positions open to men.[32] Prepared by their lyceum experience, in the local or "subordinate" Granges New England women frequently stepped into the role of Lecturer and took responsibility for organizing the literary and musical programs.

Most of the village Granges met at first in local school-houses—another lyceum echo—and some, for a few years, included in their programs an editress's production of a hand-written paper. According to its record book, when the Mount Vernon (ME) Grange was organized in 1876, a committee of three was appointed "to furnish a Paper for the Grange," and minutes through the summer noted votes of thanks to the editresses. Thereafter, papers are not mentioned.[33] During the 1890s the records of the Cornish (NH) Grange make occasional reference to a "Grange paper" read sometimes by a woman and sometimes by a man. In some cases editing the paper might even have reflected a family tradition. In Fryeburg, Maine, Hattie Adams, daughter of my great-grandmother Maria Gordon Adams who had edited the *Toll Bridge Journal* in 1870, edited some numbers of a paper called the *Grange Echo* for the Fryeburg Grange in about 1895, when she would have been seventeen years old. She might have had her mother's guidance; certainly the *Grange Echo* maintained the mixture of prose and poetry, laced with humor, typical of the earlier *Toll Bridge Journal* and even included contributions from Lovell lawyer John Hobbs, whose wry wit had enlivened Maria's paper a quarter of a century before.

Not surprisingly, the Grange papers focus more heavily on farming than do the lyceum papers. Matching the contemporary movement toward specialized knowledge, Grange authors argued for the professionalism of farming:

> There is no profession that needs to be more thoroughly educated than that of agriculture. I trust that we shall eventually duly impress ourselves with this fact. There is good warrent for calling it a "profession." It involves exact knowledge on as many points as does law, medicine, or theology. The man who is attempting to farm without such knowledge bears the same relation to the profession of agriculture as does the quack to medicine and the pettifogger to law or the mere spouter to theology.[34]

The Grange papers also seem to reflect a trend away from training the mind, so central to the mission of the village lyceums. This is evident in editress Detta Goodhue's issues of the *Golden Harvester* for the Webster (NH) Grange between 1885 and 1889, although those papers mention some activities akin to those in the Webster Lyceum.

But of what good has the Grange been to the people of Webster?

The discussion of questions relating to farming, stock raising, poultry raising, and the dairy, as well as of matters that affect the state and country, have brought out new ideas, and been the means of awakening an interest in all that is going on about us.

It has been of benefit to the young people as the means of continuing the recitations and declamations which are so often dropped on leaving school.

It has also made friends of those who were strangers and would have remained so but for the Grange, and more than all else it has made the people more social, which was something much to be desired, therefore we say, "May the Grange live long and be prospered."[35]

Grange programs emphasized sociability and hard work; mottos on the covers of the *Golden Harvester* include *"Always do your best," "Whatever is worth doing, is worth doing well,"* and *"Be always ready to lend a hand."*[36] According to the minutes of the January 25, 1895, meeting of the Moosilauke Grange in East Haverhill, New Hampshire, the day's literary program included "A Grange paper . . . composed and read by the Worthy Lecturer." But this is the only mention of a paper in the entire record book; at the previous monthly meeting, the literary program had been quite different:

> The Lecturer gave a programme for the next meeting as follows. The ladies are to exchange fancy cooking recipes. The gentlemen that are farmers are to tell the most profitable and the most unprofitable crop raised this year and the reasons. The rest are to give a Bible quotation relating to farm life. Those not taking part in the programme are to pay a fine of five cents.[37]

The heartfelt words of Hattie Adams's editorial for the *Grange Echo* emphasized the paper's mission of comfort and support:

I hope my paper may contain some word, may drop some thought, that may be a help to someone. We aim to do good, and to make it instructive as well as amusing.

We hope to speak some word that may cheer some desponding Bro. or Sister, that may give them courage for the "Battle of Life." If we are able to do this we shall feel satisfied, we shall feel like the poor widow who cast in her two mites, we have done what we could.[38]

Sociability and community maintenance, not mental improvement, were uppermost. These words from the daughter of a lyceum editress make it clear that times had changed.

Lyceums in the form of debating societies did continue as activities in high schools and academies. In 1891 the *Youth's Companion* magazine founded a national organization, the Lyceum League of America, "to cultivate good citizenship among the young men of America." Hailing the advent of the new organization as a revival of old traditions, the *Vermont Phoenix* of Brattleboro commented: "One of the great molding forces of the last generation was the old lyceum or debating club. . . . It ought never to have fallen into desuetude."[39] But the League revived nothing of the "old lyceum" but its debates, and its standardized chapters did not encourage papers or other kinds of community participation. The magazine's central board in Boston issued uniform charters, badges, meeting rituals, subjects for debates, and a library for each branch of the League.[40] Those who remembered the village lyceums clearly recognized that the newer youth lyceums were different institutions As M. O. Howe in Newfane, Vermont, wrote in 1907:

Besides the younger people, there were for many years in the little village of West Wardsboro a class of older persons who were permanent residents always ready to take part in the debates and to help maintain the lyceum. The village including the whole of the school district, had at its best only about two hundred inhabitants. Where now is there such a lyceum in such a place?[41]

Where, indeed? Those cherished New England societies could not ultimately stem the tide of history. Nonetheless, even today they offer timely and valuable models of community life. I admire those gatherings where diverse opinions were attentively heard and evidence was weighed carefully. (One common instruction to nineteenth-century debaters: "Listen to your opponent as though he might be right.") I am reminded that art is not only the province of the elite. I hear clearly the message that human relationships must transcend technology, lest we embody the detached, enfeebled future that the centennial author of *"The Three Centuries"* named *"1976."* And I am cautioned over and over again that I am responsible for my own—and my community's—improvement. We cannot revive the old village lyceums, but we can admire their vibrant ambition, resilience, and creativity.

"COMING HERE AMONG STRANGERS"

I end as I began, with my great-grandmother, Maria Eliza Gordon, whose *Toll Bridge Journal* in that Fryeburg attic launched me on this quest. Maria's life changed dramatically after her marriage in December 1872. Twenty-four years old, she moved from her childhood home to the new National Asylum for Disabled Volunteer Soldiers in Togus, Maine, where her husband Edgar Adams, himself a Civil War veteran, had been hired as chief engineer.

Her first letter to her mother reflected the shock of leaving her lifelong neighborhood. "The Asylum is a very big thing. . . . I couldn't go alone unless I had a piece of chalk to mark where I went for I never could find my way back." Discounting the hundreds of soldiers living in the same building, she commented with dismay, "No people live out here." In those new institutional buildings, arranged in a massive square, she felt alien. Time and again in that first letter home she pulled herself back from the brink of loneliness by admiring the technology. "The rooms and halls are all carpeted, and the floors are just so warm to your feet—the steam pipes run all round under the floors so any one never has cold feet. You would like living here, it is so warm." She opines bravely, "I guess we shall get round all right in the course of time." Meanwhile, she consoles herself with technological novelty. "Where I get my hot and cold water and go out back is the next door to my room. It is a nice bath-room."

In that first homesick letter Maria sent greetings to individual family members, but asked for news about only one specific aspect of Toll Bridge: "Tell me everything about the Lyceum paper." Of all she must have yearned for, why did she select only the lyceum paper—not even the lyceum as a whole? I think the paper conjured what she most valued about the entire lyceum, signifying the essentials of her home village. It would have evoked the varied voices of her relatives and neighbors, laughing, lamenting, arguing, teasing, proclaiming. It would have suggested what Maria had lost with the move to Togus: the recognition of her acumen and stature as a woman in the public space of the community. It would have called to mind the intellectual and aesthetic challenge of writing and speaking, the fun of holding and guessing secrets, the dance and drama, the pains and pleasures of being known.

In 1872 Maria could not have guessed that the Toll Bridge Lyceum's days were numbered. She believed in the lyceum tradition and loved creating its papers so much that two decades later, when that lyceum was no more, she inspired her daughter Hattie to carry on a similar editing practice for the local Grange. But by the time of Maria's death in 1926, lyceums and papers had been long gone and generally forgotten. Instead of recording neighborhood gatherings like those of her youth, the diaries of her old age mention days when she went driving around Fryeburg with her brother-in-law, Horace Greeley Adams, first behind Queenie the horse and later, by 1913, in his Model T. Her daughters had moved on into the larger world, and one of them (my grandmother Josephine) had graduated from Wellesley College. Her granddaughters would attend universities, study abroad, and maintain their own careers.

The cosmopolitan swirl of the century since Maria's death has obscured those tiny village lyceums with their face-to-face exchanges and handwritten artistry. All too often nowadays we meet one another screen to screen, our "documents" impersonal, intangible electronic records. I am deeply grateful that Maria's fondness for the lyceums of her youth led her to squirrel away some Toll Bridge writings. It is a gift to be able to hold those tattered scraps in my hands today, to imagine their lively performance, and to listen, however distantly, to the buoyant voices of that inventive community. Though most of New England's lyceum papers have now vanished, many of the graceful connected farmsteads where their writers once lived still remain, calling to mind the village wit and wisdom of my great-grandmother's time.

FIGURE 12. Maria Gordon Adams and her brother-in-law, Horace Greeley Adams, ready to set out on a drive in Fryeburg, c. 1910. They are standing in front of the house in which I found the *Toll Bridge Journal*. Collection of the author.

ACKNOWLEDGMENTS

It has been many years since I first realized that the peculiar manuscript from my great-grandmother's attic had unsuspected kindred in archives and attics all over northern New England. I will never forget my astonishment when I showed the *Toll Bridge Journal* to Stan Howe, then director of the Bethel (ME) Historical Society, and he responded, "Oh! I have something like that in my attic in East Bethel!"—and sent me photocopied pages that were indeed "something like that." This happenstance launched my research, which has been squeezed in among other obligations for decades. Along the way I have received inestimable assistance from fellowships, local and regional historical societies, curators and archivists, academic colleagues, independent scholars and community historians, and many friends and hearteners.

Support from the New England Regional Fellowship Consortium allowed me to travel to major archives in New England to find a critical mass of documents. At the New Hampshire Historical Society, Donna-Belle Garvin, librarians Bill Copeley and Phil Abbott, and manuscript curator David Smolen patiently oriented me to collections, catalogs, and procedures. Volunteer researcher Peter Burr took pains to help me identify lyceum members. At the Vermont Historical Society library, Paul Carnahan and Marjorie Strong kindly shared their expertise. Christopher Hartman was my guide at the New England Historic Genealogical Society. In Providence, Rick Stattler at the Rhode Island Historical Society, Joyce Botelho at the John Nicholas Brown Center, and Mark Brown and Tim Engels at the Hay Library were very helpful. Donald Friary, director of Historic Deerfield, and his wife Grace provided kind hospitality and introduced me to museum curators and nearby academic historians. At the Memorial Libraries of the Pocumtuck Valley Memorial Association I was fortunate to have the expert assistance of David Bosse and Martha Noblick. William D. Barry and Stephanie Philbrick at the Maine Historical Society were generous guides.

In the most recent stages of the project, Elizabeth Hamlin-Morin and Sarah E. Galligan at New Hampshire Historical Society and Tiffany Link at Maine Historical Society have provided support. I would also like to thank Betsy Paradis at the Bangor (ME) Public Library and the staffs of the Special Collections Department of the Fogler Library, University of Maine, Orono, and the Maine Women Writers Collection at the University of New England in Portland, Maine.

Nine months as a Mellon Postdoctoral Research Fellow at the American Antiquarian Society let me make a deep dive into the historical context of the lyceums: nineteenth-century journalism, the culture of oratory and forensics, education and self-education, popular poetry, and women's social and intellectual history. I often drew on the patience and beyond-the-call-of-duty diligence of Marie Lamoureux and the skillful reader services team and appreciated the advice of Joanne Chaison and Caroline Sloat. The gifted area specialists—Thomas G. Knoles, Dennis Laurie, Philip J. Lampi, Gigi Barnhill, Laura Wasowicz—always found the perfect, necessary documents, even in the midst of a major institutional construction project. My fellow researchers at the American Antiquarian Society, particularly Altina Waller, Ben Reiss, David Silverman, and Robert Forrant, made a community of scholars with whom it was a joy to labor. I thank The American University for granting me a leave of absence to do this work.

Because village lyceums were ubiquitous in northern New England, many essential clues and pieces have turned up in local historical societies. I am particularly grateful to these resourceful historical society individuals: John Harris and Paul Tuller, Dublin, New Hampshire; Stanley R. Howe, Randall Bennett, and William F. Chapman, Bethel, Maine: Roberta Chandler, Irene Dunham, Catherine Stone, and Marcia Storkerson, Lovell, Maine; Winnie Moore, Denmark, Maine; Roger Lane, Fayette, Maine; Diane Jones and Linda Drew, Fryeburg, Maine; Sean Minear, Weld, Maine; Matthew E. Thomas, Fremont, New Hampshire; Meredith Marcinkewizc, Shirley, Massachusetts; Peter Dannenberg, Cabot, Vermont; Sue Black, Bridgton, Maine;

Carol Dolan, Embden, Maine; Jeanne Eastman, Chatham, New Hampshire; also Billie Gammon, Washburn-Norlands Living History Center; Earle G. Shettleworth, Maine State Historian; Kathleen Farrar, Hazen Memorial Library, Shirley, Massachusetts; and Clyde G. Berry, Master of the Maine State Grange.

Without the generous collaboration of independent scholars and community historians, I could never have found or understood many of the surviving lyceum papers. In particular, I thank Patricia P. Pickard, Bangor, Maine; Susan Schnare, Andover, New Hampshire; Dennis Stires, North Livermore, Maine; Don Buzzell, Jo Buzzell, and Diane Towle, Fryeburg, Maine; and Dorothy Berry Mason, Dixfield, Maine.

Academic colleagues have also been crucial in this project. Margaret E. Yocom of George Mason University has been a wise companion from the start, reading, questioning, speculating, offering her folkloristic experience and understanding. Leo Marx of the Massachusetts Institute of Technology took interest in the project early; his breadth of vision helped me believe in the value of what I had found, and his suggestions took me in important, unexpected directions. The work of Joseph Conforti of the University of Southern Maine on New England cultural history was a guidepost; I thank him also, as one of the readers for the press, for his careful and generous insights into this book. Thomas C. Hubka's penetrating cultural analysis of New England connected farm buildings brought me to a major realization, as I saw the parallels between the material culture and the intellectual inventions of lyceum participants. I also thank Jane Kamensky of Harvard University and Jere Daniell of Dartmouth College for their guidance.

I have been blessed with more hearteners and helpers along the way than I could ever name. Emily Joseph's patient transcriptions of the first documents helped me see lyceum papers whole. My energy has been sustained over the years by the enthusiasm of dozens of New England community audiences, particularly those reached through the Humanities to Go program of New Hampshire Humanities. I send special thanks to friends who read sections of the work, asked pertinent

questions when I was puzzled, pushed when I needed pushing, and were genuinely interested in the story of the lyceum
tradition: Michael Parent, Meg Gilman, Susan Gordon, Clare
Cuddy, Barbara Lipke, Linda Havel, Maria Puzzanghero, Kate
Carney, Judith Black, Diane Edgecomb, Lani Peterson, Frances
Malino, Deborah Waber, Dianne Lior, and Gail Pressberg, and
our granddaughter, Mia Kelley-Lanser.

At the end of this book's long trail, I have been blessed by
the kindness of the staff at the University of Massachusetts
Press. Brian Halley's generosity, encouragement, and keen
editorial insights have been vital. I have also appreciated the
guidance of Rachael DeShano and Sally Nichols. Dawn Potter,
who has a poet's ear for language, is surely the most perspicacious, thorough, and graceful copyeditor this side of the moon.

My gratitude to my family is centuries deep. Were it not for
my New England packrat ancestry and my great-grandmother
Maria's hoard in that attic, this project would never have begun.
Were it not for my family's recurrent interest in family history
since that time, I would never have been moved to dig into
the dusty heaps. I am delighted that Joshua and Jack Radner,
caring and resourceful sons, have maintained curiosity about
their heritage and interest in this project.

It was, finally, the enforced isolation and reduced work
demand during the Covid-19 pandemic that gave me the time
to finish this book. But no amount of uncluttered time, no
army of researchers and helpers could have made that happen,
had it not been for Sue Lanser's long and tenacious belief in
the project, and in me. Her keen reader's eye, her unparalleled
editorial acumen, and her generous enjoyment of the subject
have filled this undertaking with pleasure.

APPENDIX A

LYCEUM PAPERS CONSULTED

This table lists, in chronological order, all of the manuscript papers I have seen that I am fairly confident were produced for rural lyceums. Blank spaces indicate that information was unknown at time of publication.

Village	State	Lyceum	Paper Title	Vol.	No.	Date	Editor(s)	Location	Notes
Dublin	NH	Dublin Lyceum	Dublin Rural Repository	2	9	2/7/1840	Dexter Mason	Dublin Historical Society	
Dublin	NH	Dublin Lyceum	Dublin Rural Repository	3	8	2/7/1841	L[evi] W. Leonard	Dublin Historical Society	
Dublin	NH	Dublin Lyceum	Dublin Rural Repository	3	10	3/17/1841	C[harles] A. Hamilton	Dublin Historical Society	
Dublin	NH	Dublin Lyceum	Dublin Rural Repository	4	1	11/10/1841	L[evi] W. Leonard	Dublin Historical Society	
Dublin	NH	Young People's Society for Mutual Improvement	Ladies' Miscellany	4	9	1/15/1842	Betsy E. Mason	Dublin Historical Society	Record book for 1837–45 also at Dublin Historical Society
Dublin	NH	Young People's Society for Mutual Improvement	Ladies' Miscellany	5	4	11/1/1842	Eliza Gleason	Dublin Historical Society	

Town	State	Society	Newspaper	Vol.	No.	Date	Editor	Repository	Notes
Dublin	NH	Young People's Society for Mutual Improvement	Ladies' Miscellany	5	6	12/7/1842	Mary E. Morse	Dublin Historical Society	
Dublin	NH	Young People's Society for Mutual Improvement	Ladies' Miscellany	6	8	11/29/1843	F[idelia] P. Mason	Dublin Historical Society	
Dublin	NH	Young People's Society for Mutual Improvement	Ladies' Miscellany	7	2	11/13/1844	M. Gleason	Dublin Historical Society	
Dublin	NH	Young People's Society for Mutual Improvement	Ladies' Miscellany	7	4	12/11/1844	E. M. Piper	Dublin Historical Society	
Dublin	NH	Young People's Society for Mutual Improvement	Ladies' Miscellany	7	6	1/8/1845	B. E. Mason	Dublin Historical Society	
Dublin	NH	Young People's Society for Mutual Improvement	[Ladies'] Miscellany	[7]	7	1/22/1845		Dublin Historical Society	Cover reads "Vol. 6" but publication date indicates this was an error
Dublin	NH	Young People's Society for Mutual Improvement	Wednesday Evening Post	6		2/7/1844	C[harles] W. Gowing	Dublin Historical Society	
Dublin	NH	Young People's Society for Mutual Improvement	Scrap Gatherer	1	4	11/8/1854		Dublin Historical Society	
East Andover	NH	East Andover Social Lyceum	Kearsarge Fountain			1/12/1848		New Hampshire Historical Society	Cover missing, date estimated from internal evidence
East Andover	NH	East Andover Social Lyceum	Kearsarge Fountain	1	7	2/16/1848	George Edwin Emery	New Hampshire Historical Society	
East Andover	NH	East Andover Social Lyceum	Kearsarge Fountain	2	1	12/6/1848		New Hampshire Historical Society	

Location	State	Organization	Paper	Vol.	No.	Date	Editor	Repository	Notes
East Andover	NH	East Andover Mountain Club	Kearsarge Fountain	2	3	1/24/1849	George E. Emery	New Hampshire Historical Society	Cover also reads "New Series, Whole No. 11"
East Andover	NH		Kearsarge Fountain	2	4	2/14/1849	William A. Bachelder	New Hampshire Historical Society	
East Andover	NH	Mountain Club	Kearsarge Fountain	3	12	12/19/1849	George E. Emery	New Hampshire Historical Society	
East Andover	NH	Mountain Club	Kearsarge Fountain	4	4	n.d.	Mary E. Bachelder	New Hampshire Historical Society	Cover also reads "Whole No. 20"
East Andover	NH	Mountain Club	Kearsarge Fountain	6	5	n.d.	Mary E. Bachelder	New Hampshire Historical Society	Cover also reads "Whole No. 31"
East Andover	NH	Mountain Club	Kearsarge Fountain		16	3/15/1850	Mary E. Bachelder	New Hampshire Historical Society	
Landaff	NH		Experiment	2	6	12/24/1852	[Unnamed woman]	New Hampshire Historical Society	Editor addressed in a letter in this paper as "Miss Editress"
Mont Vernon	NH	Young Men's Literary Club	Literary Banner	1	5	1/7/1858	S[arah] E. Batchelder	New Hampshire Historical Society	
Mont Vernon	NH	Young Men's Literary Club	Literary Banner	1	6	1/14/1858	S[arah] E. Batchelder	New Hampshire Historical Society	
Mont Vernon	NH	Young Men's Literary Club	Literary Banner	2	7	1/20/1859	S[arah] E. Batchelder	New Hampshire Historical Society	
Mont Vernon	NH	Young Men's Literary Club	Literary Banner	2	8	1/27/1859	S[arah] E. Batchelder	New Hampshire Historical Society	

South Freeport	ME	South Freeport Mutual Improvement Society	Cruiser	1	1	1/20/1859	Talbot and Shaw, no first names	Freeport Historical Society	Accessed through Maine Memory Network, Maine Historical Society
South Freeport	ME	South Freeport Mutual Improvement Society	Cruiser	1	3	2/12/1859	Talbot and Shaw, no first names	Freeport Historical Society	Accessed through Maine Memory Network, Maine Historical Society
South Freeport	ME	South Freeport Mutual Improvement Society	Cruiser	1	4	2/19/1859	Talbot and Shaw, no first names	Freeport Historical Society	Accessed through Maine Memory Network, Maine Historical Society
South Freeport	ME	South Freeport Mutual Improvement Society	Cruiser	1	6	3/27/1859	Talbot and Shaw, no first names	Freeport Historical Society	Accessed through Maine Memory Network, Maine Historical Society
South Freeport	ME	South Freeport Mutual Improvement Society	Cruiser	1		4/9/1859	Talbot and Shaw, no first names	Freeport Historical Society	Accessed through Maine Memory Network, Maine Historical Society
South Freeport	ME	South Freeport Mutual Improvement Society	Cruiser	1	8	4/30/1859	Talbot and Shaw, no first names	Freeport Historical Society	Accessed through Maine Memory Network, Maine Historical Society
Landaff	NH	[Landaff Lyceum]	Emblem	1	3	1/20/1860	L[uke] B. Chandler, J. A. Chandler, M[artha] M. Eastman	New Hampshire Historical Society	
Landaff	NH	[Landaff Lyceum]	Emblem	1	4	1/27/1860	J[ohn] E. Hall, S[arah] J. Chandler, M[artha] M. Eastman	New Hampshire Historical Society	Cover date reads 1/20/1859 but was corrected by internal evidence

Town	State	Lyceum	Paper	Vol.	No.	Date	Editor(s)	Repository	Notes
Landaff	NH	[Landaff Lyceum]	Emblem	1	8	2/25/1860		New Hampshire Historical Society	
Landaff	NH	[Landaff Lyceum]	Emblem			c. 1860		New Hampshire Historical Society	No cover
Fryeburg	ME	Toll Bridge Lyceum	Toll Bridge Journal	6	3	3/12/1870	Maria Eliza Gordon	Private collection; photocopy at Fryeburg Historical Society	Editor identified by handwriting
Bow Lake Village, Strafford	NH	Bow Lake Village Social Association	Bow Lake Journal	1	2	c. January 1875	Abbie S. Jewell, Elsie M. Hanson	New Hampshire Historical Society	Date estimated from internal evidence
Bow Lake Village, Strafford	NH	Bow Lake Lyceum	Bow Lake Journal	2	4		Elsie M. Hanson	New Hampshire Historical Society	No date on cover
Carthage	ME		Mystic Tie	1	1		D. Frank Holt, Bettie Holt	Weld Historical Society	Editors identified by handwriting
Carthage	ME		Mystic Tie	1	3	c. January or February 1875	D. Frank Holt, Bettie Holt	Weld Historical Society	Editors identified by handwriting; date estimated from internal evidence
Veazie	ME	Veazie Lyceum	Veazie Light			1/22/1877	Mrs. Katie Shaw	Bangor Public Library, Collection MS043	
Beans Corner, Jay	ME	Bean's Corner Lyceum	Bean's Corner Sunbeam	1		1/16/1877	George E. Childs, Mary E. Webster	Weld Historical Society	
Beans Corner, Jay	ME	Bean's Corner Lyceum	Bean's Corner Sunbeam			c. 1877		Weld Historical Society	No cover; date estimated from internal evidence

Beans Corner, Jay	ME	Bean's Corner Lyceum	Bean's Corner Sunbeam					Weld Historical Society	Cover missing; issue possibly not intact
Beans Corner, Jay	ME	Bean's Corner Lyceum	Bean's Corner Sunbeam	3	11	3/20/1879	Horace Ranger, Mary E. Webster	Weld Historical Society	
East Bethel	ME					c. December 1877		Private collection	Eight loose pages; no cover; date estimated from internal evidence
East Cabot	VT	East Cabot Debating Club	Monitor	1	3	1/9/1878	Charles Howe, Mrs. Laura Glidden, Mrs. Snattie Howe	Vermont Historical Society	
East Cabot	VT	East Cabot Debating Club	Monitor	1	6	1/30/1878	Henry L. Hill, Lizzie M. Abbott, Laura C. Glidden	Vermont Historical Society	
East Cabot	VT	East Cabot Debating Club	Monitor	1	11	2/27/1878	James A. R. Glidden, Laura C. Glidden, Lizzie M. Abbott	Vermont Historical Society	
East Cabot	VT	East Cabot Debating Club	Monitor			c. February or March 1879		Vermont Historical Society	No cover; date estimated from internal evidence
West Plymouth	NH	West Plymouth Literary Association	Gem of the Valley		1	11/30/1878	Alma Harriman	New Hampshire Historical Society	This version of lyceum name appears in 1870–80 record book
West Plymouth	NH	West Plymouth Literary Association	Gem of the Valley	3	6	1/22/1880	Emily Harriman	New Hampshire Historical Society	
West Plymouth	NH	West Plymouth Lyceum	Gem of the Valley	3	10	2/26/1880	Alma Harriman	New Hampshire Historical Society	Cover of this issue reads "Published weekly by the West Plymouth Lyceum"

Location	State	Society/Club	Paper			Date	Names	Collection	Notes
Fremont	NH	Fremont Literary Society	Poplin Herald			12/16/1879		Fremont Historical Society	
Fremont	NH	Fremont Literary Society	Poplin Herald			2/17/1880		Fremont Historical Society	
Carthage	ME					c. 1880		Private collection	No cover; "1880" in pencil on top page.
Carthage	ME		Carthage Notes[?]					Private collection	No cover; "Carthage Notes" in different hand on top page; clearly related to other Carthage paper
South Levant	ME	South Levant Reading Club	Independent	1	7	3/23/1881	Inez McLaughlin, Nancy Read	Bangor Public Library Collection #MS043	
Webster	NH	Webster Lyceum	Scrap Book			c. January 1882	Govuetta Goodhue	Private collection	No cover; date estimated from internal evidence; editor identified by handwriting
West Danville	VT	West Danville Debating Club	Enterprise	1	1	1/24/1884	William D. Glidden, Mrs. George Merrel, Mrs. William Glidden	Vermont Historical Society	
Kenduskeag	ME	Kenduskeag Lyceum	Meteor	1	6	11/15/1884		Bangor Public Library Collection, MS043	
Kenduskeag	ME	Kenduskeag Lyceum	[Meteor]			c. late 1884 or early 1885		Bangor Public Library Collection #MS043	No cover; date estimated from internal evidence
Antrim	NH	Literary Club	Literary News	1	7	7/6/1883	Olive Buchanan	New Hampshire Historical Society	Editor's name suggested by internal evidence

Antrim	NH		Literary News	2	1	1/2/1886	Gertrude Hastings	New Hampshire Historical Society	Editor's name suggested by internal evidence
Fryeburg	ME		Toll Bridge Graphic			c. 1886	Mary E. Buzzell?	Private collection; photocopy at Fryeburg Historical Society	Date and editor suggested by collector's local knowledge
Dublin	NH	Dublin Literary and Social Union	Miscellany	3	3	12/3/1886		Dublin Historical Society	1884–95 record book also at Dublin Historical Society
North Foyette	ME	North Foyette Lyceum	Firefly	5	7	c. 1887	Lester R. Fellows, Carrie M. Wing	Foyette Historical Society	Contents of all four issues scrambled; date estimated from internal evidence
North Foyette	ME	North Foyette Lyceum	Firefly	5	8	c. 1887	Lester R. Fellows, Carrie M. Wing	Foyette Historical Society	
North Foyette	ME	North Foyette Lyceum	Firefly	6	9	c. 1887	Lester R. Fellows, Carrie M. Wing	Foyette Historical Society	
South Bethel	ME	South Bethel Debating Society	Gazette	5	2	November 1889		Bethel Historical Society	
Embden	ME		Emden Center Times			11/29/1893		Embden Historical Society	Possibly a school paper open to the community

1870 CONSTITUTION

The Literary Association of West Plymouth, New Hampshire

ARTICLE I   PLEDGE

We the Undersigned, Individually and unitedly agree that we will take a part in the Lyceum to be held in this place the present season. We also promise that we will do our best to make the same pleasant and profitable. [Thirty-seven signatures follow.] . . .

ARTICLE II

SEC. I   OFFICERS AND THEIR TERMS

The officers of this Association shall consist of a President, Vice President, Secretary, Assistant Secretary, Editor, Editress, and Guard.

Which shall be chosen by vote of the members of this association once in two weeks.

ARTICLE III   DUTIES OF OFFICERS

SEC. I

It shall be the duty of the President to preside over all meetings and enforce the due observance of the Constitution and By-Laws. To see that all Officers perform their respective duties. To appoint committees. To appoint officers to fill vacancies temporarily. To give the casting vote in case of a tie and see that good order is kept during meetings.

SEC. 2

It shall be the duty of Vice President to render the President such assistance as he may need. In the absence of the President to perform his duties.

SEC. 3

It shall be the duty of the Secretary to keep a true account of the proceeding of each meeting. At the opening of the meeting call the role and read the report of last meeting and appoint meetings when orderd to do so by the President.

SEC. 4

It shall be the duty of Assistant Secretary to perform the Secretary duties in his absence and render him such assistance as he may need.

SEC. 5

It shall be the duty of the Editor to furnish and read a paper before the society at each regular meeting. Contributions for the paper shall in no case be allowed to change except for the purpose of making them grammatical.

SEC. 6

It shall be the duty of the Editress to perform the same duty as the Editor.

SEC. 7

It shall be the duty of Guard to see that no person enters without the pass-word and Signal.

ARTICLE IV
SEC. I

No person shall be admitted as a member of this association except by vote of the society which shall in all cases be decided by ballot, after the Organization and if not more than three shall vote against them they shall be admitted as members of the society.

ARTICLE V
SEC. I

Any member which shall violate our laws shall be expelled from the society.

ARTICLE IV [VI]
SEC. I

In case of the absence of President and Vice President the latter President shall preside over the meeting.

ARTICLE VII
SEC. I

No alteration or addition shall be made, unless by a two thirds vote of members present at any regular meeting.

ARTICLE VIII
SEC. I

No person shall be admitted as a member of this society under ten years of age unless by a three forths vote of the members present at any regular meeting.

ARTICLE IX
SEC. I

Every person on becoming a member of this society shall sign the Constitution.

EMBLEM (LANDAFF, NH) 1, NO. 8, FEBRUARY 25, 1860[1]

The Emblem

Saturday eve. Feb. 25th 1860

Vol. 1st   No. 8

Devoted to every thing good.

A type of truth may it ever appear
Of friendship and joy and kindly cheer
To honor and virtue be its pages given
Moving our spirits nearer to Heaven

Editorial.

In presenting to you this the 8th number of the Emblem we
take a deep interest in presenting to you through its columns a
variety of such matter as we think best calculated to improve
the mind in all the various duties in which it is called to act,
and such as will tend to cultivate our intellectual, social and
moral faculties with the principles of virtue, which are the
foundation of every well regulated society. Taking this as
our standard and keeping in view as nearly as possible the
object of our mission, we lay before you our productions and
those of our valued correspondents with the assuredness that

---

1   The *Emblem* was the paper of the Landaff Lyceum. Although the editors
are not mentioned on its cover, it is likely that this issue, like two previous
surviving issues of the *Emblem* from the winter of 1860, had three editors—a
man and two women—and that one of the editresses was Martha M. Eastman, twenty-four years old and (according to the 1860 census) a teacher, who
was probably the keeper of the surviving *Emblems*. Eastman was named as
an editress of the two earlier issues, and Luke B. Chandler, named editor of
vol. 1, no. 3, became her husband in 1866. Given the editorial's reference to
"twice filling the editorial chair," Chandler might also have edited this issue.

we have fulfilled our duties to the best of the abilities which a kind providence has bestowed upon us. If some that deem themselves members of this fraternity would feel as deeply as we do the importance of performing the post devolving upon them, this Society would flourish like an exuberant plant beneath the burning rays of a tropical sun. We again express our deep gratitude to our kind friends and patrons for past favors shown us, and beg your forbearance while we lay before you our ill-developped sheet. We trust that twice filling the editorial chair will be a sure guarantee to our friends of our inability to conduct a journal that increases in confidence and circulation like the Emblem.

"Tis infamy to die and not be missed."

In the universal mission of mankind each has a task to perform. The great drama of action is yet unfinished. And in the progressing unfinished drama, as truly has every one a part assigned him, as if the programme was marked out before him; as if he could view the length of the scene that is left for him to act. For this purpose alone has he come upon the stage. The great framer of the scheme saw that none else could perform the work. If he acts well his part he shall pass away in honor bearing on his brow a crown: but if he does it not well, it will still remain undone. The influence it was given him to shed, to brighten the pathway of the future, will be unfelt forever, and vacant will be the place for which he was designed, in the universe of life and thought. Let each one remember that until the now enthralled children of earth, shall go free; until the world shall be released from the darkening way of error; until vice shall cease to stalk forth at noonday; until the satanic war whoop shall no longer ring upon the air; until the foul breath of drunkenness shall no more go up to pollute the skies; until horrid profanity shall cease to fill the ears of Heaven with its unhallowed curses; until truth shall have purified the earth & every clime shall have gladened under the peaceful reign of righteousness; until the drawing millennium shall proclaim that the beaming rays of the Son of righteousness have

brightened the dark recesses of the ransomed earth; there is
a work to do, and it is infamy to die and not have hastened
it on, one day at least, towards its final glorious completion
and perfection.

Conundrums.

Why is R. H. Noyes like a dejected man?
Because his spirits are gone.

Why are the cars the most durable
things in the world?
Because you can brake them without damage.

Why is a member of this society like a
fop in Broadway?
Because he practices the latest fashions.

Why are certain persons in this town who
attend the meetings of this society but re-
fuse to join or take part in them, like a
barking cur? Because when they are
outside they are ready to bark, but inside
never a word.

Old Maids

Old maids! old maids: we hear it oft
From the lips of those disposed to scoff
Tis spoken with a heartless jeer
Which to our ears sounds very queer
As if it were a great disgrace
To keep the happy maidens place
As if it were a monstrous sin
To live without the wedlock ring
Ah! thoughtless scoffer dost thou know
Thou art adding to a weight of woe
Art conscious that these cruel sneers
Have filled our world with womans tears

Full many a maid of blessed life
Becomes a ruined wretched wife
Because she dares not brave the shame
Which clingeth to an old maids name.
Her present weal she'd fain maintain
Till she a happier lot might gain
Would sooner live a single life
Than be a worthless husband's wife
But no! Ah! no alack she sighs
Tis fashion to do other wise
Hence they try all men to please
And the first chance for marriage seize
And thus to certain ruin run
The dreaded name Old Maid to shun
O, scoffers, if by justice laws
Ye answer for the woes ye cause
If tears for tears your eyes must shed
If drop for drop your hearts be bled
Eternity its course must longer keep
To give full time for you to weep.

M. J. Noyes

A Will.

I, Orlando W. Garvin being weak in body but sound and perfect in mind, do make and publish this my last will and testament, in manner and form following.

First I give and bequeath to my beloved wife Lizzie all my personal property and real estate. I do also give and bequeath to my eldest son Benj. Morrill my best pair of thin boots. I do also give and bequeath to my two younger sons R. H. Noyes and R. T. Gordon my old hats to be divided equaly between them. I do also give & bequeath to my eldest daughter Laura J. Sherman one square foot of ground on which to raise beans for her especial benefit. I do also give and bequeath to my intended son-in-law Wm. H. Webber my new coat hoping he will make good use of it. I do also give and bequeath to my remaining daughter Martha Taylor the only brass kettle the family ever posesed. I do also give and bequeath to my great-uncle Foster Hall my iron bowed spectacles. I do also give and bequeath to my great grandfather Alson Little my new pair of cow hide boots. I do also give and bequeath to my aunt Ann L. Gordon my best go-to-meeting pants which she can make over for my cousin Benji. Cline. I do also give and bequeath to my sister in law Lomira my shawl which she can use for a bed or horse blanket as may be convenient. I do also give and bequeath to my grand mother Ann Young my best feather bed without the tick. I do also give and bequeath to my grand father J. E. Hall my old great coat which will be an exact fit. I do also give and bequeath to my father Orrin Young the only vest I ever possessed, and lastly as to the residue and remainder of my goods and chattels I give and bequeath the same to my said beloved wife Lizzie, whom I hereby appoint the sole executrix of this my last will and testament hereby revoking all other wills made by me.

In witness whereof I have hereunto set my hand and seal this 25th day of Feb. in the year of our Lord 1860.

Orlando W. Garvin

Signed Sealed published and declared by the above named Orlando W. Garvin to be his last will and testament; in the presence of us, who here unto subscribed our names as witnesses in the presence of the testator

H. H. Noyes

M. A. Flint

G. W. Gordon

Married

At Sugar Hill, February 22nd by Rev. J. H. Shipman. Mr. James S. Webster of Landaff to Miss Emily Bowls of Sugar Hill.

Accompaning the above was a liberal slice of cake for which we return our sincere and heartfelt thanks, wishing the happy ones long life and much joy.

Our latest Wish

That gold dollars like scandal
might grow big by circulation.

The Car of Education

Here's the car of Education
In its motion steady
And it stops at every station
Taking who are ready;
Step on board and claim a seat
Or you'll fall behind it;
Nothing can with this compete
And so you'll surely find it.

In the Car are friends of learning
Zealous all and prudent;
Each his reputation earning
As a faithful student;
Take the tickets Time and study
Haste! the bell is ringing
Soon beyond your reach will be
Its way right onward winging.

Here you'll meet the hoary headed
Ardent still and active,
To the car they're firmly wedded
Finding it attractive.
Soon they'll pass beyond the goal
Never more returning
But their virtues we enrol
Upon the alter burning.

Here is manhood in his power
Vigor and ambition
Gathering laurels every hour
By his erudition

See them toiling side by side
Each in his vocation
Spreading knowledge far and wide
In this growing nation.

Here's the rising generation
Thoughtful and aspiring
On the car of education
Never never tiring
See them with an active zeal
And a true devotion
Counting it their greatest weal
To keep the car in motion.

Come and join the grand procession
All are now invited
Come whatever your profession
Let us be united.
Keep the car upon the track
Free from all disaster
And if there's no holding back
In time 'twill roll the faster.

Capra

Forty Years Ago

Forty years ago! That's quite a ways to look back on life's journey, 40 years ago I was—let me see well no matter how old I was. I did not intend to tell my age—only to tell you young people about the girls and boys when I was young. no I didn't mean just that for I am not old, no indeed, not by any manner of means, yet I have lived long enough to receive many flattering invitations to become Mrs. just as though I would change my name for that of any man living or dead either. Not I indeed. Well as I was saying, I will tell you about the young people 40 years ago. It was in the good old town of Landaff in the winter of 59 and 60 that the young people gentlemen

and laidies concluded that it would be for their good to have
a Lyceum and it is of these same young people that I will tell
you. There was R. H. Noyes who kept store across the street
from the church, when he died left his store to his son Frank
with Chandler an old bachelor for his clerk. Then R. T. Gordon
who with Noyes owned the starch factory, being there at work
one hot day in mid-summer, the water being so low it could
hardly be seen above the rocks, it was supposed he fell in and
was drowned. His body was found the next day but having lain
so long it was impossible to identify it. J. E. Hall having been
mittened[2] by a Miss Dexter went crazy and wandering about
was finally lost. Search was made in all directions but he was
nowhere to be found. The next spring he was found behind Mr.
Dexter's woodpile in a stove pipe hat covered up with leaves.
It was supposed he had wandered to that place in hopes of
meeting his lost love and night overtaking him he had crawled
into the hat and froze to death. Sarah Jane Chandler long since
settled down quietly with Foster Hall. Luella Quimby united
her fortunes with one of the Flints which I cannot remember.
The other Flint placed his head and heart in keeping of Ann
Young. Lizzie Noyes after securing alternately the attentions
of Moses Chandler M. A. Flint and O. H. Garvin concluded
to accept the flattering invitations of Chas. King and became
his wife. O. H. Garvin concluded it was not good for him to
marry and therefore like a sensible man lived all his days in
single blessedness, but died a few years ago of enlargement of
the heart—supposed to have been caused by seeing the min-
iature of a pretty girl. Geo. Gordon married Elvira Lovejoy
but not living in peace and tranquility ran away and the last
that was heard of him he was teaching school in China. Fred
Noyes studied law and was admitted to the bar but broke
down in the middle of his maiden speech and left in disgust.
He afterwards became a minister and at last account was a
saint among the mormons with 16 wives and 50 children. Ben

---

2   A woman who refused a man's attentions was said to "give him the mitten."

Glines studied medicine and was loved by all for the skillful manner in which he sent his patients out of the world. Lamira Noyes married a merchant and resides in Boston. But time would fail me to speak of the Webbers and Clarks and Noyes innumerable. I fear I have wearied your patience already by talking so long but when I get to talking of old times I hardly know when and where to stop. O! 40 years ago.

APPENDIX D

"THE THREE CENTURIES"[3]

Once upon a time the people of three generations met to talk over affairs. 1776-1876-1976 They met on friendly terms but out of respect to the oldest 1776 commenced the meeting. They talked a long time; it seemed so strange to the modern people of the 18th and 19th [19th and 20th] centuries to listen to so strange a tale. First it spoke of its old fire places when each could conviently sit in the corners. How gladly they hailed the tin kitchen and the baker; they thought themselvs happy when such conveniences were added to their store. They spoke of their flax and wool carded and spun by their industrious Daughters and taught by their careful Mothers. The others interupted them, "You do not mean that your Daughters worked in those days! Why, our Daughters only learn the fine arts." The old Lady raised her head in surprise. "Why, our Daughters were a great help in all the household affairs; they were perfect in all the industries of the age, to card and spin, weave, knit and sew untill our houses were clothed with the industry of our hands."

I was pained to see the look of disgust on the faces of her listeners, but as 1876 had the floor we were soon interested in her story. She asked the old lady if she did not think Traveling had improved much in the last century. She merely said she did not think there used to be so many accidents in her day; if a stage coach was slower than the modern steam cars or steam boats, it was pretty safe. "Well, you must remember all our improvements in agriculture, all our sewing machines, our machines of all kinds for farming; and the advances in science, our telegraphs, all these are the products of the 18th [19th] century." I thought I could see a look of exultant pride on the face of the speaker. She turned to the old Lady: "Surely you did not have a Centennial in your day. Look to Philiadelphia where we have sent all the specimens of our improved age." "True," she replied, "but

---

3   *Bean's Corner Sunbeam* (Jay, Maine) 1, January 16, 1877. Editors were George E. Childs and Mary E. Webster. (Punctuation edited for clarity.)

we with our Noble Fathers gave you the fredom you now enjoy. We left to our Children a united and free land; we fought nobly that you might have peace." The old Lady paused; a look of pain pased over her features. It stired old memories in her heart: it stired up the memories of Bunker hill, of Lexington, and Concord, and the long and bloody war. But 1876, not abashed, said, "If you speak of war, our own people have been brave in battle as those before us. Look at our last war. We took the Country from your hands with liberty on our banners while our country was writhing in the bonds of slavery. We felt that in the sacred cause of liberty we could send our sons to battle to finish the work you so gloriously commenced."

The old lady bowed and turning to 1976, a lady of great talent seeming much younger than the others, said she would like to hear what she had to say of the improved age in which she lived. 1976, taking the floor, said it seemed almost presumption to speak after listening to their storys, but as they had met to compare the talents of the ages it become her to speak of their wonderful age. It seemed a great effort to speak as all of their work was done by machinery, also all their Education was done by that process. "We do not learn any thing. We have only to look at our wonderfull machine—it gives us a look into the future. It tells us the result of our inquiries and realy leaves us nothing to do but to enjoy or amuse ourselves as we think best. Our music is all arranged and by changeing a little we have whatever tune we desire. I think our wonderful moniters of war would quell any rebellion of the land without sending our friends to battle. Of course we need directors to that and it gives more dignity to have a government, but a look into these machines tells us just who to Vote for and what their political life will be, so that saves the trouble of sending orators to rouse the public spirit, and stump speeches are out of place here." "But don't you think Women begin to have their rights more than before?" "Why, nearly all the Ladies scarcely know their own Children, they spend so much of their time abroad, and with their friends. But we know just when our friends are coming and all is arranged on such a perfect plan you can but see we realy live in a wonderful age. We scarcely need the improvements of the last century."

She seemed exhausted with the effort and the others feeling a little behind the times kindly invited her to sit down.

NOTES

INTRODUCTION

1   Ronald J. Zboray and Mary Saracino Zboray, *Everyday Ideas: Socioliterary Experience among Antebellum New Englanders* (Knoxville: University of Tennessee Press, 2006), xxi.

2   See Carl Bode, *The American Lyceum: Town Meeting of the Mind* (New York: Oxford University Press, 1956); and Angela G. Ray, *The Lyceum and Public Culture in the Nineteenth-Century United States* (East Lansing: Michigan State University Press, 2005). Although in its early decades the American Lyceum aimed for "mutual instruction" and included in its programs public debates as well as invited lectures and readings, its dominant form quickly became the subscription lecture, usually by a celebrity speaker from outside the town. After the Civil War, commercial lecture bureaus marketed increasingly entertaining programs, and the early educational focus of the lyceum movement waned.

3   *Gazette* (South Bethel, ME) 5, no. 2, November 1889.

4   Joseph F. Kett, *The Pursuit of Knowledge under Difficulties: From Self-Improvement to Adult Education in America, 1750–1990* (Stanford, CA: Stanford University Press, 1994), 45. The term *lyceum* was used generically in nineteenth-century rural New England. For example, in the *Cold River Journal* (Alstead, NH), October 21, 1887, the local Acworth columnist reported: "Our schools are progressing finely. The students of the grammar school will give *a literary entertainment, or lyceum,* at Eagle hall [*sic*] on Friday evening of this week. Everybody is invited."

5   See Ray's excellent discussion of the word *lyceum* in *The Lyceum and Public Culture,* 3–6.

6   Edmund Clarence Stedman, *Poets of America* (Boston: Houghton, Mifflin, 1886), 99.

7   James L. Hill, "Formative Influences in Early Iowa," *Annals of Iowa,* ser. 3, 10 (1912): 216.

8   *Gazette and Courier* (Greenfield, MA), February 5, 1882.

9   Although Todd Steven Gernes's study of nineteenth-century women's ephemeral writings did not include village lyceum papers, his discussion of the idea that "the performative aspect of the culture of ephemera . . . is its most defining characteristic" is relevant here ("Recasting the Culture of Ephemera: Young Women's Literary Culture in Nineteenth-Century America" [PhD diss., Brown University, 1992], 35).

10 Ray, *The Lyceum and Public Culture,* 6.

CHAPTER 1: "REPORT OF LAST LYCEUM"

1   Glanders is a contagious disease, chiefly of horses and mules but communicable to humans, caused by the bacterium *Pseudomonas mallei* and characterized by swellings beneath the jaw and a profuse mucous discharge from the nostrils.

2   This entry, of course, raised more mysteries for me: How did the March 12, 1870, *Toll Bridge Journal* wind up among Maria's papers, when she did not

even attend the lyceum that night? It is the only intact gathering among the papers, but I found it in the midst of other separate pieces. (I did *not* find the February 12 paper she told her diary that she actually produced herself and read to Sam Frye, though four of the miscellaneous pieces in the pile can be dated, on internal evidence, to the period prior to March 12 and some may have been part of Maria's earlier creation.) Perhaps, because of Willard Barker's death, Maria had *not* read the intended paper at the March 12 lyceum. As I learned later when I discovered more lyceum papers from other New England villages, it was the editorial custom to make a fair copy of the pieces submitted, to facilitate reading to the assembled audience. The March 12, 1870, gathering of pieces would have been preliminary to the copying—a valuable example of the way in which an editor deliberately arranged the pieces submitted by the neighbors. Maria's final copying of the paper might have been prevented by her cousin's death.

3 Margaret K. Nelson, "Vermont Female Schoolteachers in the Nineteenth Century," *Vermont History* 49 (1981): 20. Catherine E. Kelly also mentions that, for women, teaching "proved less a vocation for most of them than a job" (*In the New England Fashion: Reshaping Women's Lives in the Nineteenth Century* [Ithaca, NY: Cornell University Press, 1999], 117).

4 Maria's experience in spelling and writing schools as well as her own portrayal of herself as teacher testifies that Karen V. Hansen's observation about antebellum customs held true in the small villages of northern New England well into the latter part of the century: "the *social* includes that range of behaviors that mediates public and private activities, linking households to neighbors and individuals to institutions" (*A Very Social Time: Crafting Community in Antebellum New England* [Berkeley: University of California Press, 1994], 8).

5 Hannah Chase, listed as age twenty-eight in the 1870 census, was living as "domestic servant" in the household of house carpenter Enoch S. Chase, age thirty-six; his wife Mary; his parents Thomas, age seventy-one, and Mary, age sixty-one; and a resident named Josiah, age twenty-one, who may have been Enoch's brother. They lived next door to Isaac Abbott. Augusta Wiley (c. 1852–1900) was a daughter of Enoch Wiley and Miranda Jones and a younger sister of Lizzie, Hazen, and Harriet (Albion Gordon's wife).

6 Bachelors in general seemed to be targets of teasing. Taking a clue from the names that appeared regularly in Maria Gordon's diary, I guessed that the victim of the *Toll Bridge Journal*'s tormenting rhymes in "*Sam's Soliloquy*" would have been Samuel Frye of Center Fryeburg, who was listed in the 1870 census as a forty-year-old bachelor farmer keeping house for his elderly parents and uncle.

7 This would have been Charlotte Farrington, listed as age seventeen in the 1870 census and a daughter of James W. R. Farrington, age sixty-one, and his wife Abigail A., age fifty-seven. Flora Temple was a world-famous trotting horse, foaled in 1845. Perhaps the writer was comparing Charlotte's singing voice to whinnying?

CHAPTER 2: "A CROWN OF WISDOM WEAVE"

1 I use a variety of terms to refer to the areas in which the rural lyceums were located, including neighborhood, district, hill town, hamlet, and village.

Unlike towns and cities, these locales had no official boundaries but were nonetheless clearly distinguished in the minds of their residents.

2 *Dublin (NH) Rural Repository* 4, no. 1, November 10, 1841.

3 *Kearsarge Fountain* (East Andover, NH) 2, no. 4, February 14, 1849.

4 Bridgton Historical Society, *History of Bridgton, Maine, 1768–1994*, 2nd ed. (Camden, ME: Picton, 1993), 594–95.

5 Charles Morley, *A Guide to Forming and Conducting Lyceums, Debating Societies, &C. With Outlines of Discussions and Essays, and an Appendix, Containing an Epitome of Rhetoric, Logic, &C.* (New York: Wright, 1841), 5. There were many such guides, among them *How to Behave: A Pocket Manual of Republican Etiquette and Guide to Correct Personal Habits, with Rules for Debating Societies and Deliberative Assemblies* (New York: Fowler and Wells, 1857); and *Beadle's Dime Debater and Chairman's Guide: Comprising Suggestions for the Formation of Debating Societies; Laws and Rules for Their Government; the Art of Debate; How to Acquire It; Questions for Debate; Debates in Full and in Brief; Also, the Rules of Order*, Speaker Series, vol. 11 (New York: Beadle and Company, 1869).

6 *Poplin Herald* (Fremont, NH), December 16, 1879. Needless to say, the village of Fremont never boasted an actual brazen temple. See also the chronicle-style piece about the founding of the Young People's Society for Mutual Improvement: *Wednesday Evening Post* (Dublin, NH) 6, February 7, 1844. Chronicle-style descriptions of a previous meeting are found in *Literary Banner* (Mont Vernon, NH) 1, no. 6, January 14, 1858; and *Literary News* (Antrim, NH) 1, no. 7, July 6, 1885; 2, no. 1, January 2, 1886.

7 "A Condensed History of our Lyceum," *Gem of the Valley* (West Plymouth, NH) 1, November 30, 1878. See appendix B for the transcript of the constitution, which was hardly more elaborate than most.

8 Morley, *A Guide*, 7–9. For another generic constitution and bylaws, see *How to Talk: A Pocket Manual of Conversation, and Debating*, Hand-Books for Home Improvement, vol. 2 (New York: Fowler and Wells, 1857), 153–54.

9 "Condensed History."

10 "Prelude," *Emblem* (Landaff, NH) 1, no. 3, January 20, 1860.

11 "Our Society," *Cruiser* (South Freeport, ME) 1, no. 1, January 20, 1859.

12 Catherine Kelly, *In the New England Fashion: Reshaping Women's Lives in the Nineteenth Century* (Ithaca, NY: Cornell University Press, 1999), 170.

13 Chester (VT) Village Lyceum, record book, 1857–58, University of Vermont Library, Burlington.

14 Thaddeus Perry Mason, "Report on the History of the Young People's Society for Mutual Improvement," *Thaddeus Perry Mason Papers*, 1842, box 3, Historic Deerfield Library, Deerfield, MA. Mason reported the "stormy debate" at the meeting in his diary, November 10, 1837 (*Mason Papers*, box 1).

15 Alice Cary, "The Grand House and Its Owner," in *From Year to Year*, ed. Alice Cary and Phoebe Cary (Chicago: Belford, Clarke, 1889), 17, 21. Born in 1820, Alice Cary was raised on a farm in Ohio in a family that exemplified the New England diaspora (and this lyceum, too, belonged to that diaspora).

16 *Maine Teacher and School Officer* 3, no. 3 (September 1860): 73.

17 *Vermont Record* (Brandon, VT), February 11, 1865.

18 Edward Calver, *Heath, Massachusetts: A History and Guidebook* (Heath, MA: Heath Historical Society, 1979), 194.

19 L. F. Society (Westminster, VT), "The Constitution for the L. F. Society," December 1845, in L. F. Society record book, 1845–47, University of Vermont Library, Burlington.

20 Enoch Emory, *Myself: A Romance of New England Life* (Philadelphia: Lippincott, 1872), 73ff.

21 *Grafton County Journal* (Plymouth, NH), February 7, 1880.

22 *Ladies' Miscellany* (Dublin, NH) 5, no. 4, November 1, 1842.

23 "When time has left its changes," *Independent* (South Levant, ME) 1, no. 7, March 23, 1881.

24 *Cold River Journal* (Alstead, NH), December 12, 1884.

25 Zuar E. Jameson, diary entry, January 27, 1856, in diaries 1855–64, Vermont Historical Society, Barre.

26 One instance of a willingness to travel: "*Henry Hill went out to Lyceum at West Danville with Mae Howe and her brother.*" In 1870 Henry Hill lived in Calais, Vermont, to the west of Cabot and West Danville, so this journey would have been close to twenty miles one way ("Mind Your Own Business," *Monitor* [East Cabot, VT] 1, no. 6, January 30, 1878).

27 "Condensed History."

28 Tunbridge (VT) Lyceum, minutes, January 10, 1844, records, 1838–44, Vermont Historical Society, Barre.

29 William Sweetzer Heywood, *History of Westminster Massachusetts* (Lowell, MA: Vox Populi, 1893), 263.

30 *Enterprise and Vermonter* (Vergennes, VT), February 14, 1862; *Brandon (VT) Gazette*, April 24, 1862; *Bellows Falls (VT) Times*, February 13, 1863.

31 *Barre (VT) Gazette*, March 18, 1864.

CHAPTER 3: "THE GREAT WORK OF SELF-CULTURE"

1 J[ohn] L[everett] Merrill, *History of Acworth, with the Proceedings of the Centennial Anniversary, Genealogical Records, and Register of Farms* (Springfield, MA: Bowles, 1869), 104; Thomas Gustafson, *Representative Words: Politics, Literature, and the American Language, 1776–1865* (Cambridge: Cambridge University Press, 1992); Joseph F. Kett, *The Pursuit of Knowledge under Difficulties: From Self-Improvement to Adult Education in America, 1750–1990* (Stanford, CA: Stanford University Press, 1994); Thomas S. Harding, *College Literary Societies: Their Contribution to Higher Education in the United States, 1815–1876* (New York: Pageant Press International, 1971).

2 Silas R. Coburn, *History of Dracut Massachusetts* (Lowell, MA: Press of the Courier-Citizen Company, 1922).

3 Angela G. Ray, *The Lyceum and Public Culture in the Nineteenth-Century United States* (East Lansing: Michigan State University Press, 2005); Carl Bode, *The American Lyceum: Town Meeting of the Mind* (New York: Oxford University Press, 1956); Barbara Allen Hinds, "The Lyceum Movement in Maine" (MA thesis, University of Maine, 1949).

4 The New Hampshire Historical Society has nine issues of East Andover's lyceum paper, the *Kearsarge Fountain*, dating between January 1848 and March 1850. The surviving issues were edited by George E. Emery, who served as founding secretary of the East Andover High School Association (which established the Highland Lake Institute) in 1850; William A. Bachelder, who

succeeded Emery as secretary in 1852; and Bachelder's sister Mary, who married George Emery in 1851. The first catalog of the institute lists the Mountain Club as one of the school's three literary societies.

5 Two record books, 1868–72 and 1874–82, and two issues of the *Gazette* from 1879 and 1880 are in the collection of the Dublin Historical Society.

6 Lynne Benoit-Vachon, "Education and the Rural Middle Class: Limington Academy, 1848–1860," *Maine History* 38, no. 2 (1998): 122.

7 As early as the beginning of the nineteenth century, academy lyceums were often closely connected with townspeople. Harriet Marr points to the example of Hebron, Maine, where in 1802 the teachers of the district schools formed a society. In 1804 Hebron Academy was established, and in 1806 academy students were included in the local society. Gradually the society became more closely attached to the academy as the Tyro-Adelphoi, but it still allowed young men of the town (though not, at this early date, young women) to become members (*The Old New England Academies Founded before 1826* [New York: Comet Press Books, 1959], 146–47).

8 Timothy Dwight, *Travels in New England and New York* (1921–22; reprint, Cambridge, MA: Harvard University Press, 1969), 4:253.

9 See Kett, *The Pursuit of Knowledge under Difficulties.*

10 "Our Common Schools—Their Influence Upon Community," *Vermont School Journal and Family Visitor* 3, no. 9 (1861): 257–61. Crowing that "a perfected system of common schools is at once the peculiarity and glory of New England," this author contrasts the enlightenment of the North with the state of the slaveowning South, which "has nourished the scorpion of ignorance" but might have been saved had common-school education taken hold.

11 Mrs. Rachel C. Mather, "The True Mission of the Teacher," *Massachusetts Teacher, and Journal of Home and School Education* 9, nos. 2–5 (February–May 1856): 148, 150.

12 *Experiment* (Landaff, NH) 2, no. 6, December 24, 1852.

13 S. K., "Clubs and Associations," *Vermont School Journal and Family Visitor*, new ser., I, no. I (1866): 10–11.

14 *How to Talk: A Pocket Manual of Conversation, and Debating*, Hand-Books for Home Improvement Series, vol. 2 (New York: Fowler and Wells, 1857), 129.

15 Isaac Watts, *The Improvement of the Mind; to Which Are Added, Questions Adapted to the Work; for the Use of Schools and Academies* (1741; reprint, Boston: Loring, 1821), 105.

16 John Quincy Adams, *Lectures on Rhetoric and Oratory* (Cambridge, MA: Hilliard and Metcalf, 1810), 1:72, quoted in Thomas Gustafson, *Representative Words: Politics, Literature, and the American Language, 1776–1865* (Cambridge: Cambridge University Press, 1992), 97–98.

17 George M. Wadsworth reported this debate topic at the Franklin, Massachusetts, lyceum in his January 2, 1858, diary entry ("The Diaries of George M. Wadsworth, 1857–1893. Compiled, Transcribed and Annotated by Gail V. Lembo and Donated to the People of the Town of Franklin through the Franklin Town Library and the Friends of the Franklin Library" [Franklin, MA, 1998]). See also Morley, *Guide to Forming and Conducting Lyceums*, 58: "Does the orator exert a greater influence than the poet?"

18 C. P. Bronson, *Abstract of Elocution and Music, in Accordance with the Principles of Physiology and the Laws of Life, for the development of Body and Mind* (Auburn, MA: Oliphant, 1842), 48.

19 Ralph Waldo Emerson, "Eloquence," in *Letters and Social Aims* (Boston: Osgood, 1876), 107.

20 *Beadle's Dime Debater and Chairman's Guide: Comprising Suggestions for the Formation of Debating Societies; Laws and Rules for Their Government; the Art of Debate; How to Acquire It; Questions for Debate; Debates in Full and in Brief; Also, the Rules of Order*, Speaker Series, vol. 11 (New York: Beadle , 1869), 9.

21 South Acworth (NH) Association for Mental Improvement Public Lyceum and Select Club, records, 1850–65, New Hampshire Historical Society, Concord.

22 *The History of the Town of Amherst, Massachusetts* (Amherst, MA: Carpenter and Morehouse, 1896), 356.

23 *Herald and News* (West Randolph, VT), December 6, 1888, reporting the first meeting of the Pomfret (VT) Lyceum.

24 Edwin Harris Burlingame, *1853 Journal of Edwin Harris Burlingame, Transcribed from the Original by Richard Veit* (South Portland, ME: Vermont Historical Society, Leahy Library, 1998).

25 John N. Norton, *The Boy Who Was Trained up to Be a Clergyman* (Philadelphia: Hooker, 1854); N. P. Lasselle, *Hope Marshall, or, Government and Its Offices* (Washington, DC: Lasselle, 1859); Elizabeth Doten, "Women and Wisdom," *My Affinity: And Other Stories* (Boston: William White, 1870), 85–108.

26 Francis Dana Gage, *Elsie Magoun, or, the Old Still-House in the Hollow* (Philadelphia: Lippincott, 1867); T. S. Arthur, *Woman to the Rescue, a Story of the New Crusade* (Philadelphia: Cottage Library Publishing House, 1872).

27 Mrs. E. E. Boyd, *The "P.D.S."* (Philadelphia: Martien, 1873).

28 David D. Hall, "Introduction: The Uses of Literacy in New England, 1600–1850," in *Printing and Society in Early America*, ed. William L. Joyce, David D. Hall, Richard D. Brown and John B. Hench (Worcester, MA: American Antiquarian Society, 1983), 1–47.

29 "Composition and Declamation," *Maine Teacher* 2, no. 3 (1859): 88.

30 G. Francis Robinson, "Debates in School," *Maine Normal* 2, no. 12 (1868): 449–51.

31 E. Foster Bailey, "Reminiscences of the Old Town Hall," *Proceedings of the Fitchburg Historical Society* 4 (1908): 74.

32 Union Lyceum (Duttonsville, VT), records, 1841–44, Vermont Historical Society, Barre.

33 *Aurora of the Valley* (Windsor, VT), March 6, 1872.

34 *Beadle's Dime Debater*, 10.

35 *Milford (MA) Enterprise*, March 19, 1875, and March 26, 1875.

36 *Woonsocket (RI) Patriot*, January 28, 1859.

37 Similar topics were also debated in the college literary societies; see Harding, *College Literary Societies.*

38 *Pittsfield (MA) Sun*, November 11, 1874.

39 *Milford (MA) Enterprise*, October 13, 1874.

40 Oliver Bell Bunce, *A Bachelor's Story* (New York: Rudd and Carleton, 1859), 22.

41 "Jimtown Lyceum," *Mcbride's Comic Dialogues for School Exhibitions and Literary Entertainments*, ed. H. Elliott McBride (New York: Dick and Fitzgerald, 1873), 118–27. McBride's *All Kinds of Dialogues* included another lyceum comedy,

"Bungtown Lyceum," in which the members' jibes at each other's literary efforts and personalities lead to chaos; one man cackles, "This is jolly big fun. This here s'iety is got up for mutual improvement. Ha,ha!" (New York: Dick and Fitzgerald, 1874), 173. "

42 *Clarion* (Skowhegan, ME), November 12, 1842.

43 Silvanus Hayward, *History of the Town of Gilsum, New Hampshire from 1752 to 1879* (Manchester, NH: Clarke, 1881), 132.

44 Mrs. Kirkland, "Country Visiting," *American Agriculturalist* 4, no. 3 (1845), 95.

45 Wilson Palmer, *Reminiscences of Candia* (Cambridge, MA: Riverside, 1905), 77.

46 Morley, *A Guide to Forming and Conducting Lyceums*, 4.

47 Bronson, *Abstract of Elocution and Music*, 17.

48 "Editorial," *Mystic Tie* (Carthage, ME) 1, no. 1, n.d.; "Editorial" (poem), *Meteor* (Kenduskeag, ME) 1, no. 6, November 15, 1884.

CHAPTER 4: "THE LADIES HAVE NOBLY RESPONDED"

1 Louisa C. Tuthill, *The Young Lady at Home and in Society* (New York: Allen Brothers, 1869), 65; Ralph Waldo Emerson, "Eloquence," in *Letters and Social Aims* (Boston: Osgood, 1876), 102, 94; "Popular Eloquence," *Southern and Western Literary Messenger and Review* 13 (1847): 741; *Beadle's Dime Debater and Chairman's Guide: Comprising Suggestions for the Formation of Debating Societies; Laws and Rules for Their Government; the Art of Debate; How to Acquire It; Questions for Debate; Debates in Full and in Brief; Also, the Rules of Order* (New York: Beadle and Adams, 1879), 10.

2 Reverend J. M. Austin, *A Voice to Youth, Addressed to Young Men and Young Ladies* (Utica, NY: Grosh and Hutchinson, 1838), quoted in Anna Ferguson, *The Young Lady; or Guide to Knowledge, Virtue, and Happiness* (Nashua, NH: Fletcher, 1851), 43.

3 See Caroline Field Levander, *Voices of the Nation: Women and Public Speech in Nineteenth-Century American Literature and Culture* (Cambridge: Cambridge University Press, 1998). Nevertheless, as Granville Ganter points out, many female orators met with considerable success even before the Civil War. ("The Unexceptional Eloquence of Sarah Josepha Hale," *Proceedings of the American Antiquarian Society* 112, no. 2 [2004]: 116–36).

4 Margaret Coxe, *The Young Lady's Companion, and Token of Affection; in a Series of Letters* (Columbus, OH: Whiting, 1846), 41. On the flyleaf of the copy of Coxe's book in the collection of the American Antiquarian Society (Worcester, MA) is the following inscription, suggesting a role for such conduct books in social relationships: "A birthday gift Presented to Miss Sarah A. Newton by her affectionate friend Edward. Boston June 18th 1846."

5 Sarah Josepha Hale, *Manners; or, Happy Homes and Good Society All the Year Round* (Boston: Tilton, 1868), 233.

6 *The Book of Manners, a Guide to Social Intercourse* (New York: Carlton and Porter, 1852), 191–94.

7 Charles Butler, *The American Lady* (Philadelphia: Hogan and Thompson, 1836), 178; William A. Alcott, *The Young Woman's Guide to Excellence*, 13th ed. (Boston: Peirce, 1847), 311; the first edition appeared in 1839. Alcott was a cousin and close friend of Bronson Alcott, Louisa May Alcott's father.

8 *The Young Lady's Own Book: A Manual of Intellectual Improvement and Moral Deportment*, (Philadelphia: Key and Biddle, 1833), 184–85; William G. Crippen, "The Reign of Petticoats," in *Green Peas, Picked from the Patch of Invisible Green Esq.* (Cincinnati: Moore, Wilstach, Keys, and Overend, 1856), 265–70.

9 Evidently unaware that they were already taking part in rural lyceums, Mrs. Kirkland, writing in the "Ladies Department" of the *American Agriculturalist*, urged young rural women to include book discussions in their social visits:

> There is hardly any country village so small and unambitious, as not to have its debating society or its literary effort of some kind. Many a young man who has had good success in life, has ascribed the figure he has been able to make in court, or his reputation as a teacher, or his acceptableness in the pulpit, to an early opportunity for practice in his native village, and the taste for literature which naturally grows with such efforts.
>
> This is excellent; why then confine it to young *men*? Why should not young women, too, make some attempt at improvement, in a mode suited to their position? We should never recommend to them debating societies or lyceums, but why should they be debarred from all social literary enjoyment? . . . How advantageous then would be the introduction of well selected books into social visits!" ("Country Visiting," *American Agriculturalist* [NY] 4, no. 3 [1845]: 95).

10 Charles Morley, *A Guide to Forming and Conducting Lyceums, Debating Societies, &C. With Outlines of Discussions and Essays, and an Appendix, Containing an Epitome of Rhetoric, Logic, &C.* (New York: A.E. Wright, 1841), 3, 15.

11 See Mary Kelley, *Learning to Stand and Speak: Women, Education, and Public Life in America's Republic* (Chapel Hill: University of North Carolina Press, 2006). Kelley takes her title phrase from an 1892 letter from Lucy Stone to Antoinette Brown Blackwell in which Stone recalls what she and Blackwell had learned as members of women's literary societies: "We discussed educational, political, moral and religious questions, and especially we learned to stand and speak" (275). Women in colleges or academies also frequently formed separate women's societies. Although female academies multiplied— Kelley estimates that at least 340 had been established by 1860—they drew from a fairly high social stratum.

12 The situation in Danville, Vermont, was typical. In 1870 a women's club, the Young Ladies' Library Association, was founded in the center of Danville. The tiny hamlet of West Danville had no library or women's club, but by 1883 it did have a lyceum (and a paper, the *Enterprise*).

13 William J. Gilmore, *Reading Becomes a Necessity of Life: Material and Cultural Life in Rural New England, 1780–1835* (Knoxville: University of Tennessee Press, 1989), 49; *Godey's Lady's Book* (November 1837): 230, quoted in Patricia Okker, *Our Sister Editors: Sarah J. Hale and the Tradition of Nineteenth-Century American Women Editors* (Athens: University of Georgia Press, 1995), 123; Susan K. Harris, "Responding to the Text(s): Women Readers and the Quest for Higher Education," in *Readers in History: Nineteenth-Century American Literature and* *the Contexts of Response*, ed. James L. Machor (Baltimore: Johns Hopkins University Press, 1993), 259–82.

14 Mrs. E. Little, "What Are the Rights of Woman?," in *The Ladies' Wreath*, ed. Mrs. S. T. Martyn (New York: Martin and Ely, 1848–49), 2:133; "What Are Woman's Rights?," *New Dominion Monthly* 1, no. 1 (1867): 39. In this last article, someone, probably the editor, has appended a note: "It is to be hoped that men are not excluded from these rights." I am grateful to Betsy Hedler for pointing out these analogues to the lyceum poem.

15 Whether this poem was originally composed for the *Gem of the Valley* is unclear—though its decisive "Good Night" at the end of the issue suggests editorial strategy—but it seems at least to have been written nearby, according to a note at its beginning: "From the Fern Leaves of the Pemigewassett Valley." Plymouth is in the Pemigewassett Valley, and "Fern Leaves" might have been a vanished local publication, the title of another lyceum's paper, or an invention of the poem's author.

16 West Plymouth (NH) Literary Association, minutes, February 12, 1880, records, 1870–80, New Hampshire Historical Society, Concord.

17 Joel Perlmann and Robert A. Margo, *Women's Work? American Schoolteachers, 1650–1920* (Chicago: University of Chicago Press, 2001), 22.

18 Richard M. Bernard and Maris A. Vinovskis, "The Female School Teacher in Ante-Bellum Massachusetts," *Journal of Social History* 10 (1977): 333.

19 Shirley (MA) Institute, minutes, March 9, 1866, records, 1861–71, American Antiquarian Society, Worcester, MA.

20 *Franklin County Times*, January 8, 1875. B. I. Wheeler's diary from East Montpelier, Vermont (in the collection of the Vermont Historical Society, Barre) gives extensive information about the lyceums he attended in 1858, including the names of every critic; both men and women served in this office in 1875.

21 David B. Tyack and Elizabeth Hansot, *Learning Together: A History of Coeducation in American Public Schools* (New Haven, CT: Yale University Press, 1990), 66–67, 46; [no first name] Lessur, "Female Culture," *Vermont School Journal and Family Visitor*, new ser., 1, no. 1 (1866): 21–22.

22 Duttonsville (VT) Lyceum, records, 1841–45, Vermont Historical Society, Barre.

23 *Gazette and Courier* (Greenfield, MA), February 13, 1882.

24 *Emblem* (Landaff, NH) 1, no. 3, January 20, 1860.

25 To avoid criticism earlier in the century, educator Emma Willard sometimes wrote out her lectures to be read by male friends. See Anne Firor Scott, "What, Then, Is the American: This New Woman?," *Journal of American History* 65, no. 3 (1978): 679–703.

26 South Acworth (NH) Public Lyceum, records, 1850–65, New Hampshire Historical Society, Concord.

27 *Grafton County (NH) Journal*, January 13, 1880.

28 Kenduskeag (ME) Literary Association, reports, October 11, 18, 25, 1884, collection MS043, Bangor Public Library, Bangor, ME.

29 *Herald and News* (West Randolph, VT), October 25, 1888.

30 Cyrus Platt, *Life and Letters of Mrs. Jeanette H. Platt* (Philadelphia: Claxton, 1882), 363.

31 Beth Ann Rothermel, "A Sphere of Noble Action: Gender, Rhetoric, and Influence at a Nineteenth-Century Massachusetts State Normal School," *Rhetoric Society Quarterly* 33, no. 1 (2002): 35–64.

32 Arthur O. Norton, ed., *The First State Normal School in America: The Journals of Cyrus Peirce and Mary Swift* (Cambridge, MA: Harvard University Press, 1926). Coeducational debating was not universal in normal schools, however. In the first years of the Illinois State Normal University, women did not take part in the debates in the students' Philadelphian and Wrightonian societies, founded in 1857 and 1858. In 1887 the women organized their own Sapphonian Society, which met weekly and featured debates as well as music, recitations, declamations, orations, and essay readings. The topics for the women's debates often included subjects relating to gender roles, such as whether women should compete with men in all vocations. But they also took up other topics, and it seemed easier for them to debate when the audience was all women. See Sandra D. Harmon, "'The Voice, Pen and Influence of Our Women Are Abroad in the Land': Women and the Illinois State Normal University, 1857–1899," in *Nineteenth-Century Women Learn to Write*, ed. Catherine Hobbs (Charlottesville: University Press of Virginia, 1995), 84–102.

33 Shawomet (RI) Lyceum, record book, December 14, 1860–February 11, 1862, Rhode Island Historical Society, Providence.

34 Young Ladies' and Gentlemen's Lyceum of Wrightsville (VT), constitution, bylaws, and minutes, 1858–59, Vermont Historical Society, Barre.

35 *Bridgton (ME) News*, April 7, 1876.

36 Harriet Webster Marr, *The Old New England Academies Founded before 1826* (New York: Comet Press Books, 1959), 150.

37 *Gazette and Courier* (Greenfield, MA), February 1, 1882.

CHAPTER 5: "WHO WILL SUSTAIN THE PAPER?"

1 Thaddeus Perry Mason, diary entries, March 25, 1840, and March 30, 1842, Thaddeus Perry Mason Papers, box 1, Historic Deerfield Library, Deerfield, MA.

2 *Monitor* (East Cabot, NH) 1, no. 11, February 27, 1878. As East Cabot never had a Glidden Street or a High Street, I assume that the actual reference is to the home of James or to his daughter-in-law Laura Glidden, two of the three editors of this issue; the third editress was Lizzie M. Abbott.

3 *Veazie (ME) Light*, January 22, 1877.

4 *Gem of the Valley* (West Plymouth, NH) 3, no. 10, February 26, 1880.

5 Silvanus Hayward, *History of the Town of Gilsum, New Hampshire from 1752 to 1879* (Manchester, NH: Clarke, 1881), 135.

6 Franklin Lyceum, minutes, October 4, 1852, and October 15, 1852, "Records of the Franklin Lyceum," 1852–58, New Hampshire Historical Society, Concord. No papers have survived from the Franklin Lyceum, so the meaning of this note is uncertain. Did the lyceum have a paper only once in four weeks? Or was the same woman appointed to serve as editor for more than one issue? Both situations would have been unusual.

7 *Literary Banner* (Mont Vernon, NH) 2, no. 7, January 20, 1859.

8 *Dublin Rural Repository* (Dublin, NH) 3, no. 10, March 17, 1841.

9 *Kearsarge Fountain* (East Andover, NH) 3, no. 12, December 19, 1849.

10 *Kenduskeag (ME) Meteor* 1, no. 6, November 15, 1884.

11 The *Casket* was evidently a Sunday-school paper, not a lyceum paper, so I have not included it in the table in appendix A. However, several lyceum-style pieces and allusions to a lyceum occur in the *Casket,* three issues of which are among the Bronson Family Papers (New Hampshire Historical Society, Concord). This archive includes miscellaneous examples of several handwritten papers from Landaff lyceums and church groups. It is clear that the same writers contributed to these papers and sometimes borrowed pieces from one to use in another.

12 Sophie May [Rebecca Sophia Clarke], *The Doctor's Daughter* (Boston: Lee and Shepard, 1871).

13 *Emblem* (Landaff, NH) 1, no. 4, January 27, 1860.

14 William A. Bachelder of East Andover, New Hampshire, apparently had a gift for deadpan wit. When he edited the *Kearsarge Fountain* (2, no. 4, February 14, 1849), he created a playful piece titled *"Kissing—By the Editor."*: *"We do not mean when we speak of 'kissing by the editor' that either the writer or editor whoever they may be ever did or ever intends to perform any such thing but it is intended only to express that the present article was written by somebody who may be designated by the fictitious name of Editor."* Evidently fond of this piece, he (or his sister Mary and her husband George Emery, other editors) must have kept the issue. At the top of the page is a penciled note by Bachelder, "Read at Grange Oct. 28, 1884," and an edited version of the essay, on different paper, is tucked into the *Kearsarge Fountain.*

15 "How a Man Helps His Wife" was frequently reprinted in the 1870s, including in the *Rockland County (NY) Journal,* July 18, 1874, available at https://news.hrvh.org.

16 Most antebellum papers contain at most a single item copied from a published source, but a few (was this editorial choice or local convention?) are dense with previously published poetry. For instance, such reprints appear in multiple issues of the *Cruiser* (South Freeport, ME) in and after vol. 1, no. 4 (1859) but not in earlier issues. However, reprints appear in just one of the four issues of the *Emblem* (Landaff, NH) that I have seen (1, no. 8, February 25, 1860).

17 *Bow Lake Journal* (Strafford, NH), 2, no. 4, c. 1875.

18 "Reading" [by "a School-Committee Man"], *Common School Journal* 1, no. 10 (1839): 158.

19 David D. Hall calls this earlier stage of New England history "traditional literacy," when children "came to literacy by the road of recitation and reading aloud" ("Introduction: The Uses of Literacy in New England, 1600–1850," in *Printing and Society in Early America*, ed. William L. Joyce, David D. Hall, Richard D. Brown and John B. Hench [Worcester, MA: American Antiquarian Society, 1983], 23–24).

20 William J. Gilmore points to genre paintings as evidence of community newspaper reading, citing Richard Caton Woodville's *War News from Mexico* (1848) and William Sidney Mount's *California News* (1850). See his *Reading Becomes a Necessity of Life: Material and Cultural Life in Rural New England, 1780–1835* (Knoxville: University of Tennessee Press, 1989), 378.

21 "Lectures and Lecturing," *Harper's Monthly Magazine* 14 (1856), quoted in James Perrin Warren, *Culture of Eloquence: Oratory and Reform in Antebellum America* (University Park: Pennsylvania State University Press, 1999), 18.

22 Quoted in Anna U. Russell, *The Young Ladies' Elocutionary Reader; Containing a Selection of Reading Lessons; with Introductory Rules and Exercises in Elocution, Adapted to Female Readers, by William Russell* (Boston: Munroe, 1845), 17.

23 See the discussion in Patricia Okker, "Women's Reading," in *Our Sister Editors: Sarah J. Hale and the Tradition of Nineteenth-Century American Women Editors* (Athens: University of Georgia Press, 1995), chap. 5.

24 As Barbara Finkelstein puts it, "learning to read and write in such rural schools was a 'process of communal exposure' in which children exhibited what they had learned in a 'face-to-face community of oral discourse'" ("Reading, Writing, and the Acquisition of Identity in the United States: 1790–1860," in *Regulated Children/Liberated Children: Education in Psychohistorical Perspective*, ed. Barbara Finkelstein (New York: Psychohistory Press, 1979), 114–39.

25 Mary Frances Hodsdon, diary entries, January 29 and February 19, 1866, Special Collections, Fogler Library, University of Maine, Orono. Reading skill might well have had social advantages; witness this scene in the 1875 diary of schoolgirl Emily Luther McKenney of Bethel, Maine: "Went up to the spelling school at the school-house this evening and had a rather good time. The boys spoke pieces and Sybil read a Candle Lecture, and I read 'The Echo' Volume 1st, No. 3. There was quite a crowd out. . . . When I came to my seat after reading the paper, Elmer Waterhouse whispered 'I swanny! You read the paper nice.' I am sure I thank him for the compliment" (diary entry, February 23, 1875, Bethel Historical Society, Bethel, ME).

26 *Aurora of the Valley* (Claremont, NH), October 26, 1872; *Literary Banner* (Mont Vernon, NH) 1, no. 6, January 14, 1858.

CHAPTER 6: "EFFULGENT IN WISDOM AND SPARKLING WITH WIT"

1 William J. Gilmore, "Literacy, the Rise of an Age of Reading, and the Cultural Grammar of Print Communications in America, 1735–1850," *Communication* 11 (1988): 25; Ronald J. Zboray and Mary Saracino Zboray, *Everyday Ideas: Socioliterary Experience among Antebellum New Englanders* (Knoxville: University of Tennessee Press, 2006), 1.

2 Lyceum authors manipulated styles and genres strategically and often ironically, juxtaposing their original contexts with the immediate situation in the lyceum community. As Katherine Arens points out, "each genre is not just an aesthetic form but also the enactment of communication in a particular situation, a set of meanings transacted within a horizon of expectation for communication, part of a group's social contract" ("When Comparative Literature Becomes Cultural Studies: Teaching Cultures through Genre," *Comparatist* 29 [2005]: 128).

3 *Meteor* (Kenduskeag, ME), c. 1884–85.

4 For more discussion of children's early literary experience, see Zboray and Zboray, *Everyday Ideas.*

5 Salem Town and Nelson M. Holbrook, review of *The Progressive Fifth or Elocutionary Reader*, in *Massachusetts Teacher and Journal of Home and School Education* 10 (January 1857): 47–48.

6 N. G., "'How Shall I Write?' The Student's Greatest Trouble," *Vermont School Journal and Family Visitor* 1, no. 10 (January 1860): 240–41.

7 The Bronson Family Papers from Landaff (New Hampshire Historical Society, Concord) contain versions of pieces that appear in some of the lyceum papers, perhaps providing examples of how young people revised compositions for the lyceum papers.

8 Two of the papers Gavuetta "Detta" Goodhue of East Andover, New Hampshire, created for her common-school pupils have survived: the *Sweatt's Mills Journal* (Webster, NH), October 22, 1886; and the *North Road Journal* (Salisbury, NH), June 1889. Each contains a similar range of typical lyceum-paper pieces including moral essays, poetry, alphabetical rhymes, maxims, mock advertisements, and so on, all with a genteel didactic emphasis and no doubt composed by Detta herself. Each begins with an identical editorial addressed to *"Dear Scholars,"* explaining Detta's three goals in writing the paper: *"First. to show you that I take an interest in you all, and want you all to do the best you can. Second. the hope that you might be more ready to learn the lessons given you, and be more willing to do as I would like to have you. Third: the wish that in the years to come when you think of the North Road Journal* [or *Sweatt's Mills Journal*], *it may bring to your minds memories of one of the pleasantest terms of school you ever attended."*

9 Unnamed paper, no cover page (Carthage, ME), c. 1880.

10 *Mystic Tie* (Carthage, ME) 1, no. 3, c. 1875.

11 *Bean's Corner Sunbeam* (Jay, ME), n.d.

12 "Alphabetical Jumble," *Gazette* (South Bethel, ME) 5, no. 2, November 1889.

13 *Emblem* (Landaff, NH) 1, no. 4, January 27, 1860.

14 *Monitor* (East Cabot, VT) , 1, no. 11, February 27, 1878.

15 Unnamed paper, no cover page (East Bethel, ME), c. December 1877.

16 *Kearsarge Fountain* (East Andover, NH) 2, no. 3, January 24, 1849. As promised, the next issue (2, no. 4, February 14, 1849) provided the answer: *"Nightingale."*

17 *Emblem* (Landaff, NH) 1, no. 4, January 27, 1860. See also the *Gem of the Valley* (West Plymouth, NH) vol. unknown, issue 1, November 30, 1878; *Literary Banner* (Mont Vernon, NH) 1, no. 6, January 14, 1858; and *Experiment* (Landaff, NH) 2, no. 6, December 24, 1852.

18 *Bean's Corner Sunbeam,* (Jay, ME) 3, no. 11, March 20, 1879.

19 *Poplin Herald* (Fremont, NH), December 16, 1879.

20 *Literary Banner* (Mont Vernon, NH) 1, no. 6, January 14, 1858.

21 Historical Address for Sweden's Centennial, August 26, 1913, quoted in Philip W. Richards, *Sweden, Maine History*, vol. 2, *Adversity and Determination* (Sweden, ME: Richards, 1989), 4–5.

22 *Mystic Tie* (Carthage, ME) 1, no. 3, c. 1875.

23 Another *"Chronicle"* piece about the founding of a lyceum appears in *Wednesday Evening Post* (Dublin, NH) 6, February 7, 1844. *"Chronicle"* pieces describing the previous lyceum meeting are in the *Literary Banner* (Mont Vernon, NH) 1, no. 6, January 14, 1858; and *Literary News* (Antrim, NH) 1, no. 7, July 6, 1885; and 2, no. 1, January 2, 1886.

24 *Kearsarge Fountain* (East Andover, NH) 2, no. 3, January 24, 1849. Jared W. Williams served as governor of New Hampshire from June 3, 1847, to June 7, 1849.

25 *Kearsarge Fountain* (East Andover, NH), perhaps October 1850. That date is suggested in the opening of "Chronicles Chapt. 13th": *"Moreover it came to pass in the third month of the reign of Filmore (Dinsmore meantime being governor of New Hamp.)."* Millard Fillmore assumed the office of U.S. president on July 9, 1850, after the death of Zachary Taylor. Samuel Dinsmore, Jr., was governor of New Hampshire from June 7, 1849, to June 3, 1852.

26 Unnamed paper, no cover page (East Bethel, ME), c. December 1877.

27 *Emblem* (Landaff, NH) 1, no. 8, February 25, 1860. The full text of this issue can be found in appendix C.

28 *Bean's Corner Sunbeam* (Jay, ME) 1, January 16, 1877. See also *"Aunt Jerusha's Will,"* Beans Corner Sunbeam 3, no. 11, March 20, 1879; and *"Our Grandmother's Will,"* lyceum paper from Carthage, Maine, no cover page, c. 1880. A similar style of versified will in the *Independent* (South Levant, ME) 1, no. 7, March 23, 1881, makes its "bequests" not to couples but to single young people in the community:

> *L. S. McLaughlin who has forsaken the Reading School to attend the masquerade at West Hampden thought he would dispose of his property before leaving for fear of being smitten with some fair one and be persuaded to stop in Hermon! Know ye all men by these presents that I L. S. McLaughlin of the town of Levant State of Maine County of Penobscot do will and bequeath my property as follows.*
>
> > *To Emma Shaw so smart and good*
> > *An old tin pail and cord of wood,*
> > *To Llewellyn Mc who has bought a farm*
> > *I will to him a shed and barn*
> > *To Walter Shaw a tall young chap*
> > *My linen duster and old fur cap*
> > *To Benjamin Lufkin who likes to laugh*
> > *A broken plow and yellow calf.*

29 "The Return of Spring," *Kearsarge Fountain* (East Andover, NH) 2, no. 3, January 24, 1849.

30 "To Lizzie Staples," *Mystic Tie* (Carthage, ME) 1, no. 3, c. 1875.

31 *Dublin (NH) Rural Repository* 3, no. 8, February 17, 1841.

32 *Experiment* (Landaff, NH) 2, no. 6, December 24, 1852.

33 *Wednesday Evening Post* (Dublin, NH) 6, February 7, 1844; *Monitor* (East Cabot, VT) 1, no. 6, January 30, 1878.

34 Abby Maria Hemenway, *The Vermont Historical Gazetteer: A Magazine, Embracing a History of Each Town, Civil, Ecclesiastical, Biographical and Military*. 5 vols. (Burlington, VT, 1877), 3:899.

35 *Dublin (NH) Rural Repository* 4, no. 1, November 10, 1841.

36 *Cruiser* (South Freeport, ME) 1, no. 3, February 12, 1859.

37 Unnamed paper, Fryeburg, ME., n.d. Consider also this jest, archived in the Bronson Family Papers, which appeared in the *Casket* (Landaff, NH), n.d.: *"Why are old maids like honest politicians? Because they go for principles not men"* (New Hampshire Historical Society, Concord).

38 Hal S. Barron, *Mixed Harvest: The Second Great Transformation in the Rural North, 1870–1930* (Chapel Hill: University of North Carolina Press, 1997), 15.

39 *Scrap Gatherer* (Dublin, NH), November 8, 1854.

40 *Kearsarge Fountain* (East Andover, NH) 2, no. 4, February 14, 1849. "Milo" is one of the common author pseudonyms in the *Fountain*.

41 *Emblem* (Landaff, NH) 1, no. 3, January 20, 1860.

42 *Emblem* (Landaff, NH), c. 1860. Although the poem refers to no specific earth-quake, contemporary papers often reported these sensational phenomena, and the disastrous Basilicata Earthquake (or Great Neapolitan Earthquake) of December 1857 had received considerable press in New England.

43 *Kearsarge Fountain* (East Andover, NH) 2, no. 4, February 14, 1849.

44 *Dublin (NH) Rural Repository* (Dublin, NH) 3, no. 8, February 17, 1841.

45 "The Passing Cloud," *Literary Banner* (Mont Vernon, NH) 2, no. 7, January 20, 1859.

46 *Mystic Tie*, (Carthage, ME) 1, no. 3, c. 1875.

47 *Gazette* (South Bethel, ME) 5, no 2, November 1889.

48 *Emblem* (Landaff, NH), c. 1860. I am assuming that, as with the other three issues of the *Emblem* I have seen, this one had multiple editors, one man and two women.

49 *Monitor* (East Cabot, VT) 1, no. 11, February 27, 1878.

50 *Gazette* (So. Bethel, ME) 5, no. 2, November 1889.

51 *Kearsarge Fountain* (East Andover, NH) 3, no. 12, December 19, 1849.

52 *Emblem* (Landaff, NH) 1, no. 3, January 20, 1860. The poem might have been composed by the editor, Luke B. Chandler, the twenty-six-year-old son of a farmer, working at the time as a clerk in a local store.

53 *Bean's Corner Sunbeam* (Jay, ME), n.d.

54 Pauline Greenhill, *True Poetry: Traditional and Popular Verse in Ontario* (Montreal: McGill-Queen's University Press, 1989), 10, 18.

55 "Other People's Spectacles," *Harper's Bazaar*, March 9, 1872, 170.

56 *Cruiser* (South Freeport, ME) 1, no. 1, January 20, 1859.

57 My identifications of lyceum pieces as original local compositions may occasionally be wrong. Although digitization of nineteenth-century popular literature has advanced enormously in recent years, and many of the pieces copied into lyceum papers can now be discovered online, the databases are still incomplete and searches are not fully reliable. However, I believe that the general trends I have outlined are correct.

58 *Literary Banner* 2 (Mont Vernon, NH) 2, no. 8, January 27, 1859.

59 *Gem of the Valley* (West Plymouth, NH) 3, no. 10, February 26, 1880. "The Wife" was widely published in newspapers as early as the spring of 1857 and was reprinted in *Gleason's Literary Companion* (Boston, MA), April 7, 1866, 215.

60 The original authorship of this song is unclear. See Augustus Meves, lyricist, "Wake, Lady, Wake," sheet music (1832); and Mrs. J. C. W. Smith, lyricist, "Serenade: Wake, Lady, Wake," sheet music (1848). The song was also published as a poem by J. Day Barron, in *Ballou's Monthly Magazine* (1855), with different lyrics but the same refrain.

61 *Kearsarge Fountain* (East Andover, NH), February 16, 1848.

62 Paper from Carthage, ME, no cover page, c. 1880. Verses quoted from the *Crimson* also appear in *Yale Literary Magazine* 44 (1879).

63 *Enterprise* (West Danville, VT) 1, no. 1, January 24, 1884.
64 *Monitor* (East Cabot, VT) 1, no. 3, January 9, 1878.
65 *Kearsarge Fountain* (East Andover, NH) 3, no. 12, December 18, 1849.

CHAPTER 7: "READ BY SO MANY EAGER SUBSCRIBERS"

1 George P. Rowell, ed., *Geo. P. Rowell & Co.'s American Newspaper Directory* (New York: Rowell, 1873), 15, quoted in E. C. Jerry, "The Role of Newspapers in the Nineteenth-Century Women's Movement," in *A Voice of Their Own*, ed. M. M. Solomon (Tuscaloosa: University of Alabama Press, 1991), 18. The mushroom growth of the press in the nineteenth century has been well studied: see, for example, Gerald J. Baldasty, *The Commercialization of News in the Nineteenth Century* (Madison: University of Wisconsin Press, 1992); Richard D. Brown, *Knowledge Is Power: The Diffusion of Information in Early America, 1700–1865* (New York: Oxford University Press, 1989); William Charvat, *Literary Publishing in America* (Amherst: University of Massachusetts Press, 1993); Edward E. Chielens, *The Literary Journal in America to 1900: A Guide to Information Sources* (Detroit: Gale Research, 1975); David D. Hall, "Introduction: The Uses of Literacy in New England, 1600–1850," in *Printing and Society in Early America*, ed. William L. Joyce, David D. Hall, Richard D. Brown, and John B. Hench (Worcester, MA: American Antiquarian Society, 1983), 1–47; Thomas C. Leonard, "News at the Hearth: A Drama of Reading in Nineteenth-Century America," *Proceedings of the American Antiquarian Society* 102, no. 2 (1993), 379–401;David J. Russo, *The Origins of Local News in the U.S. Country Press, 1840s–1870s*, ed. Bruce H. Westley, Journalism Monographs, vol. 65 (Lexington, KY: Association for Education in Journalism, 1980); Mary P. Ryan, *The Empire of the Mother, American Writing about Domesticity, 1830–1860* (New York: Institute for Research in History; Haworth Press, 1982); Michael Schudson, *Discovering the News: A Social History of American Newspapers* (New York: Basic Books, 1978); Michael Schudson, *The Power of News* (Cambridge, MA: Harvard University Press, 1995); and M. M. Solomon, "The Role of the Suffrage Press in the Woman's Rights Movement," in Solomon, *A Voice of Their Own*, 1–16.

2 Allan R. Pred, *Urban Growth and the Circulation of Information: The United States System of Cities, 1790–1840* (Cambridge, MA: Harvard University Press, 1973).

3 Jerry, "The Role of Newspapers," 18.

4 Samuel Goodrich, *Recollections of a Lifetime*, 2 vols. (New York: 1857) vol. 1, 75, quoted in Hall, "Introduction," 21.

5 M. F. Sweetser, "What the People Read," in *Hints for Home Reading, a Series of Chapters on Books and Their Use*, ed. Lyman Abbott (New York: Putnam, 1880), 6.

6 *Grafton County (NH) Journal*, February 14, 1880. Even oratory seemed to be threatened by the newspaper explosion. In "Is Oratory a Lost Art?" William Mathews acknowledged the cost of mass written communications: "It is evident that oratory no longer occupies the place which it once did, before the discovery of 'the art preservative of arts,' and the general diffusion of knowledge . . . Is it, indeed, true that the orator's occupation has gone,—that the newspaper has killed him,—that his speech is forestalled by the daily

editorial, which, flying on the wings of steam, addresses fifty thousand men, while he speaks to five hundred? By no means. Eloquence is not, and never will be, a useless art" (*Oratory and Orators* [Chicago: Griggs, 1879], 49–50).

7 See, for instance, Truman J. Spencer, *The History of Amateur Journalism* (New York: Fossils, 1957); Truman J. Spencer, *A Cyclopedia of the Literature of Amateur Journalism* (New Britain, CT: Adkins, 1891); and Harlan H. Ballard, "Amateur Newspapers," *St. Nicholas Magazine* 9, no. 9 (1882): 717–27. Before the marketing of the affordable Novelty Press in 1867, home-produced amateur newspapers were sometimes painstakingly pen-printed by hand in imitation of typescript. The American Antiquarian Society (Worcester, MA) has several of these pen-printed papers as well as what must be the largest collection of mechanically printed amateur newspapers in the United States. For an interesting account of the career of a pen printer of amateur newspapers, see Robert W. G. Vail, "James Johns, Vermont Pen Printer," *Papers of the Bibliographical Society of America* 27, no. 1 (1933), 89–109. For a comprehensive contemporary history of the movement and a personal account of experiencing it, see Thomas G. Harrison, *The Career and Reminiscences of an Amateur Journalist, and a History of Amateur Journalism* (Indianapolis, 1883).

8 "Amateur journalism," writes Truman J. Spencer, "forms . . . a vast literary society, whose members express their opinions, and comment, criticize, or commend the work of one another's pen and press" (*The History of Amateur Journalism*, 3). Lucille M. Schultz discusses the extracurricular school newspapers produced by students at nineteenth-century private secondary schools. Produced with some faculty oversight, such papers contained fuller content than the amateur newspapers did; but as the century wore on, they shared with amateurdom the tradition of exchanging papers among schools and publishing comments about other papers (*The Young Composers: Composition's Beginnings in Nineteenth-Century Schools* [Carbondale: Southern Illinois University Press, 1999], 135–43).

9 Jessica Isaac, "Youthful Enterprises: Amateur Newspapers and the Pre-History of Adolescence, 1867–1883," *American Periodicals* 22, no. 2 (2012): 158–77. See also Lara Langer Cohen, "The Emancipation of Boyhood: Postbellum Teenage Subculture and the Amateur Press," *Commonplace* 14 (February 2013), http://commonplace.online.

10 Aunt Carrie [Mrs. Caroline L. Smith], *Popular Pastimes for Field and Fireside; or, Amusements for Young and Old* (Springfield, MA: Milton Bradley, 1867), 216–17; Oliver Optic [William Taylor Adams], *Sports and Pastimes for in-Doors and Out* (Boston: Cottrell, 1863), 109–10; Lucretia Peabody Hale, *Fagots for the Fireside; a Collection of More Than One Hundred Entertaining Games for Evenings at Home and Social Parties* (Boston: Ticknor, 1889), 222–31. In this volume, Hale, whose "Fagots" had previously appeared separately in *Good Housekeeping*, printed an entire sample "Impromptu Newspaper," making it clear that humor, especially wordplay, should combine with serious literary effort in this form of recreation. Her sample issue is titled "No More," its motto is "One is enough," and it includes a review of the current exhibit at the Fine Arts Club, a "Poet's Corner," some "Pleasantries" (brief jokes), and a "weather" report on Boston social circles ("Cold, at freezing-point, thawing on rare occasions").

11 *Cold River Budget* (Chatham, NH), 1, no. 1, "*Published at Chatham, Dec. 25th, 1887*," Chatham Historical Society. I thank Jeanne Eastman for bringing this paper to my attention.

12 *Bristol (NH) Wild Flowers*, October 21, 1856, and November 11, 1856, New Hampshire Historical Society, Concord.

13 *Ladie's Enterprise* (Sweden, ME), May 10, 1877, Sweden Historical Society.

14 *Hampton (NH) Budget*, October 20, 1847, New Hampshire Historical Society, Concord.

15 *Temperance Herald* (Carthage, ME), March 16, 1882, private collection. This was the paper of the Webbs River Lodge of Good Templars.

16 The Bronson Family Papers (New Hampshire Historical Society, Concord) demonstrate the variety of manuscript papers with which one family or family member could be associated as well as the relationship among different kinds of papers. The archive reveals the family's activities between 1852 and 1860 in Landaff, New Hampshire. It includes thirteen different issues of four named manuscript papers: the *Experiment* (2, no. 6, December 24, 1852), which seems comparable in style and contents to the Dublin, New Hampshire, *Ladies' Miscellany* (no local names or references except for initials, various literary epideictic pieces and reflections on transitory life, no editors named); the *Garland* (a women's Sunday school paper, "Published weekly by the Laidies Union Society"); the *Casket* (a Sunday school paper, with many different pieces, mostly on religious topics and some generic conundrums and puns, but no local topics or named editors); and the *Emblem* (a lyceum paper, with editor and editresses, local jokes, and allusions to the debates, very like the Dublin *Wednesday Evening Post* in content). The Bronson Family Papers also include many examples of one young person's drafts of essays, pieces for the paper, and debate arguments.

Sometimes the same pieces appear in different papers; *Casket* 1, no. 11, contains what is clearly a lyceum poem that does not match the style of much of the rest of the issue and mentions "the Lyceum band." Family members (as judged by handwriting) sometimes put pieces from one paper into another. *Casket* 1, no. 10, even has a little poem urging listeners to write for the *Emblem*. Evidently the Bronson family was involved in papers beyond those that appear in the archive. A miscellaneous folder contains a piece titled "Conversation" on which someone has written, at the top, "For the Excelsior." Another group of papers in the folder is evidently a large portion of a new church paper; it ends with an editorial ("The first number of our little Semi Monthly is before you").

17 Untitled lyceum paper (Carthage, ME), c. 1880. I have seen two copies of this paper, neither with a cover that identifies it by name.

18 *League Scrap Basket* (Webster, NH), July 31, 1895 ("Filled with manuscripts and clippings from the Ladies of the League"); *Golden Harvester* (Webster, NH), various issues, 1885–88. School papers include *Corser Hill Journal* (Webster, NH), December 9, 1885 ("Edited by the Fun Club . . . Motto—Laugh and be merry"); *Sweatt's Mills Journal* (Webster, NH), October 22, 1886 ("Motto—Always do your best."); and *North Road Journal* (Salisbury, NH), June 1889 ("Motto—Whatever is worth doing, is worth doing well"). All are archived in a private collection.

19 *Scholars' Gazette* (Dublin, NH), December 21, 1840, Thaddeus Perry Mason Papers, box 3, Historic Deerfield Library, Deerfield, MA. Mason believed so strongly in the intellectual virtues of community lyceums that he not only encouraged his common-school pupils to attend lyceums but he also escorted them. On December 27, 1843, when he was engaged as teacher in Peterborough, New Hampshire, he noted in his diary that he took his students five miles to attend the weekly meeting of the Dublin Young People's Society for Mutual Improvement (Mason Papers, box 1).

20 *Haney's Guide to Authorship, Intended as an Aid to All Who Desire to Engage in Literary Pursuits for Pleasure or Profit* (New York: Haney, 1867) 89, 94. *Haney's* prescription is echoed by the editor of the *Grafton County (NH) Journal* ("A Live Local and Family Newspaper"), February 21, 1880, in a long paragraph of "Instructions to Correspondents" who were sending in information from towns in the region. It included a list of topics for "especial attention": "births, marriages and deaths, new enterprises, crimes, casualties, fires, religious, industrial and farming facts, entertainments, announcements of what will take place, suggestions for improvement, historical matters and personals." Regular reports of local news did not begin to appear in U.S. papers until the 1840s, then became somewhat more regular in the 1850s, and were quite common in the 1860s and 1870s (Russo, *The Origins of Local News*).

21 *Haney's Guide*, 92–93.

22 For an example of an extensive letter to the editress of a lyceum paper, see *"The Closing Year," Experiment* (Landaff, NH) 2, no. 6, December 24, 1852. Michael Schudson suggests that the nineteenth-century newspaper was far more amateur in its contents, far more reflective of community conversation, than is the press today (*The Power of News*, 50–51).

23 *Mystic Tie* (Carthage, ME) 1, no. 3, c. January 1875.

24 Rufus Fowler's argument was delivered in Barre, Vermont. A draft appears in the back of the ledger book containing the records of the Blackstone Literary Association (Northbridge, MA), American Antiquarian Society, Worcester, MA.

25 *Independent* (South Levant, ME) 1, no. 7, March 23, 1881.

26 *Literary Banner* (Mont Vernon, NH) 1, no. 6, January 14, 1858.

27 *Literary Banner* (Mont Vernon, NH) 2, no. 8, January 27, 1859.

28 *Haney's Guide*, 92.

29 Russo, *The Origins of Local News*, 23.

30 *Independent* (South Levant, ME) 1, no. 7, March 23, 1881.

31 *Gazette* (South Bethel, ME) 5, no. 2, November 1889. Columbus F. Kimball, born in 1862, was a farmer in Woodstock, Maine, adjacent to Bethel; he was married on September 26, 1887.

32 *Independent* (South Levant, ME) 1, no. 7, March 23, 1881.

33 *"An Afternoon in the Monitor Office," Monitor* (East Cabot, VT) 1, no. 6, January 30, 1878.

34 *Haney's Guide*, 84. For a general discussion, see Baldasty, *The Commercialization of News*; and David Paul Nord, "The Business Values of American Newspapers: The Nineteenth-Century Watershed," in *Communities of Journalism: A History of American Newspapers and Their Readers* (Urbana: University of Illinois Press, 2001), 133–51.

35 Tamara Plakins Thornton, *Handwriting in America: A Cultural History* (New Haven, CT: Yale University Press, 1996), xiii.

36 Bridgewater (MA) Normal School, *Normal Offering* 1 (January 1870).

37 Mary Douglas, "Jokes," in *Implicit Meanings: Essays in Anthropology* (London: Routledge and Kegan Paul, 1979), 104, 96.

38 Silvanus Hayward, *History of the Town of Gilsum, New Hampshire from 1752 to 1879* (Manchester, NH: Clarke, 1881), 148. Gilsum nourished a number of local lyceums throughout the century.

39 Michael Warner, *The Letters of the Republic: Publication and the Public Sphere in Eighteenth-Century America* (Cambridge, MA: Harvard University Press, 1990), xiii. In the nineteenth century, says Schudson, "reading the newspaper became a part of what it meant to be civilized in America" (*The Power of News*, 48).

40 Philip Gilbert Hamerton, "On the Reading of Newspapers," *Scribner's Monthly* 5, no. 3 (1873): 318–19. Furthermore, to *write* for a newspaper was to join a powerful fraternity. In 1850 a Waterville, Maine, newspaper, quoting a piece from the *Boston Chronotype*, proclaimed that "it is the newspaper that does nine-tenths of the teaching, preaching and governing" ("The Newspaper," *Eastern Mail*, February 14, 1850). Looking back at the 1860s, when she edited her high school's lyceum paper, a Rhode Island woman recalled "our feelings of admiration and awe for the people who earned their living by the daily use of the pen" (*Bohemian* [Medway, RI], March 2, 1880; this handwritten paper is in the collection of the American Antiquarian Society, Worcester, MA).

41 *Piscataquis Observer* (Dover, ME), December 7, 1865; *Beadle's Dime Humorous Speaker: A New Collection of What Is Amusing and Droll in American Wit, Humor, and Burlesque*, Speaker Series, vol. 6 (New York: Beadle, 1866), 80.

42 Toll Bridge Lyceum (Fryeburg, ME), miscellaneous papers, private collection.

43 Gilmore, "Literacy," 41, 42.

44 Steven Feld, quoted in Tad Tuleja, ed., *Usable Pasts: Traditions and Group Expressions in North America* (Logan: Utah State University Press, 1997), 9.

CHAPTER 8: "THE SPEAKING EYE AND THE LISTENING EAR"

1 Quoted in Michael Schudson, *Discovering the News: A Social History of American Newspapers* (New York: Basic Books, 1978), 21.

2 *Kearsarge Fountain* (East Andover, NH) 3, no. 12, December 19, 1849. Emery made another expostulation following *"An Adventure,"* a story in which, after a life of traveling, the speaker returns to his beloved village as an old man, comes to his favorite spot on the edge of the lake, and sees an unutterably beautiful woman sitting there. He approaches her: *"She raised her head and I met the thrilling glance of those deep blue eyes—the ruby lips parted and she said in silver tones, 'Mister hain't you seen nothin of dads old Hoss?'"* Emery grumbled: *"To the author of this we would say—it is a* sin *to create such a vision of beauty, and then annihilate it with a dash of* common reality. *Ed—"*

3 Reverend Carlos Wilcox, "The Religion of Taste," in *Remains of the Rev. Carlos Wilcox . . . : With a Memoir of His Life* (Hartford, CT: Hopkins, 1828), 177–208. See also James Hazen, "Carlos Wilcox (1794–1827)," in *Encyclopedia of American Poetry: The Nineteenth Century*, ed. Eric L. Haralson (Chicago: Fitzroy Dearborn, 1998), 487–89.

4 "Our Latest Wish," in *The Student and Family Miscellany*, ed. N. A. Calkins (New York: Calkins, 1855), 70.

5 *Scholar's Penny Gazette* (Boston), March 23, 1850, 156.

6 *Casket* (March 1855), in Bronson Family Papers, New Hampshire Historical Society, Concord. Although the *Casket* was a Sunday school paper, it was one of the many manuscript papers produced by members of the Bronson family, who tended to copy pieces from one paper into another. Like other items, this poem in the *Casket* was probably originally composed for one of the family's lyceum papers.

7 Occasionally editors did juxtapose pieces on similar topics. The *Emblem* (Landaff, NH), c. 1860, contains contrasting, adjacent pieces on the sorrows or joys of bachelorhood. In one issue of the *Dublin (NH) Rural Repository* (3, no. 8, February 17, 1841), the editor prefaced a poem on intemperance with an apology, saying that, had the piece not come in late, it would have followed an earlier letter to the editor on the need for a drunkards' asylum. However, such concurrences are unusual.

8 Thaddeus Perry Mason, diary entries, March 25, 1840, and March 30, 1842, Thaddeus Perry Mason Papers, box 1, Historic Deerfield Library, Deerfield, MA.

9 *Kearsarge Fountain* (East Andover, NH) 3, no. 12, December 19, 1849.

10 A description of the Wilton Lyceum appeared in the *Milford (NH) Enterprise*, January 8, 1877: "The people [evidently the paper's title] by Miss Myrta M. Jones was excellent and original, one of the pieces bringing in all of the places of business in town, in a very mirthful and pleasing manner. It was enthusiastically and loudly cheered." Mention of another lyceum appeared in the *Aurora of the Valley* (Claremont, NH), March 2, 1872: "FELCHVILLE.— The tenth number of the Village Gem was read by Miss Kate Stearns and Miss L. K. Fletcher, and was received with tremendous applause."

11 An analogous situation obtained in the Semi-Colon Club, founded by Harriet Beecher Stowe and other New England expatriates in Cincinnati in the 1830s, in which both women and men wrote anonymous compositions that were read aloud. Women, who organized the meetings and kept the club going, took advantage of the anonymity to write intellectual and humorous pieces beyond "womanly" expectations. See Nicole Tonkovich, "Writing in Circles: Harriet Beecher Stowe, the Semi-Colon Club, and the Construction of Women's Authorship," in *Nineteenth-Century Women Learn to Write*, ed. Catherine Hobbs (Charlottesville: University Press of Virginia, 1995), 145–75.

12 William Russell, *Primary Reader: A Selections of Easy Reading Lessons, with Introductory Exercises in Articulation, for Young Children* (Boston: Tappan and Dennet, 1843), 5.

13 *Scrap Book* (Webster, NH), c. January 1882; *Cruiser* (South Freeport, ME) 1, no. 3, February 12, 1859. The issue *that* evidently contained the critics' objections (*Cruiser* 1, no. 2) is not in the collection of the Maine Historical Society, Portland.

14 *Bean's Corner Sunbeam* (Jay, ME), c. 1877. Lyceum papers often mentioned "getting hit." Another example is quoted in the opening epigraph of this book.

15 *Monitor* (East Cabot, VT), c. February or March 1879.

16 Sophie May [Rebecca Sophia Clarke], *The Doctor's Daughter* (Boston: Lee and Shepard, 1871).

17 T[haddeus] P[erry] Mason, "Report upon the condition of The Young People's Society for Mutual Improvement, Nov. 1843," Thaddeus Perry Mason Papers, box 3, Historic Deerfield Library, Deerfield, MA. As far as I can tell from the surviving issues, papers for the Dublin, New Hampshire, lyceums in the 1840s generally avoided personal teasing.

18 *Independent* (South Levant, ME) 1, no. 7, March 23, 1881.

19 *Bean's Corner Sunbeam* (Jay, ME), c. 1877.

20 See Catherine E. Kelly, *In the New England Fashion: Reshaping Women's Lives in the Nineteenth Century* (Ithaca, NY: Cornell University Press, 1999).

21 Mikhail Bakhtin, "Carnival and Carnivalesque," trans. Caryl Emerson, in *Cultural Theory and Popular Culture: A Reader*, ed. John Storey (Atlanta: University of Georgia Press, 1998), 251.

22 Toll Bridge Lyceum (Fryeburg, ME), "*Continuations of Kelsey's Diary, 1871*," miscellaneous papers, private collection.

23 Barnet Baskerville, *The People's Voice: The Orator in American Society* (Lexington: University Press of Kentucky, 1979); Gregory Clark and S. Michael Halloran, eds., *Oratorical Culture in America: Essays on the Transformation of Nineteenth-Century Rhetoric* (Carbondale: Southern Illinois University Press, 1993); Nan Johnson, *Nineteenth-Century Rhetoric in North America* (Carbondale: Southern Illinois University Press, 1991); James Perrin Warren, *Culture of Eloquence: Oratory and Reform in Antebellum America* (University Park: Pennsylvania State University Press, 1999).

24 Donald M. Scott, "The Popular Lecture and the Creation of a Public in Mid-Nineteenth-Century America," *Journal of American History* 66, no. 4 (1980): 295.

CHAPTER 9: "HOW SHALL WE WIN BACK LOST GROUND?"

1 On the positive images, see Joseph A. Conforti, "Regional Identity and New England Landscapes," in *A Landscape History of New England*, ed. Blake Harrison and Richard W. Judd (Cambridge, MA: MIT Press, 2011), 17–34; and Joseph A. Conforti, *Imagining New England: Explorations of Regional Identity from the Pilgrims to the Mid-Twentieth Century* (Chapel Hill: University of North Carolina Press, 2001). On the decline, see Rudyard Kipling, *Something of Myself* (London: Macmillan, 1964); Philip Morgan, "The Problems of Rural New England: A Remote Village" *Atlantic Monthly* 79, no. 475 (1897): 577–87; Alvan F. Sanborn, "The Problems of Rural New England: A Farming Community," *Atlantic Monthly* 79, no. 476 (1897): 588–98; Alvan F. Sanborn, "The Future of Rural New England, *Atlantic Monthly* 80, no. 477 (1897): 74–83; Rollin Lynde Hartt, "A New England Hill Town. 1. Its Condition," *Atlantic Monthly* 83, no. 498 (1899): 561–74; and Rollin Lynde Hartt, "A New England Hill Town. 2. Its Revival," *Atlantic Monthly* 83, no. 499 (1899): 712–20.

2 Roger B. Stein, "After the War: Constructing a Rural Past" in *Picturing Old New England: Image and Memory*, ed. William H. Truettner and Roger B. Stein (Washington, DC: National Museum of American Art, Smithsonian Institution, 1999), 21; Roberta Smith Favis, "Home Again: Worthington Whittredge's Domestic Interiors," *American Art* 9, no. 1 (1995): 24–25.

3 Edwin Arlington Robinson, *Collected Poems: The Children of the Night and Captain Craig* (New York: Macmillan, 1927), 28.

4 *Gazette* (South Bethel, ME) 5, no. 2, November 1889.

5 Tad Tuleja, ed., *Usable Pasts: Traditions and Group Expressions in North America* (Logan: Utah State University Press, 1997), 9.

6 *Scrap Book* (Webster, NH), c. January 1882.

7 *Mystic Tie* (Carthage, ME) 1, no. 3, January 8, 1875.

8 Unnamed lyceum paper (East Bethel, ME), c. December 1877.

9 *Scrap Book* (Webster, NH), c. January 1882.

10 Harold Fisher Wilson, *The Hill Country of Northern New England, Its Social and Economic History, 1790–1930* (New York: Columbia University Press, 1936); John Donald Black, *The Rural Economy of New England: A Regional Study* (Cambridge, MA: Harvard University Press, 1950); Hal S. Barron, *Those Who Stayed Behind: Rural Society in Nineteenth-Century New England* (Cambridge: Cambridge University Press, 1984); Hal S. Barron, *Mixed Harvest: The Second Great Transformation in the Rural North, 1870–1930* (Chapel Hill: University of North Carolina Press, 1997); Jan Albers, *Hands on the Land: A History of the Vermont Landscape* (Cambridge, MA: MIT Press, 2000), 173; Lance Newman, "Class Struggle in New England," in *Our Common Dwelling: Henry Thoreau, Transcendentalism, and the Class Politics of Nature* (New York: Palgrave Macmillan, 2005), 25–34.

11 Barron, *Those Who Stayed Behind*.

12 *Dublin (NH) Rural Repository* 3, no. 10, March 17, 1841; and 2, no. 9, February 7, 1840.

13 *Literary News* (Antrim, NH) 1, no. 7, July 6, 1885. The Antrim lyceum is the only one I have found that ever met in the summer.

14 *Literary Banner* (Mont Vernon, NH) 2, no. 7, January 20, 1859.

15 *Bean's Corner Sunbeam* (Jay, ME) 3, no. 11, March 20, 1879.

16 *Emblem* (Landaff, NH) 1, no. 8, February 25, 1860.

17 *Veazie (ME) Light*, January 22, 1877.

18 *Bean's Corner Sunbeam* (Jay, ME), c. 1877.

19 *Monitor* (East Cabot, VT), c. February or March 1879.

20 *Literary News* (Antrim, NH) 2, no. 1, January 2, 1886.

21 *Veazie (ME) Light*, January 22, 1877. The corruptions of consumer culture had been of concern in New England for decades, as Catherine E. Kelly points out in "'Joining anon in fashion's noisy din,'" in *In the New England Fashion: Reshaping Women's Lives in the Nineteenth Century* (Ithaca, NY: Cornell University Press, 1999), 214–41.

22 *Bean's Corner Sunbeam* (Jay, ME) 3, no. 11, March 20, 1879.

23 *Cold River Journal* (Alstead, NH), October 21, 1887, and December 9, 1887.

24 Thomas C. Hubka, *Big House, Little House, Back House, Barn: The Connected Farm Buildings of New England* (1984; reprint, Waltham, MA: Brandeis University Press, 2004), 120, 178.

25 Joseph F. Kett, *The Pursuit of Knowledge under Difficulties: From Self-Improvement to Adult Education in America, 1750–1990* (Stanford, CA: Stanford University Press, 1994), 144–45. See also Anne Ruggles Gere, *Writing Groups: History, Theory, and Implications* (Carbondale: Southern Illinois University Press, 1987), 14; and Gregory Clark and S. Michael Halloran, eds., *Oratorical Culture*

in Nineteenth-Century America: Transformations in the Theory and Practice of Rhetoric (Carbondale: Southern Illinois University Press, 1993).

26 Among the rare notices, the *Deerfield Valley Times* (Wilmington, VT) reported occasional lyceums in the villages of Sherman, Grove, and Dummerston in the 1890s, some with papers.

27 One possible exception is the *Emden (ME) Center Times,* November 29, 1893, perhaps a hybrid school and village paper, which was clearly devoted to local teasing. There is no internal evidence as to where the paper was read or on what occasion. According to Carol Dolan of the Embden Historical Society, the paper was found in the late 1980s in the wall of a house that was being renovated.

28 See, for example, "Revive the Old Lyceum," in which the author recollects how "bi-partisan discussion gives all an opportunity to hear both sides, to weigh one argument against another" (*St. Albans (VT) Daily Messenger,* February 21, 1902, quoting the *Montpelier (VT) Argus*).

29 *Deerfield Valley Times* (Wilmington, VT), March 27, 1908.

30 *Herald and News* (Randolph, VT), February 25, 1909.

31 Albion F. Watson, diary entry, December 9, 1881, Fayette Historical Society, Fayette, ME. Starling Hall, the Grange building, was completed in 1879.

32 Jean F. Hankins, "Women in the Grange," *Courier* 34, no. 1 (2010): 4–9.

33 Mount Vernon (ME) Grange, record book, 1876–82, Maine Historical Society, Portland.

34 *Grange Echo* (Fryeburg, ME), c. 1895, private collection.

35 *Golden Harvester* (Webster, NH), c. spring 1888, private collection.

36 *Golden Harvester* (Webster, NH), c. December 1885, August 7, 1888, and February 5, 1889, private collection.

37 Moosilauke Grange (Haverhill, NH), minutes, December 14, 1894, records, 1894–98, New Hampshire Historical Society, Concord.

38 *Grange Echo* (Fryeburg, ME), c. 1895.

39 *Vermont Phoenix* (Brattleboro, VT), October 16, 1891.

40 "Education in Citizenship," *Lend a Hand* 10 (January–June 1893): 37–41.

41 *St. Albans (VT) Daily Messenger,* March 18, 1907.

INDEX

Abbott, Isaac, 18, 25
Abbott, Joseph, 58
Adams, Hattie, 187–89, 192
Adams, John Quincy, 60
Adams, Maria Eliza Gordon. *See*
    Gordon, Maria Eliza
Alcott, Louisa May (*Little Women*),
    6, 137
Alcott, William A., 74–75
amateur newspapers: compared
    to school newspapers, 239n8;
    movement ("amateurdom"),
    136–37; pen-printed, 239n7
American Lyceum, 4, 9, 56, 223n2.
    See also lyceum movement
anonymity, 148, 161–65, 243n11
Antrim, New Hampshire. See
    Literary News
Arthur, T. S. (*Woman to the Rescue*),
    63
Athol, Massachusetts: New
    Sherburne Literary Association
    and Union Lyceum in, 52
Aunt Carrie (Mrs. Caroline L.
    Smith), 137–38
Austin, Rev. J. M., 73

bachelors, 24, 33, 47, 121, 159, 168,
    224n6
Barker, Willard, 29
Barre, Vermont, 141
Barron, Hal, 116, 173
Beadle's Dime Debater, 66–67, 72, 80
Beadle's Dime Humorous Speaker, 152
Bean's Corner Sunbeam (Jay, Maine),
    87, 107, 109, 113, 115, 125, 134, 164,
    167, 176–80, 203–4, 221–22
Bennett, James Gordon, 154
Bennett Hill Lyceum (Petersham,
    Massachusetts), 52
Bethel, Maine, 138. *See also* East
    Bethel; South Bethel
Boyd, Mrs. E. E. (*The "P.D.S."*), 63–64
Bow Lake Journal (Strafford, New
    Hampshire), 99–100, 203

Brandon (VT) Lyceum, 54
Bridgewater, Massachusetts, 79;
    Bridgewater Normal School,
    149; *Normal Offering*, 149
Bridgewater (NH) Lyceum, 82, 136
Bridgton (ME) High School lyceum,
    84
Bristol, New Hampshire: *Bristol
    Wild Flowers*, 138
Bronson, C[harles]. P. (*Abstract of
    Elocution and Music*), 70
Bunce, Oliver Bell (*A Bachelor's
    Story*), 68
Buswell [Buzzell], Frank, 23
Butler [Charles], 74

Calver, Edward, 47
Candia (NH) Lyceum, 69–70
Carthage, Maine: Berry's Mills,
    172–73; *Mystic Tie*, 87–88, 95, 107,
    110, 114, 121, 129, 164, 172, 203;
    papers with covers missing, 205;
    temperance paper, 139
Cary, Alice, 45
Casket (Landaff, New Hampshire),
    93, 159–60, 233n11
Centennial Gazette (paper of the
    South Levant [ME] High
    School), 175
Chatham, New Hampshire, 138
Cherokees, 116
Chester (VT) Village Lyceum, 42
circles, 32–34, 224n7
common schools, 16; coeducation
    in, 80–81; compositions in, 101,
    105–6; elocution in, 64–65; exhi-
    bitions, 65, 106; lyceum papers
    for, 106, 139, 235n8; lyceums in,
    65; in New England, 227n10;
    pupils attending village lyceums,
    241n19; reading in, 100; recita-
    tions in, 101; and self-education,
    58; teaching in, 30–32; women
    teachers in, 78–79, 158–59, 224n4;
    visiting, 30–32

INDEX

women (*continued*)
coeducation on, 83–84; lyceum critics, 79; lyceum officers, 85; mental capacity of, 74–75, 79–80; "old maids," 47, 121, 129–30, 158, 236n37; participation in Grange, 186–89; reading and study clubs for, 75–76, 230n9, 230n12; reading in lyceums, 101–3; schoolteachers, 78–79; women's rights, 77–78, 179–80, 231n14

Young People's Society for Mutual Improvement (Dublin, New Hampshire), 7, 43–44, 106, 162–63

Zboray, Mary and Ronald, 3, 104
Zoar (MA) Lyceum, 5